T0319802

Strategic Behaviour in Network Industries

Strategic Behaviour in Network Industries

A Multidisciplinary Approach

Ernst ten Heuvelhof

Martin de Jong

Mirjam Kars

Helen Stout

Delft University of Technology, The Netherlands

Edward Elgar

Cheltenham, UK • Northampton, MA, USA

Published by
Edward Elgar Publishing Limited
The Lypiatts
15 Lansdown Road
Cheltenham
Glos GL50 2JA
UK

Edward Elgar Publishing, Inc.
William Pratt House
9 Dewey Court
Northampton
Massachusetts 01060
USA

A catalogue record for this book is available from the British Library

Library of Congress Control Number: 2009904799

Mixed Sources
Product group from well-managed forests and other controlled sources
www.fsc.org Cert no. SA-COC-1565
© 1996 Forest Stewardship Council

ISBN 978 1 84720 610 7

Printed and bound by MPG Books Group, UK

Contents

Figures

Tables

Foreword

Strategic behaviour in the various utilities has presented governments, firms and consumers with considerable problems in the past few years. The consequences of clever interventions, sly misuse of technical capabilities, foul financial play and deceit when providing information to others have often been quite substantial. And yet, apart from some economic studies in which game-theoretic models have been applied, very little actual empirical research has been conducted on the what, how and why of strategic behaviour. This is not all that surprising, because the subjects under study may be quite reluctant to collaborate in telling researchers the full story. Also, the existence of strategic behaviour is sometimes exceedingly difficult to prove. Perhaps journalists may write that wherever there is smoke, there is fire, but for judges and investigators, serious evidence is required to make that point. The authors of this book therefore utilized a great variety of research methods to gather insights worked out into demonstrative and convincing case studies.

It is with pride and pleasure that one of the research groups of the Next Generation Infrastructures Foundation of which I am scientific director, has, after several years of theoretically and empirically studying the subject, now managed to get a book out in which the background, breeding grounds and mechanisms of this phenomenon are elaborately explained, five meaningful and characteristic empirical cases are described from different utility sectors and different countries, and credible suggestions are given to counter the downsides of this phenomenon. Moreover, it is written in a clear and accessible style, making this very useful study material not only for academics in the field (politics, policy, economics, law, systems engineering), but also for master's students. May this book prove useful for students, professionals and academics for many years in seeing through situations and circumstances plagued by strategic behaviour and in undertaking appropriate action.

Margot Weijnen
Scientific Director, Next Generation Infrastructures Foundation

Acknowledgements

When putting this book together, the authors have leaned on the support of various people and organizations and are intellectually as well as practically endebted to many. A small number of them have really proven indispensable. Rather than mentioning a wide range of names, we would like to emphasize only a few here.

First of all, we would like to thank the following two organizations: the contributions of Helen Stout were made possible by the financial support of the Royal Netherlands Academy of Arts and Science (KNAW); furthermore, for all authors, the preparation of this book would not have been possible without the financial support of the Next Generation Infrastructures Foundation.

One person who we would like to thank for his contribution is Mark de Bruijne. Although he had no role to play in compiling the book or the brainstorms leading to the conceptual framework underlying it, he was willing to provide us with an invaluable chapter on Enron, which according to the anonymous reviewer of our book, was among the best documented that he had seen.

We are also endebted to Edward Elgar's anonymous reviewer who, while having a very sympathetic view of the approach we chose, provided us with constructive and useful suggestions to sharpen our theoretical and methodological choices and justifications.

Another person that we would like to mention here is Krispijn van Gasteren, a student of ours but at the same time much more than merely a student. His diligence and timeliness in arranging the format of the book, working on our editorial changes and sending it to the publisher in the right shape, indicate that he saw through our theoretical scribbles without requiring additional clarification on our part. Good student-assistants are young academics and secretaries at the same time. This is more than any one of the four authors can say of themselves.

Finally, we are immensely grateful to Hans de Waard, our conscientious translator, who ensured that large parts of the book were written in an English that both native and non-native speakers can feel comfortable with. It is with sadness that we heard he passed away after completing the work for this book but before seeing it in published form. We cherish the idea that he was proud to work for Delft University of Technology in general and for us in particular. Hans, we will remember you with fondness.

Ernst ten Heuvelhof, Martin de Jong,
Mirjam Kars and Helen Stout

1. Introduction

1.1 INFRASTRUCTURES

Infrastructures are the backbone of the economy and of society. In particular the network-based infrastructures (for example energy, water, information and telecommunication infrastructures and transport infrastructures for freight and passengers) provide essential services that are enabling for almost every type of economic and social activity. The annual expenditure of households and enterprises in OECD countries for services delivered over the infrastructures is relatively high, some thousands of euros per year per inhabitant. The annual investments of the infra operators and service providers are correspondingly high. The current changes in the economic structure make the crucial role of the infrastructures even more evident. The infrastructures are crucial as enablers of the present service-oriented economy. Hence, they are often labelled 'critical' infrastructures. The economy and society as a whole gain by well-functioning and well-performing infrastructures. This is why anything that hampers the optimal functioning of network-based industries deserves attention.

1.2 CHANGES IN NETWORK-BASED INDUSTRIES

Until recently, this world of infrastructures and utility services was a quiet world. Stable public-owned companies delivered the same products and services year in, year out. However, technological developments, liberalization, privatization, commercialization and internationalization have turned this world upside down. The changes in infrastructure-based sectors have been immense. To mention a few examples:

- The telecommunication sector has changed rapidly: until recently, this was a stable sector. Most countries had one vertically integrated provider, in most cases publicly owned, which offered a limited number of services. A few years on, this sector has changed completely. There are far more services in the market than before. The technological developments are highly dynamic. Convergence with other types of infrastructure has completely changed the relations in this sector. There is considerable competition. The sector is predominantly private and the market is fully internationalized.

- The market for energy has changed beyond recognition in a short time. Producers, network managers and suppliers have been unbundled, competition has been introduced in many links of the chain, and some companies have been privatized. A consolidation battle is taking place at the international level, resulting in gigantic companies, and the markets retain their oligopolistic character.
- Cable companies that used to deliver a respectable package of channels to living rooms anonymously for little money have become aggressive listed companies, developing new products and services for commercial reasons.

Many were highly optimistic about the consequences of the transitions. Companies were believed to become more customer-oriented, to realize great innovations, their services were expected to become cheaper and consumers would have more options. Although some of these advantages have indeed been realized, the changes are heavily criticized. The positive consequences are less visible than was hoped and disadvantages are manifesting themselves. At times, the once so peaceful utility world seems to have changed into a battlefield where companies, regulators, governments and politicians are making each other's lives miserable. This often reaches the point where the behaviour goes beyond the limits of fair play. Some examples are:

- Computer giant Microsoft made the operation of Windows Client Personal Computer Operating System conditional on the simultaneous acquisition of Windows Media Player software, thus stifling competing providers.
- AT&T, the powerful telecoms firm, was able to retain its hegemony for a long time by denying interconnection to competing firms.
- In a short time, Enron changed from a reputable energy company into a cynically operating one where deceit and window dressing were the order of the day.
- Versatel, the Dutch telecoms firm, participated in the bidding at the Universal Mobile Telecommunications System (UMTS) auction merely to drive up prices for competitors, without having serious ambitions itself to secure frequencies.

This book elaborates the idea that, although the changes in network-based sectors may potentially have positive effects, these advantages seldom materialize completely in practice. One of the reasons for these disappointing results is the 'strategic behaviour' of the players involved. For brevity's sake, strategic behaviour can be defined here as actor behaviour in interaction settings aimed at a very one-sided realization of this actor's own interest. Since infrastructures are so important for a country, particularly for its inhabitants and for its economy, strategic behaviour that negatively affects the quality of the infrastructures and the services transmitted over them might have major adverse economic and social effects. This is sufficient reason for highlighting strategic behaviour.

Although these aspects of strategic behaviour are intuitively clear, the fact remains that scientific clarity about this concept is imperative. Research into strategic behaviour presents a specific methodological problem. Strategic behaviour is difficult to detect. There are at least two reasons for this. The first is that particular actions seem strategic from one perspective, but are not so from another perspective or at any rate are not consciously intended to be so. The second is that the actors displaying strategic behaviour will usually deny acting strategically, which makes furnishing conclusive evidence for its existence almost impossible. Strategic behaviour is surrounded by a haze of blameworthiness, causing a tendency for actors to distance themselves from such a qualification. This means that many methods of social-scientific research do not lend themselves to exploring strategic behaviour, because the respondents that are a source of information about their own behaviour in normal research may hardly be a source of information in this type of research.

1.3 PROBLEM DEFINITION OF THIS BOOK

In this book we define, describe and analyse this strategic behaviour. We do not study strategic behaviour in the world of network-based industries as an isolated phenomenon, but place it in the wider context of strategic behaviour in general. The problem definition is as follows: *What examples and types of strategic behaviour can be observed in the world of network-based industries and what arrangements are conceivable to counter it?*

The following subquestions are relevant:

- What is strategic behaviour in general?
- How does strategic behaviour arise and persist?
- What forms of strategic behaviour are present in the liberalizing and privatizing network-based industries?
- What counterarrangements are conceivable?

In the academic literature, much has been written about strategic behaviour. We should point out here that this literature is relatively one-sided.

Strategic behaviour has been profoundly analysed at the level of abstract theory, especially from an economic and a game-theoretic perspective (Joskow and Klevorick, 1979; Milgrom and Roberts, 1987; Schelling, 1978; Schmalensee, 1981; Williamson, 1977). Many of these analyses are model-oriented and present a theoretical and model-oriented exploration of particular forms of strategic behaviour. These studies do not limit themselves to the network-based industries, but essentially relate to the economy as a whole and, even more widely, to all processes and games between actors in them. Actors, then, are not only companies, but also other organizations, or even countries.

This book focuses on strategic behaviour of actors in the network-based industries. On the one hand, network-based industries are ordinary industries. The companies in these network industries will therefore behave in a way similar to that of companies from other industries. The strategic behaviour that companies display in those ordinary industries can also be expected to feature in the network-based industries. On the other hand, the network-based industries have some special characteristics that may influence the intensity and the nature of the strategic behaviour in these sectors. This might lead to other strategic behaviour, in addition to the regular strategic behaviour.

1.4   STRUCTURE AND APPROACH

This book starts in Chapter 2 with a description of strategic behaviour in general. What are the general characteristics?

In Chapter 3 we explore the general literature about strategic behaviour, focusing on two questions: what is its origin; in other words, what are the breeding grounds for strategic behaviour? And what concrete strategic behaviour can thrive on these breeding grounds?

Chapter 4 zooms in on the network-based industries. It describes in more detail what this world looks like and what changes are taking place in it. We will then discuss six different opportunities for strategic behaviour, which may help to identify the ways in which actors employ strategic behaviour. These are the strategic use of rules, strong ties with the government, bottleneck facilities, the essential and indispensable nature of infrastructure utilities, the strategic use of the factor time and the use of financial resources.

In Chapters 5 to 9 we present five highly diverse empirical case studies in which several forms of strategic behaviour occur, thriving in the three different types of general breeding grounds and employing one or more of the six infrastructure-specific opportunities to display this strategic behaviour.

In each of these chapters, we first describe the events and interpret and identify the strategic actions, and at the end we always set out in a table what they were and what opportunity or opportunities were chosen for this behaviour.

. In selecting the case studies, we opted for a spread over various economic sectors: aviation (open skies), telecommunications (AT&T and UMTS), electricity (Enron) and IT (Microsoft).[1] In addition, the selection is based on variety as regards the geographical setting of the case studies. The events discussed in the five chapters take place in, for instance, the United States, the European Union, the Netherlands, Germany and Austria. In addition, the case studies are marked by a great diversity of actors. We not only look at the interests and behaviours of national governments and former monopolists, but also deal with the actions and reactions of, for example, the European Commission, national regulators and new market entrants.

In Chapter 10 we present an analysis based on the empirical findings from our case studies. First, we will discuss what dominant pictures of strategic behaviour in the network-based industries have emerged from our empirical material. Then, we will compare our empirical findings with the theoretical literature on strategic behaviour. This will result in a theoretical overview of strategic behaviours in the network-based industries.

Finally, in Chapter 11 we present a number of potential counter-arrangements. These arrangements can be employed to counter strategic behaviour or mitigate its effects. We will subsequently discuss three traditional counterarrangements (competition engineering, skimming returns and consumer protection) and two alternative arrangements (hybrid governance and regulators).

NOTE

1. Microsoft may not be the most obvious case study in the context of a book on strategic behaviour in network-based industries, because one would usually associate network-based industries with sectors like transport or electricity. Nevertheless, we believe that this case study makes a valuable contribution to our research. Besides, in our view, the industry of which Microsoft is a part can most definitely qualify as a network-based industry. In the first place, this industry fills a distinct utility function. Computers have a key function in today's society and are indispensable for the functioning of the economy as a whole. Besides, the industry can also most clearly qualify as a network-based industry as regards technological features. Here, we would like to point in particular to the bottleneck character of the service. Emmons also points out that Microsoft's current operating system can be characterized as a basic infrastructure. According to Emmons, the fact that Microsoft has, in the course of time, increasingly faced pressure from government regulators can be explained by the 'increasing perception among the public

– both individual consumers and corporate clients – that Microsoft's operating system has become a type of basic infrastructure. Hence, Microsoft now confronts the type of scrutiny traditionally faced by companies with near monopoly control of access to essential facilities like rail systems, telecommunications networks, and electricity transmission systems' (Emmons, 2000, p. 7).

REFERENCES

Emmons, W. (2000), *The Evolving Bargain. Strategic Implications of Deregulation and Privatization*, Boston, MA: Harvard Business School Press.

Joskow, P.L. and A.K. Klevorick (1979), 'A framework for analyzing predatory pricing policy', *The Yale Law Journal*, **89**(2), 213–69.

Milgrom, P. and J. Roberts (1987), 'Predation, reputation, and entry deterrence', *Journal of Economic Theory*, **27**(2), 280–312.

Schelling, T.C. (1978), 'Altruism, meanness, and other potentially strategic behaviors', *American Economic Review*, Princeton American Economic Association, **68**(2), 229–30.

Schmalensee, R. (1981), 'Economies of scale and barriers to entry', *Journal of Political Economy*, **89**(6), 1228–38.

Williamson, O.E. (1977), 'Predatory pricing: a strategic and welfare analysis', *The Yale Law Journal*, **87**(2), 284–340.

2.   Defining strategic behaviour

2.1   THE CONCEPT 'STRATEGIC BEHAVIOUR'

Strategic behaviour is a frequently used concept. Sometimes authors refer to strategic behaviour when they attempt to explain why the results of institutional changes such as privatization and liberalization can be so disappointing. Expected positive effects such as lower prices, innovation and better services fail to materialize. The number of competitors in network industries is usually low. Consequently, one of the explanations given in such cases is 'strategic actor behaviour' of one or more of the players involved. In such cases, the concept 'strategic behaviour' is used comparatively loosely and associatively, without defining it clearly or separating it from other modes of behaviour. However, in spite of this lack of clarity it appears to be a socially and scientifically relevant phenomenon.

Within the academic world, economists make the most rigorous use of the concept, calling it either strategic behaviour or opportunistic behaviour, and often do so in a stylized manner. Although academically rigorous, economic publications often restrict themselves to analytical descriptions of fictitious situations or stylized, generic interpretations of real-life situations (Hurwicz and Reiter, 2006; Dixit and Nalebuff, 1993; Kreps, 1990). This is a very good starting point, but not complete for our purposes. Since this book attempts to get much closer to 'what happens on the ground' and to actually see what strategic behaviour means in practice and how it evolves, we will depart from the economic 'rational choice' game-theoretic notions and then systematically expand on those and add characteristics to develop the concept towards a more inter-disciplinary definition. One of the notions on which we continue to build is the lasting effect of the concept of self-interest. The essence of strategic behaviour is that strategists do what they do to serve their own interest. They do so in a sly, opportunistic manner, by camouflaging their intentions. They do so by using the ambiguity of their behaviour. The reason is that it appears possible in many cases to give two meanings to their behaviour: the first meaning being that with their behaviour they serve their narrow self-interest. Meaning two is that, instead, with their behaviour, they serve a broader interest. Strategists will consistently refer to this second meaning and indignantly reject other interpretations (see for more details the last part of this chapter); in other words rationalization and motive diverge. All actors concerned may display such strategic behaviour. To mention just a few: incumbents, (potential) entrants, regulators, ministries, administrators, government officials, public interest groups, and so on.

This chapter examines the concept of strategic behaviour more closely. It will begin with the main insights derived from game theory and rational choice theory, as well as outlining its limitations. Subsequently, six additional characteristics of strategic behaviour 'in the real world' will be given.

2.2 GAME THEORY AND RATIONAL CHOICE THEORY: FEATURES AND LIMITATIONS

Game theory was introduced in a famous and agenda-shaping publication by Von Neumann and Morgenstern (1944). Its central theme is always the reasoning that in multi-actor environments with a game character, actors adopt a self-seeking attitude and try to pursue their goals rationally. They do this in interaction (anticipation and reaction) with other actors in their environment. The preferences of these actors and the values from which they originate are clearly defined. Today there is a large group of these theories, which employ advanced mathematics, but whose link with developments in practice is at least problematic. Assumptions underlying the calculations are properly set out at the beginning, but the outcomes fail to use the 'wealth of empirical reality', nor can they be retranslated to them (Scharpf, 1997, p. 2). Their most important value is a different one, that is showing basic economic heuristics behind emergent phenomena. Theories of this kind introduce distinctions that may be fertile theoretically but that soon fade in practice. For example, they distinguish between sequential games (i.e. players only make moves in succession) and synchronous ones (i.e. players are allowed to make moves simultaneously) (Friedman, 1983 and 1990). Of course, games in reality can contain both elements. Evolutionary game theory as developed in biology often remains closer to empirical evidence than in economics, but the level of complexity in the world of animals is far lower than among humans and the artefacts constructed around them (Maynard Smith, 1982; Axelrod, 1984).

It is very important to keep a close eye on the actual world here, which is full of uncertainties and where different games criss-cross. In this actual world, it is usually wise not to rely on just one strategy. Thus, we in fact encounter the core message that results from the confrontation between theory and practice: misunderstandings, misinterpretations and miscommunications are untreatable in the mathematical models, but for game theory to be actually applicable we should also take into account the world of the literally incalculable events. This is already the case when organizational behaviour is interpreted by means of evolutionary camouflage and mimicry phenomena in financial reporting (de Jong, 2001). It is even more true when such strategic conduct occurs around modern complex socio-technical systems such as network-bound infrastructures. In such systems conceptual learning is often key to success, and the mathematical models cannot cope with such complexity.

Another reason to put the merits of mathematical computations of game theory somewhat into perspective for the analysis of strategic behaviour is the following. In general, mathematical models require the game to be delimited. The question must have been answered as to which players participate in the game and which players are part of the game's environment. That also goes for the rules that apply in the game. They, too, must have been described and laid down. The question is, of course, to what extent strategical actors are prepared to stick to this delimitation. They are unlikely to do so unless it suits them. They will try to involve other actors in the game and they will try to change the rules of the game if they feel it serves their interest and see possibilities for doing so (Nalebuff and Brandenburger, 1996, p. 195; Weimer, 1995; Tsebelis, 1991). With their behaviour, they exceed, so to say, the input of the mathematically modelled game, after which their behaviour as it really develops ends up beyond the reach of the game. In other words, it may be an actor's strategy to change the limits of the game (Crozier and Friedberg, 1980, p. 67; Dixit, 1996, p. 30).

Scharpf also sees and values the analytical power of game theory, but adds the call to make this theory match empirical evidence as closely as possible (Scharpf, 1997, p. 2).

Rational choice theory has two assumptions that we regard as essential and want to problematize: the assumption of complete information and rationality, and the assumption of reliability and consistency.

From Complete Information as a Rational Ideal to Bounded Rationality and Ambiguity

An assumption of game-theoretic analyses in rational choice theory is that actors are rational. They are able to survey the various alternatives and to understand and predict the behaviour of other actors. They are also familiar with the developments in the context. Herbert Simon argues that rationality requires decision makers to have all the available information and to fully realize all the consequences of the decisions they can take (Simon, 1947 [1976]). In reality, this knowledge is very limited and fragmented.

Rationality also requires decision makers to choose from all possible behaviours that are theoretically conceivable. In reality, they only contemplate a limited number of alternatives. This is why Simon prefers to speak of bounded rationality. He also states that decision makers are, at some stage, satisfied with a solution without being prepared to keep looking for a better one. This behaviour is called 'satisficing' and is the opposite of what he sees as 'optimizing', which would presuppose complete rationality. If their level of satisfaction about the course of events falls below a particular threshold value, decision makers decide to carry out more research in order to approach their ideal of complete information more closely.

However, it appears that research cannot always play the envisaged role. In a number of cases, the confusion about the value and development of contextual factors continues to exist, despite great efforts to collect information and conduct research. In these cases, more is the matter than mere uncertainty. Even the ideal of complete information, if at all possible, will not solve the problem. In situations in which information collection and research do not help to stabilize the context, there is ambiguity. Ambiguous developments and ambiguous factors lend themselves to several interpretations and thus exclude complete information even as an ideal after research. Actors then each give their own meaning to developments and factors. There are several interpretations rather than one widely supported, unambiguous interpretation or meaning. Research alone then does not help to close the gap between these interpretations.

The context of the utility sectors has a great deal of ambiguity. A number of ever-recurrent concepts are quite frequent in the context of utilities, regulators and customers. They are not only very general concepts like 'privatization' and 'liberalization', but also more specific concepts such as 'cost price', 'universal service provision', 'innovation', 'quality', 'risks' and 'competition'. Actors repeatedly turn out to interpret such concepts each in their own way. An additional problem is that actors often assume that everybody thinks the way they do and interprets the way they do, without realizing that several interpretations co-exist. Conflicts arise about these ambiguous factors, which are not easy to solve, certainly not by mere research or information collection.

From Reliability and Consistency to Opportunism and Ambivalence

Rational choice theory describes the interactions between actors as games. The actors anticipate and react to each other's actions. They observe each other's actions, interpret them and then decide to make a move. The crucial link between mutual expectations, agreements and cooperation between parties is the assumption that parties have clearly defined options and alternatives, through which each of the parties can express their preferences. The second assumption of rational choice theory about actors is that they are able to formulate their preferences clearly and order them in relation to each other. They know what is important for them and what they will give priority in case of conflict. However, this assumption also proves to be too far removed from reality to build on. In reality, actors prove to be inconsistent in their preferences. They are irresolute and frequently redefine alternatives and preferences or fail to define them at all. They may consider different values of paramount importance at the same time. In some cases, the one is the natural consequence of the other and the two can be reconciled; in other cases, they conflict and actors have to make difficult choices, which, over time, do not always seem reliable and consistent.

At least two factors may contribute to the ambivalence of actors in the utility industries. In the first place, generally speaking, the leading actors (for example utility companies, ministries and regulators) are big and have a complex structure. They may be so big as to have a multiform composition: in utility companies, commercial departments may view problems differently from the more technology-oriented departments. In some cases, one department will dominate, in other cases the other department will. From the perspective of the utility company, this is well balanced: in some cases, one department will take priority, in other cases the other will. This may all too easily give outsiders the impression of a zigzagging enterprise.

In the second place, the actors are leavened by values between which tensions exist. Privatized utility companies will be commercial, but will also continue to cherish their traditional values. These concern, for example, technology (i.e. the quality of the network) and universal service provision (i.e. a basic package of services at a low rate, accessible to everybody). To outsiders, this ambivalence, too, leads to a zigzagging policy, although it seems well balanced and consistent from the perspective of the enterprise.

2.3 SIX CHARACTERISTICS OF STRATEGIC BEHAVIOUR 'IN THE REAL WORLD'

To deal with the caveats mentioned above and to avoid lack of clarity in definition, we have chosen six characteristics that actor behaviour in the real world should have in order to be called strategic. These are:

- Strategic behaviour is reflective.
- Strategic behaviour is relational and takes shape in interactions.

- Strategic behaviour has a time dimension.
- Strategic behaviour is aimed at narrow self-interest.
- Strategic behaviour is ambiguous.
- Strategic behaviour is intentional.

We will expand on each of these characteristics below.

Strategic Behaviour is Reflective

The behaviour of a tennis player who trains by hitting the ball against a training wall differs from that of the same player facing a flesh-and-blood opponent in a real game. Hitting balls effectively against a wall requires other skills and tactics than being successful in a match. What are the differences? They have to do with the nature of the player's 'opponent'. After all, a tennis wall is not a real opponent. The wall does not think, unlike the opponent. The wall is not reflective, unlike the opponent. The wall returns a ball hit in the same way in an always-identical way. An opponent, however, does not. He[1] will vary his strokes, knowing that this will increase his chance of winning. This difference in reflectiveness propagates and leads to a chain of differences, because the tennis player knows that the wall is not reflective whereas his opponent is. He will take this into account and adapt his behaviour to it. He anticipates his opponent's reflective behaviour. The third step is that the game between the tennis player and the wall will develop differently from the game between two players. It will be far more varied, more capricious and more unpredictable than a training session of a player against a wall.

In one sense, all behaviour of people and actors is reflective. Reflectiveness is everywhere and is always there. This is why reflectiveness in itself is meaningless for discerning strategic behaviour. However, distinguishing between different types of reflectiveness creates a relevant power of distinction. Giddens distinguishes between rationalization of action and motivation of action (Giddens, 1984, p. 5). Rationalization is the actor's reflection on his actions. Much of it takes place implicitly. It concerns the 'grounds' for action. Motives, on the other hand, refer to what prompts them. Rationalization concerns the theory behind the routine, day-to-day actions. Motivation concerns change, situations 'which in some way break with the routine'. These forms of reflectiveness take shape more or less discursively. From the perspective of strategic behaviour, we add a distinction. It is appropriate to distinguish between justification for behaviour as formulated in public and motives for behaviour that remain implicit or are only given privately. This is where justification and motives differ, the reasons mentioned in public being the justification for the behaviour, and the motives being the real incentive behind the behaviour. The reflectiveness of the behaviour lies in the fact that the actor realizes the difference.

Emphasizing the reflective character of strategic behaviour, we assume the existence of a certain freedom of will in day-to-day contact between actors, in addition, of course, to the importance of historically formed institutions that also form and condition the behaviour of actors. This assumption is in line with Scharpf's approach known as 'actor-centred institutionalism' (Scharpf, 1997; Hemerijck, 2001, p. 91).

Strategic Behaviour is Relational and Takes Shape in Interactions

The behaviour of the tennis player in the match is relational; it takes shape in interactions, in this case in interaction with his opponent. The behaviour during their training, however, is not fed by interaction and is therefore non-relational. In the following example, Tsebelis sets out how a person changes his behaviour when it changes from non-relational to relational (Tsebelis, 1989).

For a long time, Robinson Crusoe thought that, as a castaway, he was the only inhabitant of the island where he had been washed ashore. He handled his risks as well as he could. He took measures against bad weather and kept fresh water to survive times of drought, until one day he discovered a footprint on the beach. From that moment, he knew that he was not the only person on the island and that there was another thinking being around. He realized that he was no longer alone in his fight against nature, but that he also had to deal with a rationally thinking and acting being. Had Robinson Crusoe not drawn a lesson from this and had he continued to do what he was doing, he would have acted inadequately: 'the Robinson Crusoe fallacy'. However, he reacted adequately, realizing that the fight against nature is fundamentally different from the fight against a reflective being.

In this example, Robinson Crusoe will have understood that laying in too many stores might make him vulnerable to 'the other'. Instead, he might speculate that he and 'the other' would start to cooperate rather than doing everything by themselves. However this may be, from the moment Robinson Crusoe discovered the footprint, he began to see his own behaviour in a different perspective and to reflect about what the other might do. He began to anticipate the behaviour of 'the other' and respond to it. This brings us to the field of game theory. 'A game is a situation of strategic interdependence: the outcome of your choices (strategies) depends upon the choices of another person or persons acting purposively' (Dixit and Nalebuff, 1993, p. 85).

Strategic Behaviour has a Time Dimension

As we pointed out above, strategic behaviour takes shape in interactions. It is a game of anticipations, of actions and reactions. The mere fact that anticipations, actions and reactions take place at at least three different moments introduces the factor time in strategic behaviour. By definition, this game has a time dimension. In addition, the time dimension may become visible in strategic behaviour in other ways. We mention two of them.

In the first place, bounded rationality and opportunism always involve a time dimension, because bounded rationality implies that it is impossible to foresee everything. Because of bounded rationality, a contractual or institutional arrangement must remain 'incomplete' (Jensen and Meckling, 1976 [1996]; Dixit, 1996, p. 31). This makes supplements to the arrangement in the course of time inevitable. Actors will want to use this incompleteness and also 'fight' for their interest in the later supplements. This may easily trigger opportunistic behaviour. They then try to use the gaps in the arrangement that were unforeseeable. Particularly actors that made specific investments, that is investments that can no longer be used for any purpose other than implementing the provisions in the arrangement, will be vulnerable to such strategic, opportunistic behaviour, because they are less flexible in their behaviour than other actors are.

The conclusion is that incompleteness and bounded rationality make follow-up actions of the actors involved inevitable, and that actors will also want to serve their interest in these actions, which may all too easily give these actions an opportunistic touch.

Bounded rationality and opportunism are frequent, inevitable phenomena rather than exceptional ones. This is why the designers of arrangements should take bounded rationality and opportunism as their point of departure (Williamson, 1989, p. 139). It is important to realize that bounded rationality makes comprehensive contracts impossible.

In the second place, the time dimension also manifests itself in the frequently displayed positional game. In a positional game, the actor initially relinquishes direct material gain. Initially, strategists only strengthen their position or weaken their opponent's position. They do not actually strike until the second phase. In many cases, that second phase is not even necessary, and parties, experienced as they are, know enough once they have acquired the right position. We often see this aspect of strategic behaviour in chess. Chess matches are rarely won and lost by directly capturing pieces and threatening the king. The real game is to occupy positions on the chessboard, by manoeuvring pieces into a position that strengthens them later in the game rather than immediately, by heading off the opponent, preventing them from taking up particular positions, by threatening them with particular moves. The real blow in this chess game is less interesting than the moves that precede it. Nevertheless, those 'strategic moves' may look harmless in themselves and only acquire a meaning for the expert, who can estimate the value of the threat they pose. This aspect of strategic behaviour is in line with a description by Schelling, who writes that strategic behaviour 'is not concerned with the efficient application of force but with the exploitation of potential force' (Schelling, 1960, p. 5). With regard to industrial economics: 'strategic behavior has reference to efforts by established firms to take up advance positions in relation to actual or potential rivals, to introduce contrived cost disparities, and/or respond punitively to new rivalry' (Williamson, 1989, p. 176).

The conclusion is that strategic behaviour tends not to become visible until the time dimension is regarded. Only in a series of behaviours can a pattern become visible that might be strategic. An observation of all individual behaviours might have yielded no clue at all about the strategic character of the behaviour, and an analysis over time might be needed to make a pattern visible.

Strategic Behaviour is Aimed at Narrow Self-interest

The main assumption of game theory and economic theory is that actors seek to maximize their individual advantage. The classic theories also assumed that maximizing individual advantage would eventually also maximize wealth at the collective level. However, this proposition has been questioned in the more sophisticated theories and in practical policy. Katz shows how parties that each choose to serve their own interest may lower collective wealth and eventually their own wealth. Katz describes the case of an actor making an investment that only has value in its relation with another actor. This investor is vulnerable to strategic behaviour of other parties that know that the investor has nowhere to go after the investment. Of course, the investor also knows this, and it will therefore invest suboptimally. Both the investor and the other parties would have been better off if the investor had invested more and the other parties had deprived themselves of the possibility for opportunistic behaviour (Katz, 1989, p. 698). However, as long as opportunistic behaviour is possible for the other parties, this threat is imminent and investments will be suboptimal. This has given strategic behaviour a slightly more negative connotation. The pursuit of narrow self-interest might jeopardize the wider public interest (Ordover and Saloner, 1989, p. 579). Strategic behaviour is primarily aimed at self-interest, even if it might prejudice the public interest.

In this book, we follow definitions of strategic behaviour that indicate that this behaviour may conflict with the public interest. In a concrete situation, it is difficult to judge whether behaviour actually conflicts with the public interest. Tests to establish this are expensive, and in spite of this, wrong conclusions cannot be excluded.

Strategic Behaviour is Ambiguous

As we set out above, strategic behaviour is reflective, in the sense that strategists make a difference between the way they explain their behaviour in public and their reasons for their behaviour. We also suggested that strategic behaviour is aimed at narrow self-interest, even if it runs counter to the public interest. Public interest is loosely defined here as what governments would determine if they aimed at maximizing the utility of a nation's citizens or (infrastructure) customers according to a Bergson–Samuelson welfare function (Dixit, 1996). The combination of these two characteristics is obvious now. Strategists will realize reflectively that, with their behaviour, they pursue their own interest, although this may harm the public interest. However, they will deny this in public. In public, they will emphasize that their behaviour does not jeopardize the public interest, while acknowledging backstage that the behaviour does serve their own interest and that it may indeed be harmful to the public interest. This is only possible with behaviours that are ambiguous, which can be given two meanings. Compare the definition of opportunism given by Williamson: 'self-interest seeking with guile' (Ordover and Saloner, 1989, p. 539).

The one meaning is that the behaviour serves the strategist's interest; the other meaning is that it serves the public interest. There is no need to explain that the first interpretation comes from the strategist's critics, while the second interpretation will be that of the strategist themself. The strategist will indignantly reject the first interpretation. It will not be easy to find proof of the strategic character of ambiguous behaviour. It has to be proven then that the strategist speaks with two tongues, one in public and one behind the scenes and that he does so deliberately. The 'smoking gun', as decisive evidence for the existence of such strategic behaviour in a concrete case is, for example, an overheard conversation or leaked minutes. One could even claim that in some cases the actor sincerely believes he is acting in the public interest and thus there would be nothing to prove. There, it should be emphasized that only patterns of behaviour can show whether the results of actor behaviour reveal self-interest to be the real drive. In other words, analysts should focus on 'revealed preferences' rather than 'stated preferences'. In the case studies further on, we have emphatically ordered events chronologically to highlight behavioural patterns. Studying legal documents, reports, public statements and press reports are more appropriate methods of research than interviews to 'reveal preferences'.

Strategic Behaviour is Intentional

The fact that strategists' behaviour is intentional may sometimes be concluded from the fact that they make a difference between what they announce in public about their behaviour and what they say backstage. Purpose and intent should therefore be criteria in establishing whether behaviour is strategic (Crozier and Friedberg, 1980, p. 25). We should point out here that not every definition of strategic behaviour comprises this intentionality. There is a group of definitions of strategic behaviour that, inductively, infers an underlying strategy from concrete behaviour.

> The analyst can discover regularities, which make sense only relative to a strategy. This strategy, therefore, is nothing other than the inferred basis, ex post facto, for the empirically observed regularities of behavior. It follows that such a strategy is in no way synonymous with willed behavior, any more than it is necessarily conscious. (Mintzberg, 1983)

2.4 STRATEGIC BEHAVIOUR SUMMARIZED

In sum, what are the main characteristics of strategic behaviour?

- *Strategic behaviour is reflective.* Strategists reflects on their behaviour and realize that they would harm their own interest if they included the reasons for their behaviour in the reason they state in public.
- *Strategic behaviour is relational.* Strategic behaviour thrives in a constellation in which actors are aware of each other and can mutually react to each other's behaviour and anticipate it. Configurations with a limited number of actors fulfil this condition.
- *Strategic behaviour has a time dimension.* The interactive character of strategic behaviour has, by definition, a time dimension, if only because move and countermove cannot take place at the same moment, but are linked serially. Besides, there is the bounded rationality of the actors, which makes it impossible to foresee the whole future at one particular moment and lay down everything in detail in an arrangement (for example a law or an agreement). This means that arrangements always have to be supplemented and/or changed in the course of time. Finally, strategic behaviour may contain

a positional element, in the sense that strategists try to occupy a position that will be advantageous to them at a later stage.

- *Strategic behaviour is unilaterally aimed at narrow self-interest.* The core of strategic behaviour is that it serves the strategist's enlightened self-interest. This does not mean, however, that all the behaviour that serves self-interest is strategic behaviour. We speak of strategic behaviour only where strategists serve their self-interest, even if they think that this may prejudice the public interest. This may go so far as to harm other interests seriously.
- *Strategic behaviour is ambiguous.* Strategic behaviour is open to two interpretations. The first interpretation may be that the behaviour does not harm the public interest, the second view that the behaviour serves the strategist's individual interest while harming the public interest.
- *Strategic behaviour is intentional.* Strategists will realize the tension that is inherent in their behaviour. They realize the ambiguity of their behaviour and use it by emphasizing in public that their behaviour poses no harm to the public interest, while privately stating that their behaviour primarily serves their own interest. Privately, it may even be agreed to emphasize the first interpretation in public and deny that the second interpretation is relevant.

2.5 STRATEGIC BEHAVIOUR FROM A BUSINESS, LEGAL AND ECONOMIC PERSPECTIVE

Above, we have given a relatively specific elaboration of the concept of strategic behaviour. Where does this definition differ from other perspectives of strategic behaviour? To explore this question, comment on this definition from three dominant disciplines has been formulated below, followed by an indication of the added value of the approach chosen here.

1. *Business administration scholar: every company should have a strategy and behave in accordance with it. Strategic behaviour then means that the company has a strategy and behaves in accordance with it.*

   A company that formulates a strategy for the future does something completely different from a company that displays strategic behaviour. A strategy is a company's long-term vision, which, in many cases, has been laid down and is public. A company that has a strategy is valued positively. It means that the company considers its position and its future rather than operating ad hoc.

   Although strategic behaviour is semantically almost identical with strategy, it has a completely different meaning. Strategic behaviour has not been laid down. The company will always deny that it 'behaves strategically'. The valuation of strategic behaviour tends to be problematic and is ambiguous at any rate. Strategic behaviour is synonymous with operating tactically or 'politically' (de Jong and Stout, 2003).

It is quite possible for a company to have a 'strategy' while 'behaving strategically' at the same time. The strategy then consists of politically and commercially correct statements, while in reality it behaves strategically, perhaps even under the cover of the strategy.

2. *Legal scholar: Behaviour is either lawful or unlawful. This also goes for strategic behaviour. If the court has not, or not yet, declared behaviour to be unlawful, it is permitted.*

What is the relation between strategic behaviour on the one hand and behaviour contrary to the law on the other hand? Behaviour in conflict with the law comprises all forms of illegal behaviour, regardless of whether the behaviour is contrary to rules of penal, administrative or private law.

The similarities between strategic behaviour and unlawful behaviour are obvious. Both have a strongly pejorative connotation. Both the actor with strategic behaviour and the actor acting unlawfully try to obscure their behaviour from their environment. Strategic behaviour is intentional, reflective and relational. These characteristics also apply to many forms of unlawful behaviour.

However, there are also good reasons to distinguish between strategic behaviour and unlawful behaviour. A first reason has to do with the factor time. As regards unlawful behaviour, eventually the court decides whether behaviour is lawful or unlawful. Until that time, it is uncertain whether behaviour is permitted or not. Strategic behaviour is lawful until that moment. Of course, parties have opinions about the desirability of that behaviour and in some cases judicial decisions are more or less predictable, but in many other cases it is almost impossible to prove violation of written or unwritten rules of law. This is also true if, in the transition process from the old monopoly situation to the new competitive market, it is necessary to qualify behaviour quickly from a legal point of view – in real time and even in anticipation of the actual behaviour – as either permitted or not permitted. This question does not arise when behaviour has to be qualified in terms of strategic and non-strategic.

The second reason to distinguish between unlawful behaviour and strategic behaviour has to do with the ambiguity of behaviour. Strategic behaviour is by definition ambiguous. This ambiguity makes it possible to attach several meanings to concrete behaviour.

Qualifying this behaviour as lawful or unlawful ends this ambiguity, or shifts the playing field somewhere else for strategically acting actors (de Jong and Stout, 2003).

3. *Economist: the market is an arena and a good entrepreneur acts cleverly in this arena, trying to realize advantage for their enterprise, even if this harms their competitor. That is the game and it will benefit everybody in the long term.*

Good business operations are clever and strategic behaviour is also clever. Both types of action are good for the enterprise. In this sense, the two types of behaviour resemble each other. However, there is also an important difference. Strategic behaviour in the sense used here is not only clever, but above all sly. Strategic behaviour benefits the enterprise, and as such it does not differ from running a business wisely. However, strategic behaviour goes far beyond ordinary business operations. Acting strategically usually harms the public interest and, by our definition, the person who acts strategically realizes that his behaviour harms the public interest. At the same time, they realize that it may cause them reputation damage or even legal damage and they therefore deny acting strategically. In some cases, they may maintain this for a long time because of the above-mentioned ambiguity. This definition shows that we see a clear difference between an entrepreneur's ordinary, clever and aggressive behaviour and sly, strategic behaviour.

NOTE

1. Whenever the authors refer to 'he', 'him' and 'his' when addressing impersonal agents such as 'actors', 'rivals' and 'competitors', this is solely for pragmatic reasons.

REFERENCES

Axelrod, R. (1984), *The Evolution of Cooperation*, London: Basic Books.
Crozier, M. and E. Friedberg (1980), *Actors and Systems, The Politics of Collective Action*, Chicago, IL: The University of Chicago Press.
Dixit, A.K. (1996), *The Making of Economic Policy: A Transaction-Cost Politics Perspective*, Cambridge, MA: MIT Press.
Dixit, A.K. and B.J. Nalebuff (1993), *Thinking Strategically: the Competitive Edge in Business, Political and Everyday Life*, New York: W.W. Norton & Company.
Friedman, J.W. (1983), *Oligopoly Theory*, Cambridge: Cambridge University Press.
Friedman, J.W. (1990), *Game Theory with Applications to Economics*, Oxford: Oxford University Press.
Giddens, A. (1984), *The Constitution of Society*, Cambridge: Polity Press.
Hemerijck, A. (2001), 'De institutionele beleidsanalyse: naar een intentionele

verklaring van beleidsverandering' (in Dutch) ('The institutional policy analysis: towards an intentional explanation of policy change'), in T. Abma and R.J. in 't Veld (eds), *Handboek Beleidswetenschap* (in Dutch) (*A Handbook of Policy Science*), Meppel: Boom, pp. 83–95.

Hurwicz, L. and S. Reiter (2006), *Designing Economic Mechanisms*, Cambridge: Cambridge University Press.

Jensen, Michael C. and William H. Meckling (1976), 'Theory of the firm: managerial behavior, agency costs, and ownership structure', in Peter J. Buckley and Jonathan Michie (eds) (1996), *Firms, Organizations and Contracts; a Reader in Industrial Organization*, Oxford: Oxford Management Readers.

Jong, Martin de (2001), 'Manipulate tactics in budgetary games: the act and craft of getting the money you don't deserve', *Knowledge, Technology and Policy*, **14**(1), 50–66.

Jong, Martin de and Helen Stout (2003), 'Strategic behaviour and the law: how legal authorities deal with factual strategic behaviour of former monopolists', *International Journal of Technology, Policy and Management*, **3**(1), 38–55.

Katz, M.L. (1989), 'Vertical contractual relations', in R. Schmalensee and R.D. Willig (eds), *Handbook of Industrial Organization*, Amsterdam: Elsevier Science Publishers, pp. 656–724.

Kreps, D.M. (1990), *Game Theory and Economic Modelling*, Oxford: Oxford University Press.

Maynard Smith, J. (1982), *Evolution and the Theory of Games*, Cambridge: Cambridge University Press.

Mintzberg, H. (1983), *Power in and around Organizations*, Englewood Cliffs, NJ: Prentice Hall.

Nalebuff, B.J. and A.M. Brandenburger (1996), *Co-opetition*, London: HarperCollins Business.

Neumann, J. von and O. Morgenstern (1944), *The Theory of Games and Economic Behavior*, Princeton, NJ: Princeton University Press.

Ordover, J.A. and G. Saloner (1989), 'Predation, monopolization, and antitrust', in R. Schmalensee and R.D. Willig (eds), *Handbook of Industrial Organization*, Amsterdam: Elsevier Science Publishers, pp. 538–96.

Scharpf, F.W. (1997), *Games Real Actors Play. Actor-Centered Institutionalism in Policy Research*, Oxford: Westview Press.

Schelling, T.C. (1960), *The Strategy of Conflict*, Cambridge, MA: Harvard University Press.

Simon, H.A. (1947), *Administrative Behavior: A Study of Decision-Making Processes in Administrative Organization*, reprinted in H.A. Simon (1976), *Administrative Behavior: A Study of Decision-Making Processes in Administrative Organization*, New York: The Free Press.

Tsebelis, G. (1989), 'The abuse of probability in political analysis: the Robinson Crusoe fallacy', *American Political Science Review*, **83**(1), 77–91.

Tsebelis, G. (1991), *Nested Games: Rational Choice in Comparative Politics*, Los Angeles, CA: University of California Press.

Weimer, D.L. (ed.) (1995), *Institutional Design*, New York/Berlin: Springer.

Williamson, Oliver E. (1989), 'Transaction cost economics', in R. Schmalensee and R.D. Willig (eds), *Handbook of Industrial Organization*, Amsterdam: Elsevier Science Publishers, pp. 136–78.

3. General breeding grounds for strategic behaviour

In this chapter, we describe the breeding grounds of strategic behaviour in general as it occurs in any industry. Our method here is as follows. We begin with a literature scan for strategic behaviour. This yields a wide variety. We subsequently explore the backgrounds of this behaviour. In doing so, we ask the question regarding what this behaviour is based on and how it is possible that the strategist is given the opportunity to display it. We call this background the breeding ground for strategic behaviour. We will discuss three of these breeding grounds here:

1. *Fewness.* A limited number of dominant companies with a disproportionate amount of market power forms a breeding ground for strategic behaviour. Even in contexts with many players, this dominance makes checks and balances impossible.
2. *Position.* An established position, but also acquiring a new position offers possibilities for strategic behaviour.
3. *Information asymmetry.* Differences in information provision between actors present an opportunity for strategic behaviour.

The above three features mutually overlap and reinforce each other, but leaving one out would make the picture incomplete.

The structure of this chapter is as follows. In three subsequent sections, we describe the above-mentioned 'breeding grounds'. For each of them, we first describe how they can be valued and, in the second place, what concrete forms of strategic behaviour ensue from them.

3.1 BREEDING GROUND 1: FEWNESS

3.1.1 Fewness

Fewness has two famous configurations for strategic behaviour: the monopoly and the oligopoly. The most obvious breeding ground for strategic behaviour is the monopoly. A company that has a monopoly is in a comfortable position. Such a company is the only one to offer a product or service and can exploit this position.

But there are more examples of market configurations that are characterized by a limited number of players. In this context, we should mention William Fellner, the author of *Competition among the Few: Oligopoly and Similar Market Structures*. Although this book was originally published in 1949, it is still conceptually authoritative. Fellner puts it concisely:

> Fewness is an important characteristic of the contemporary economic scene. Many prices and wage rates are determined under conditions which are neither atomistic nor monopolistic. They are determined under conditions of fewness: a few decision-making units shape their policies in view of how they mutually react to each other's moves. (Fellner, 1949)

The book demonstrates that many markets are, in reality, not so easy to characterize as full competition, pure monopoly (one provider, many customers) or monopsony (many providers, one customer). In reality, there are many market forms that have just a few players, more than one, but fewer than a great many players. Some of these market forms are: oligopoly (a few providers, many customers), oligopsony (many providers, a few customers), bilateral oligopoly (a few providers, a few customers), market leadership (one dominant player besides a few lesser ones), market concentration and several combinations between them.

In oligopolistic and related market forms, actors are strongly competitor-oriented. They can be so because they have just a limited number of competitors (small-numbers rivalry). Given their interests, they react to and anticipate the steps taken by other oligopolists. Utility functions of one actor are included in those of all other actors, but as unknown variables. Any change in the behaviour of other players has to be watched closely because it may influence the realization of their own aims (Shapiro, 1989, p. 330). Every company tries aggressively to increase its market share, but if they all do so, all of them will be worse off. Realizing this, they will at the same time feel urged to cooperate with each other and make agreements. In an oligopoly, the same actors can compete and cooperate at the same time. In other words, companies in oligopolies feel divergent incentives. They will, at the same moment, feel inclined to cooperate and to compete with each other. This causes the typical dynamics in oligopolies. Because of the inherent uncertainty about what others want and do, actors have to make intelligent estimates of their own positions and possibilities and at the same time try to remain opaque to others. Fellner calls this process of anticipation and reaction between players 'conjectural interdependence'. Game theory is pre-eminently suitable for analysing the possible dynamics in this configuration (Neumann, 2001, p. 11).

3.1.2 Valuation of Monopolies and Oligopolies

Although monopolies and oligopolies are in disrepute today, they were not always so, and even today, a nuanced view of these market forms is possible.

Market and competition have two sides. On the one hand, the market stimulates companies to offer services and products that consumers need and to do so as cheaply as possible. This is the vital and innovating aspect of competition. The incentive for companies to join this game is the ousting of their competitors, which makes their position more comfortable. In this sense, allowing a monopoly is an extra incentive for effective competition. The climax of competition is monopoly, and all competition is nothing but striving for monopoly (Liefmann, 1915). Paradoxically, the process of competition can be valued positively, but its ultimate consequence, the monopoly, can be valued negatively.

On the other hand, competition has a destructive aspect. Competitors try to oust each other. Once they have been ousted, all investments relating to that market segment have been fruitless. Companies also invest parallel to each other, for example in the same innovations. This contains an element of double work. It may easily seem profitable, both from the perspective of the company and from the collective interest, to join forces and cooperate rather than driving each other out of the market through competition.

Unsurprisingly, the valuation of cartels has not always been negative. Kleinwaechter (1883) called cartels 'children of distress' (Neumann, 2001). To him, cartels were indispensable for a proper adaptation of output to a volatile demand, because, particularly in capital-intensive companies, a great deal of capital would be destroyed if companies had to be closed down because of a fall in demand, which might be temporary. Cartels thus acquired a positive connotation 'safeguarding social stability and avoiding the chaotic conditions of competition'. This stance was the basis for a decision of Germany's Reichsgericht, de facto legalizing cartels in Germany (Neumann, 2001, p. 25). But not all cartels proved to be children of distress. What appeared to be the case? At the beginning of the last century, cartels were indeed capital-intensive, but in the 1920s, labour-intensive industrial cartels also came into being. It needs no explanation that the above justification does not apply to these industries. The *children-in-distress* hypothesis assumes that cartels are born mainly in periods of depression, because in this period of the economic cycle the destruction might occur that would be so wasteful both socially and commercially. However, Sombart concluded that cartels develop mainly in times of a growing economy, which vitiated the hypothesis (Webb, 1980).

3.1.3 Strategic Behaviour on the Basis of Fewness

Monopolistic behaviour is of course the most conspicuous strategic behaviour. The monopolist is the sole provider of a product or a service, allowing them to ask relatively high prices and enabling them to earn higher profits than in a normal market. A configuration with many providers forces a company to ask a price for their products that equals the variable output costs. If they try to get more and ask a higher price, their competitor will take advantage of it, undercut their price and take away their customers. Some customers would be willing to pay a price higher than that which equals the variable costs of the product. This is called the consumer surplus and it is the prosperity increase that is created when somebody buys something at a lower price than they would be willing to pay.

In a monopoly, this process takes a different course. A monopolist can afford to ask a higher price. Although a number of potential buyers will consider the price too high and refuse to purchase, the monopolist receives the higher price from all those who do purchase. If the monopolist chooses the right price, the higher price will compensate the decreasing number of buyers and he will earn a higher profit at the expense of the consumer surplus (Teulings et al., 2005, p. 43). This type of behaviour leads to allocative inefficiency and a more uneven distribution of income between producers and consumers. Moreover, monopolies tend to show cost inefficiency (Leibenstein, 1966; Bos, 1995, p. 14); in particular bureaucratic costs may increase (Groenewegen, 2005, p. 12).

In oligopolies, companies are exposed to the temptation of colluding. The best-known form of collusion is the cartel, in which agreements are made about prices and quantities (Jacquemin and Slade, 1989, p. 424). Examples of cartels are price cartels, market-division cartels and tender cartels. In many cases, collusion results in prices that are higher and offered quantities that are lower than those companies would ask in a constellation in which there is no collusion. It needs no explanation that this is an interesting option for companies.

Collusion has an inherent tension. On the one hand, it is attractive for companies to collude, because it benefits all participants. On the other hand, the participants in the collusion nevertheless remain each other's competitors and it is an attractive option for every individual participant in the collusion to cheat his competitors despite the collusion and to undercut the agreed high price. The more the price exceeds the variable costs, the more room there is for cheating and the greater is the temptation to break the collusion. This gives rise to the non-cooperative games in oligopolistic configurations.

The optimal behaviour of player A depends on what he thinks player B will do. In his prediction, A uses the rules of the game and assumes that his opponents themselves are rational, that is that they also make predictions and maximize their own pay-off (Fudenberg and Tirole, 1989, p. 261). Companies always choose the strategy that forms the best response to the anticipated game of the opponent.

There are many types of competition in oligopoly out of which many types of equilibrium (Nash) may develop[1] (Neumann, 2001, p. 47). A first well-known one concerns the quantities that the various oligopolists put on the market. The equilibrium resulting from this competition is the Cournot equilibrium. In this model, the oligopolists each make a decision about the quantity of their product or service that they wish to put on the market. A high output means a high turnover but a low price per unit. A low output means a low turnover but a high profit per unit. Here, the companies anticipate the behaviour of the other oligopolists. The following dilemma presents itself here. Take two duopolists, A and B. If A's output is low and that of his competitors is low, too, they will receive a high price per unit, which is extremely comfortable commercially. But what happens when A decides to keep his output low and B decides to release a high output on the market? B then realizes a high turnover and, because of the former company's low output, he still receives a relatively high price per unit. The former company is doing badly here, with a low output and a moderate price per unit. Of course, A wants to avoid this situation and will raise its output to a higher level than would be optimal from the cooperation perspective. After a few rounds of adaptations to each other, the 'Cournot equilibrium' will emerge.

The Cournot equilibrium is not Pareto optimal[2] from the perspective of the companies. Each company can always change something as a result of which it is better off. Of course, this will provoke reactions from its competitors. The result is that the Cournot equilibrium has a higher output with a lower price than the collusion result (Shapiro, 1989, p. 337). Nor does the Cournot equilibrium maximize social welfare. It creates a mix of social welfare and profits.

In another type of game, the companies play with the prices of their products. The equilibrium that develops in this game is called the 'Bertrand equilibrium'. In this game, the companies do not choose the quantity, but they make decisions about the price at which they offer their products or services. If they ask high prices, the level of the demand will decrease automatically. When their prices are low, the demand will increase. Companies will adapt their prices to the price-setting behaviour of their competitors. Here, too, equilibrium will develop, known as the Bertrand equilibrium.

It is obvious how these two approaches can be combined. The productive capacity is relatively fixed after investments have been made. Given a quantity of capital goods present in the company and given a particular staff formation of an enterprise, a company is unlikely to produce fewer goods than it can in the short term. It is not easy to change capital goods and staff in the short term. This is why fluctuations in the quantity of the output cannot be expected in the short term, although such changes are possible in the longer term. However, companies can influence their prices in the short term. This creates the situation in which the price game is mainly played and the Bertrand equilibrium will be found. In the longer term, the quantity game would be played in addition and the Cournot equilibrium would become relevant.

Not all collusion is equally explicit. *Implicit (tacit) collusion* may develop. Companies may collude without ever having communicated. No binding contracts are needed for collusion. Companies behave as if they have an agreement, but that agreement does not exist. In such a situation, all companies feel that it is in the best interest of them all to behave as if there are explicit agreements. This implies that they offer goods at higher prices than is necessary or put fewer products on the market than is possible. They stick to this tacit agreement because of *a (credible) fear* that the new situation that will arise after a breach of the agreement will, after some time, be worse for them than the present situation (Fudenberg and Tirole, 1989, p. 280). The more credible it is that deviations from the 'agreement' will be punished, the smaller the risk of a breach of the 'agreement'. 'Anything . . . that makes more competitive behavior feasible or credible actually promotes collusion.' Shapiro calls this the *topsy-turvy principle of tacit collusion* (Shapiro, 1989, p. 357).

3.2 BREEDING GROUND 2: POSITION

3.2.1 Position

Positional advantage is an important issue in the game between actors, and a great deal of strategic behaviour is aimed at acquiring a good position, retaining a strong position or manoeuvring the opponent into a bad position. Once an actor is in a strong position, it is relatively easy to win concrete advantages. The positional game therefore always has at least two moves: gaining the position and capitalizing on it.

The battle for the good positions is so strategic because no directly visible advantages are attached to it. The position in itself does not create any direct gain. This makes it so difficult to prove that the strategist playing a positional game merely acts in his own interest, because the strategist can always point out that he does not benefit from it. The advantage only materializes in a later phase; so much later that it is often problematic to establish a direct link between the positional game in an earlier phase and the material profit later. The fact that this link is difficult to establish makes the positional game attractive.

The importance of position is easy to explain with an example from cycle racing. When in the last few kilometres of a course a small group of riders approaches the finish, it is usual for the likely winners of the final victory, the riders with a good sprint in their legs, to try to gain a position behind other riders, in jargon: in the wheel of other riders. This position is comfortable and therefore desirable for several reasons. In the first place, in the wheel of another rider you are out of the wind, and you are less hampered by air friction. This allows you to save your strength for the decisive sprint in the last few metres. A second advantage is that the front rider cannot see very well what the rider behind him is doing. For example, the front rider does not see immediately that the rider in the wheel is going into a sprint. The front rider does not notice this until the rider behind him comes alongside, but then it is often too late because the rider that comes from behind has already gained speed, while the rider in the lead still has to go into a sprint and try to reach full speed.

The position in the wheel is so attractive that a fierce struggle may flare up between riders as to who is to ride in the lead and who is allowed to ride in the wheel. That may even go so far that the riders come to a complete halt because neither of them wants to ride in the lead. In jargon, a 'sur place'. For the non-initiated spectator, this presents a paradoxical situation: in a sport that is all about who is the fastest rider, the fighters are standing still! But they do so to obtain a good position from which they can later strike more effectively and ride faster.

What is an attractive position in a market? We distinguish two strategically interesting positions here. The first is that of the enterprise that already occupies a position in the market and thus, in one sense, has an advantage over newcomers. The second is that of a newcomer that tries to gain a position in an existing market. This position, too, may have its advantages.

Governments, competition authorities and regulators that aim to introduce more competition in a particular market seek to create a level playing field. The reasoning can be summarized as follows. In a market with too little competition, the monopolist and the oligopolist manage to realize revenue for themselves that is higher than socially desirable. They charge prices that are higher than the incremental costs they incur. Potential entrants know this and therefore see good possibilities for themselves.

They could offer their products below the price of the vested competitors – because these prices are relatively high – relatively high, but still above the incremental costs they incur. However, this reasoning only applies if there is a level playing field, that is that vested companies and newcomers have equal opportunities in the market and can operate at equal costs. If that is not the case and the vested companies have an advantage over newcomers, the potential entrant will first have to incur costs to compensate this advantage. It remains to be seen yet to what extent he can see an attractive return for himself. In such a situation, vested companies can always continue to make a return exceeding the return they would obtain in a really open market.

It is not easy to create such a *level playing field* in formerly monopolistic or oligopolistic markets. One reason why the playing field is not level is that the former monopolist or oligopolist has a considerable advantage over the newcomers in the market. It has the technology and knows the sales market. It enjoys what is known as '*experience-related cost advantages*' (Gilbert, 1989, p. 495). These advantages result from '*learning by doing*'. Many studies show that, *ceteris paribus*, a longer presence in the market leads to lower production costs.

This alone puts the potential entrant at a disadvantage and makes it difficult to realize a level playing field. This problem becomes even more serious if the former monopolist deliberately hampers or delays the realization of the level playing field. Emmons demonstrates that the players in the world of infrastructures play their strategic game in two arenas: that of the market and that of the politicians (Emmons, 2000). The incumbent also has an advantage in the political arena. He knows the actors in the political arena and has access to the media. The politicians tend to value the continuity of the vested companies because these incumbents are traditionally national companies, to which the politicians are in a certain sense attached. In the political game, the incumbent will have many opportunities to halt or delay the realization of the level playing field, or deflect it in such a way that the game in the market becomes as convenient as possible to play.

On the other hand, the (potential) entrant is not always by definition the victim. Newcomers, too, have possibilities for strategic behaviour. They can, for example, present themselves as the underdog and appeal to politicians and the media to give them a fair chance. In other words, to obtain advantages that put them in a more favourable position than the vested companies. A second way of manoeuvring themselves into a favourable position is for entrants to evade commitments that the vested companies have undertaken in the past. These may be commitments aimed at realizing specific public interests. The costs this entailed are sometimes referred to as '*stranded costs*' (Sidak and Spulber, 1998). At the time, these companies undertook this commitment lightly because they would be able to pass on the costs, against the background that the market would remain closed to entrants. But a newcomer that does not have this commitment and consequently does not incur these costs, thus enjoys an advantage that he can exploit. A third possible advantage for an entrant is that it is not burdened with legacy technology, which is often more costly than the latest generation of technology. This also means that the entrant can shrink possible obligations linked to the legacy technology, which may put him into a comfortable position.

3.2.2   Valuation of Exploiting a Position

An important dogma of neoclassical economics is that prosperity will grow if a monopolistic or oligopolistic market is replaced by an open market with more competitors. It would benefit prosperity as a whole, and in particular the prosperity of consumers would improve because they receive products and services at a lower price. The prosperity of consumers improves, whereas that of the companies that used to operate on closed markets deteriorates.

In their policies, many governments choose to raise the prosperity of consumers. In their policies, they argue for opening up the markets, facilitating, and stimulating the arrival of more competitors. This makes vested companies envious and they will oppose these changes. Both the direction and the pace of the changes show that this resistance is successful. The policy as well as the real changes in the market, if any, tend to be incremental, that is the changes are gradual, step-by-step. Policy is seldom radical and radical changes in the market are even rarer.

This inertia in policy and reality is due to the existence of '*negative feedback processes*' (Baumgartner and Jones, 2002, p. 6). An attempt to bring about change generates a counterforce. This feedback originates from the system or the market for which the changes are meant. Bendor and Moe outline a model that provides an insight into the emergence of this negative feedback and of the force emanating from it (Bendor and Moe, 1985). In many policy fields, there are agency leaders that play a role in the existing policy, politicians that have the subject in their portfolios and interest groups with an interest in a particular policy. These three types of groups all exert their influence, lobby, and try to influence policy and reality so as to benefit. 'The result is a closed and mutually adjusting system ensuring that policies reflect the competing interests and the relative strengths of those concerned' (Baumgartner and Jones, 2002, p. 10). Vested forces will manage to influence the policy so as to serve their interests. Companies that occupy a strong position in a market will join this game and they, too, will see their efforts rewarded in just a marginal adaptation of the status quo.

This no more than incremental change can be valued in two ways. The first is that the changes in policy and market manifest themselves less successfully and quickly than was hoped and expected from a neoclassical perspective. From this perspective, this is regrettable because it withholds a certain growth in prosperity from the consumers of the companies' products, and consequently from the public.

A second angle puts the value of the changes somewhat into perspective. A status quo, however problematic, in general also harbours valuable elements. However, this may remain rather underexposed in the media and in the political debate because, generally speaking, they tend to pay more attention to problems. By focusing attention one-sidedly on these problems and advocating changes that solve these problems, such changes might also harm processes that proceed relatively well. Companies that have traditionally operated in a monopolistic or oligopolistic configuration may have sold their products at too high a price. On the other hand, in many cases it is true that they have contributed ideas to policy making and have made extra investments to help realize public interests. Quick changes in policy and the market might all too easily undo these gains.

3.2.3 Position and Strategic Behaviour

Companies that occupy a comfortable position in the market as monopolists or oligopolists and wish to retain this position have a range of strategic behaviours available. Most of these strategic behaviours are forms of *predatory behaviour. Predation* is any form of threat by enterprises to behave aggressively towards entrants with the aim of preventing their entrance (Bos, 1995, p. 21). However, not every threat has the automatic effect of potential entrants abandoning their plans to enter the market. Tension exists between threat and the actual execution of the threat. An incumbent may send potential newcomers highly threatening signals, but what will happen when the potential entrant ignores these signals and nevertheless sets up a business? Then the question is whether the threat will be executed. Realizing the threat may be unattractive to the incumbent. For example, the incumbent has to start a price war to oust the newcomer by means of low prices or an intensive marketing campaign to keep their customers away from the entrant. This is expensive. It may be far more attractive to the incumbent to regard the entrant as one of the members of the oligopoly after his entrance and involve him in the collusion. The potential entrant will of course anticipate this pragmatic and adaptive behaviour and ignore the threat. The threat will thus lose its effect. A threat therefore only makes sense if its execution is *credible*.

A threat is credible if the established firms invest in the execution of the threat (Fudenberg, 1983) visibly (Ordover and Saloner, 1989, p. 548) and irrevocably prior to the entrance (Spence, 1977). What matters here is that it is clear to the potential entrant that this investment influences the '*post-entry marginal cost curve*' in such a way that the incumbent only needs a minor investment to crack down on the entrant after their entrance (Dixit, 1980, p. 6).

Predatory behaviour tends to manifest itself in threatening with a price war. The incumbent company has held a comfortable position in the market for many years and was able to build up considerable financial reserves. The company can employ these reserves to dump its products at a low price. The newcomer facing this behaviour also has to cut its price because otherwise it would have very few possibilities for enticing customers away from the incumbent. Because the incumbent has such large reserves, it can keep up this dumping for a long time. In such a 'fight to the death', the incumbent is likely to get the best of it, but the fight will eat into its reserves. The incumbent would therefore prefer to avoid such a price war. That is why it will threaten such a war prior to the entry, hoping that the potential entrant will abandon the idea of entering. Again, the threat must be *credible*. The potential entrant who becomes acquainted with these visible financial reserves and takes the threats to dump prices seriously may decide to give up the idea of entering this market, allowing the incumbent to have his way.

However, overinvestment does not always generate the right *credible threat*. In some cases, such an investment may undo the incentive to actually react aggressively to the entrant after his entrance. To avoid this '*fat-cat effect*', the incumbent will underinvest in order to take on a '*lean and hungry look*', which also expresses considerable threat (Fudenberg and Tirole, 1984).

A second form of *predatory behaviour* is *signalling*. This is possible if the incumbent has an information advantage over the potential entrant (see the next section). The incumbent then leaks incorrect information, for example about the cost structure or the demand on the market. In many cases, the potential entrant will be unable to estimate this information at its true value because of his information disadvantage. The potential entrant will then conclude that this market is financially not attractive enough to enter.

So far, the examples of *predatory behaviour* have been mainly financial. But there are other forms of predation. Examples would be *predatory product innovation*, where the incumbent threatens to put an innovation on the market that the entrant is unable to follow. If a potential entrant markets products that should somehow be compatible with products that the incumbent is putting, or has put, in the market, the incumbent may threaten to hamper the *compatibility* of the products that the entrant will supply. This may be a reason for hesitant customers to continue their custom with the incumbent. A variant of this is that the incumbent ensures that customers who want to switch face high switching costs (Gilbert, 1989). This, too, may pose such a threat that the potential entrant abandons his plans for entrance.

Not only can vested companies use their position strategically in their behaviour. Newcomers also have possibilities of displaying strategic behaviour. One strategy for the entrant is *cream skimming* or *cherry picking* (Graham and Marvin, 1994). In the past, vested companies have often made concessions to consumer organizations and government organizations to serve also those sectors of the market that are commercially less interesting. Examples would be low-income groups or consumers based at peripheral locations. They were easily able to do so at the time, because they were able to divide the costs among their other consumers. Although the latter group had to pay higher prices, they 'did not know any better' because there was no competitor offering them lower prices. However, an entrant can ignore this. Entrants can focus on those segments of the sales market that are commercially attractive, leaving the less attractive segments to the incumbent, which is faced with the higher costs attached to serving these groups.

3.3   BREEDING GROUND 3: INFORMATION ASYMMETRY

3.3.1   Information Asymmetry

The risks posed by a market configuration with only a limited number of companies are sufficiently well known. The arrangement frequently employed to mitigate these risks is regulation, provided by, for example, a competition authority or a regulator. These regulators observe the market and intervene when their observations give rise to concern about market developments. The question is, what is the quality of their observations? To what extent are their observations valid, reliable and timely?

The observations of regulators are fed in part by information supplied by market parties. Market parties receive questions from the regulators, on the basis of which they provide information, and regulators will conduct interventions on the basis of these observations, issuing measures that will affect the companies and contain instructions for the behaviour of market parties. In this sense, the regulator is the 'principal' and the companies are 'agents' in the regulated market (Baron and Myerson, 1982; Laffont and Tirole, 1986).

Much has been written about the relationship between principal and agent. This was done in the first place for principals and agents who have a contractual relationship with each other, for example the selling homeowner as a principal and his estate agent as an agent, or the shareholder of an enterprise (principal) and the management of that enterprise (agent). Contracts between vendor and estate agent or between shareholders and management are typical agency relationships. An agency relationship is 'a contract under which one or more persons – the principal(s) – engage another person – the agent – to perform some service on their behalf that involves delegating some decision-making authority to the agent' (Jensen, 2003, p. 86). In a later phase, the scope of the principal–agent doctrine was extended to any relationship between actors in which the one actor wishes to influence the behaviour of the other actor and in which the steering actor needs information before he intervenes and wants information about the effects of his interventions. Many applications of the principal–agent model concern situations in which no decision-making power has been delegated (Jensen, 2003, p. 86). What matters is that 'the agent has some opportunity for discretionary behavior' (Neelen, 1994, p. 67).

To create a clear insight into the dynamic in the relation between principal and agent, two characteristics of the relationship between principal and agent should be pointed out (Groenewegen, 2004, p. 516). In the first place, it should be assumed that there is a conflict of interest between principal and agent. The principal wants the agent to behave in accordance with the principal's wishes and interests, whereas the agent will mainly regard their own interest as the guiding principle for their behaviour. Of course, it is in the agent's interest to comply with the principal's wishes to a certain extent.

In the second place, there is information asymmetry between principal and agent. The principal has more information than the agent has about, for example, future policy, priorities in the implementation and enforcement of current policy, and political preferences. The agent has more information than the principal has about the market, the characteristics of the technology used in a particular industry, the cost structure, and returns. By and large, the situation between principal and agent can be characterized as follows: although the principal is able to set the course and tell the agent what to do, the agent has the relevant information that is needed to plot the course and evaluate whether things are moving in the right direction. This information advantage enables the agent to use the discretionary room he has to realize his own interest, even if this harms the principal's interest. Williamson points to the room this offers for opportunistic behaviour by the agent (Williamson, 1989, p. 139). These possibilities exist because the principal lacks sufficient information to monitor every action of the agent.

3.3.2 Valuation of Information Asymmetry

The fact that an agent fails to act in accordance with a principal's interests is a problem in itself. At the collective level, it is also problematic if the agent, or the monopolist or the oligopolist, fails to act in accordance with the views of the actor representing the public interest, that is, the regulator. These societal disadvantages have been specified in types of costs (Jensen and Meckling, 1976, p. 308):

- Residual costs: 'the money equivalent of the reduction in welfare experienced by the principal due to the divergence between the agent's decisions and those decisions which would maximize the welfare of the principal' (Neelen, 1994, p. 67). This is also called shirking (Alchian and Demsetz, 1972).
- Monitoring costs: 'all expenditures the principal makes to limit those activities of the agent that diverge from the principal's interest. Monitoring refers not only to the measuring or observing of the behavior of the agent but it also includes all efforts of the principal to "control" the behavior of the agent through budget restrictions, compensation policies, operating rules', etc (Neelen, 1994, p. 72).
- Bonding costs: 'Bonding costs are all expenditures the agent makes to guarantee that he will not take certain actions which would harm the principal or to ensure that the principal will be compensated if he does take such actions' (Jensen and Meckling, 1976).

The monitoring and bonding costs together are the enforcement costs (Neelen, 1994, p. 73). The more funds are released for enforcement costs, the lower the residual costs will be. Savings on enforcement costs will usually cause a rise in residual costs. Costs will always be incurred and the highest feasible result is an optimal trade-off between enforcement costs and residual losses. This trade-off will always entail costs. In this sense, information asymmetry should be valued negatively.

Nevertheless, discretionary room and information asymmetry also have their positive aspects. Discretionary room for the agent and an information advantage for the agent counterbalance the stronger formal position of the principal. This creates a system of checks and balances between principal and agent, which will result in balanced decision making that takes account of the interests of both the principal and the agent.

A second qualification is that although the discretionary room and the large amount of information the agent has will in the first place be used in his own interest, there will also be moments when the agent avails himself of his opportunities to serve the principal's interests. This benefits both parties.

3.3.3 Strategic Behaviour Based on Information Asymmetry

Generally speaking, information asymmetry favours the agent (Hurwicz and Reiter, 2006, p. 16). In addition, in many cases the agent will be able to make the difference in information even bigger than it already is by itself. Examples would be *strategic nondisclosure, disguise,* or *distortion of information* (Williamson, 1989, p. 144). The room that the agent thus creates for himself becomes manifest in two kinds of strategic behaviour: *adverse selection* and *moral hazard.*

Adverse selection occurs during the preparation of a decision, a contract, a scheme or an arrangement. The principal or contract partner contemplates the design of an arrangement and negotiates about it with the agent. The agent has an information advantage and will keep part of it to himself (hidden information) to influence the design of the arrangement in his own favour, even if this prejudices the principal's interest. This is how an arrangement comes into being that neither maximally serves the principal's interest nor generates the optimal trade-off between the interests of principal and agent. What this may result in appears from Akerlof's famous *'lemons story'* (Akerlof, 1970).

Not all cars of a particular make and a particular year are equally good. A few cars in every year of a particular make tend to be less of a success. They show more or less serious flaws. These are lemons. Lemons cannot always be recognized at first sight, not even after a first test drive. Buyers of such a lemon will be disappointed about their purchase and be inclined to offer their car for sale soon. They will probably not do so through official, expert dealers, because these may unmask their car as a lemon, but through the informal market (for example through an advertisement). Buyers of good cars, however, will keep the cars they have bought longer and not offer them for sale. The inevitable consequence is that on the informal market more and more lemons will be offered for sale and fewer and fewer good cars. Potential buyers know this and, to be on the safe side, when making offers for cars they assume they will come across a bad car. They will therefore offer low prices. Of course, sellers of good cars will think the prices offered unacceptable. They will withdraw their car from this market and try to sell it through a different channel. As a result, the average quality will fall even more and the prices offered will collapse further, after which even more people offering relatively good cars will turn their backs on this market. The result is a market in which only cars of low quality are offered, with potential buyers that are not prepared to pay much for a car.

Moral hazard is the behaviour of the agent after the adoption and the coming into effect of the arrangement. In his behaviour, the agent manages to evade the arrangement, at any rate in part, which, generally speaking, will harm the principal's interest. He will succeed in hiding some of his actions from the principal (*hidden actions* (Neelen, 1994, p. 67)). Moral hazard is a well-known phenomenon in the world of performance measurement. The actor (agent) to whom the performance agreements apply will make sure he scores a flattering, good assessment by means of *hidden actions*, even though this performance is less satisfactory on closer inspection.

3.4 RELATION BETWEEN FEWNESS, POSITION AND INFORMATION ASYMMETRY

In this chapter, we have indicated that there are three types of breeding grounds on which strategic behaviour is likely to develop. Table 3.1 again presents these breeding grounds with the corresponding strategic behaviour.

Fewness, position and information asymmetry are related and reinforce each other. The relation proceeds along several lines, for example:

- A strong position in itself is not so valuable. A good position is a first step towards capitalizing on the profit. For example, a good position in a market automatically attracts information with which

Table 3.1   Breeding grounds for strategic behaviour

Breeding ground	Strategic behaviour
Fewness	Monopolistic behaviour/inefficiency Collusion
Position	Predatory behaviour Underdog/cherry picking
Information-asymmetry	Adverse selection Moral hazard

a company can concretely serve its interest. In addition, a good position can help a company create the conditions to benefit from a context of *fewness*.

- An information advantage helps a company defend its position. Because of its information advantage, the company will be well equipped to forecast attacks on its position, anticipate them and parry them. *Predatory behaviour* is usually based on information asymmetry (Ordover and Saloner, 1989, p. 562).
- If a company holds a strong position, operates in an oligopolistic market and has an information advantage, it has substantial market power. Basically, power is the ability to do something or not. This market power enables the company to serve its interest and to do so even in an unfair, blameworthy way. In that case, market power is abused.

3.5   VALUATION

Terms like 'market power' and particularly 'abuse of market power' have a pejorative connotation. In general, the above-mentioned breeding grounds for strategic behaviour in itself are also seen as problematic. However, this qualification requires some comment.

The introduction and intensification of competition presupposes that companies get tough on each other. They try to be innovative and represent the competitor's products as obsolete, to be cheaper than the competitor, to be better than the competitor and represent his products as inferior. For a company to be successful and survive in this context, it will have to operate cleverly, resolutely, effectively and efficiently. The assumption is that these corporate characteristics not only benefit the company, but eventually also benefit consumers and society as a whole. However, the same characteristics of companies that would be stimulated by the introduction of competition and privatization are the drivers of the strategic behaviour described above. It is doubtful to what extent it is possible to separate the desired effects (i.e. raising allocative and dynamic efficiencies) of the institutional changes from the undesired changes (strategic behaviour). At any rate, the undesired changes may, to a certain extent, be inevitable side-effects of the changes launched. The same forces that raise prosperity in part also cause strategic behaviour.

Companies that join the competition struggle aim to reinforce their own position, even when it harms other companies. They want to grow, even at the expense of their competitors. The ultimate aim is to drive the competitor out of the market. In this sense, a monopoly, once obtained, is the ultimate proof of competition. However, a monopoly obviously means the end of competition, which is undesirable. The solution then is, of course, not to allow monopolies and oligopolies, or at any rate to make sure that the barriers of entry in the event of a monopoly are limited, always leaving a threat to a monopolist that entrants for its market will appear. However, this removes the incentive for competition, because the ultimate reward, that is the monopoly, is no longer available.

Beating competitors and gaining an information advantage are the result of enterpreneurialism and clever business operations. In the competition discourse, it is appropriate that this behaviour should be rewarded. Not permitting reward, in other words prohibiting information advantage and/or not tolerating the limitation of the number of competitors deprives the market of exactly those incentives that are felt to be so necessary to reap the fruits of markets.

In some cases, a distinction can be made between entrepreneurial forms of strategic behaviour and rent-seeking forms of it. In the first case, the objective is to gain a comparative advantage over others by means of clever behaviour in a developing market or during the evolution of a new technology. In such cases, society benefits from it, because hard work and innovative impulses create something new that may bring vast societal benefits. There is no such innovation in rent-seeking versions of strategic behaviour. Here, the market has already grown up and no new product or process technologies are developed. The advantage of strategic behaviour with such a background is difficult to prove, or cannot be proved at all, to outsiders.

NOTES

1. In game theory, the Nash equilibrium is a solution concept of a game involving two or more players, in which each player is assumed to know the equilibrium strategies of the other players, and no player has anything to gain by changing only his own strategy (i.e. by changing unilaterally).
2. Given a set of alternative allocations of goods or income for a set of individuals, a movement from one allocation to another that can make at least one individual better off without making any other individual worse off is called a Pareto improvement. An allocation is Pareto-optimal when no further Pareto improvements can be made.

REFERENCES

Akerlof, G.A. (1970), 'The market for "lemons": quality, uncertainty and the market mechanism', *Quarterly Journal of Economics*, **84**(3), 488–500.

Alchian, A.A. and H. Demsetz (1972), 'Production, information costs and economic organization', *American Economic Review*, **62**(5), 777–95.

Baron, D.P. and R.B. Myerson (1982), 'Regulating a monopolist with unknown costs', *Econometrica*, **50**(4), 911–30.

Baumgartner, F.R. and B.D. Jones (eds) (2002), *Policy Dynamics*, Chicago, IL/London: University of Chicago Press.

Bendor, J. and T.M. Moe (1985), 'An adaptive model of bureaucratic politics', *The American Political Science Review*, **79**(3), 755–74.

Bos, D.I. (1995), *Marktwerking en Regulering* (in Dutch) (*Competition and Regulation*), The Hague: Ministry of Economic Affairs.

Dixit, A. (1980), 'The role of investment in entry deterrence', *The Economic Journal*, **90**(357), 95–106.

Emmons, W. (2000), *The Evolving Bargain. Strategic Implications of Deregulation and Privatization*, Boston, MA: Harvard Business School Press.

Fellner, W. (1949), *Competition among the Few. Oligopoly and Similar Market Structures*, New York: Albert A. Knopf.

Fudenberg, D. (1983), 'Capital as a commitment: strategic investment to deter mobility', *Journal of Economic Theory*, **31**(2), 227–50.

Fudenberg, D. and J. Tirole (1984), 'The fat-cat effect, the puppy-dog ploy, and the lean and hungry look', *American Economic Review*, **74**(2), 361–8.

Fudenberg, D. and J. Tirole (1989), 'Noncooperative game theory for industrial organization: an introduction and overview', in R. Schmalensee and R.D. Willig (eds), *Handbook of Industrial Organization*, Vol. 1, Amsterdam: Elsevier Science Publishers, pp. 261–305.

Gilbert, R.J. (1989), 'Mobility barriers and the value of incumbency', in R. Schmalensee and R.D. Willig (eds), *Handbook of Industrial Organization*, Amsterdam: Elsevier Science Publishers, pp. 476–535.

Graham, S. and S. Marvin (1994), 'Cherry picking and social dumping. Utilities in the 1990s', *Utilities Policy*, **4**(2), 113–19.

Groenewegen, J.P.M. (2004), 'Inzichten uit de institutionele economie (in Dutch) (Insights from institutional economics)', *Management Accounting*, **78**(11), 515–23.

Groenewegen, J.P.M. (2005), *Designing Markets in Infrastructures*, Delft: Delft University of Technology.

Hurwicz, L. and S. Reiter (2006), *Designing Economic Mechanisms*, New York: Cambridge University Press.

Jacquemin, A. and M.E. Slade (1989), 'Cartels, collusion and horizontal mergers', in R. Schmalensee and R.D. Willig (eds), *Handbook of Industrial Organization*, Vol. 1, Amsterdam: Elsevier Science Publishers, pp. 415–75.

Jensen, M.C. (2003), *A Theory of the Firm. Governance, Residual Claims and Organizational Forms*, Cambridge, MA: Harvard University Press.

Jensen, M.C. and W.H. Meckling (1976), 'Theory of the firm: managerial behavior, agency costs, and ownership structure', *Journal of Financial Economics*, **3**(4), 305–60.

Laffont, J.J. and J. Tirole (1986), 'Using cost information to regulate firms', *Journal of Political Economy*, **94**(3), 614–41.

Leibenstein, H. (1966), 'Allocative efficiency versus X-inefficiency', *American Economic Review*, **56**(3), 392–415.

Liefmann, R. (1915), 'Monopoly or competition as the basis of a government trust policy', *The Quarterly Journal of Economics*, **29**(2), 308–25.

Neelen, C.H.J.M. (1994), *Principal–agent Relations in Non-profit Organizations*, Enschede: Faculty of Public Administration and Public Policy, University of Twente.

Neumann, M. (2001), *Competition Policy*, Cheltenham, UK and Northampton, MA, USA: Edward Elgar.

Ordover, J.A. and G. Saloner (1989), 'Predation, monopolization, and antitrust', in R. Schmalensee and R.D. Willig (eds), *Handbook of Industrial Organization*, Vol. 1, Amsterdam: Elsevier Science Publishers, pp. 538–96.

Shapiro, C. (1989), 'Theories of oligopoly behavior', in R. Schmalensee and R.D. Willig (eds), *Handbook of Industrial Organization*, Amsterdam: Elsevier Science Publishers, pp. 330–414.

Sidak, J.G. and D.F. Spulber (1998), *Deregulatory Takings and the Regulatory Contract. The Competitive Transformation of Network Industries in the United States*, Cambridge: Cambridge University Press.

Spence, M. (1977), 'Entry, investment and oligopolistic pricing', *Bell Journal of Economics*, **8**(2), 534–44.

Teulings, C., L. Bovenberg and H. van Dalen (2005), *De Cirkel van Goede Intenties. De Economie van het Publiek Belang* (in Dutch) (*The Circle of Good Intentions. The Economy of the Public Interest*), Amsterdam: Amsterdam University Press.

Webb, S.B. (1980), 'Tariffs, cartels, technology and growth in the German steel industry, 1878 to 1914', *The Journal of Economic History*, **40**(2), pp. 309–30.

Williamson, O.E. (1989), 'Transaction cost economics', in R. Schmalensee and R.D. Willig (eds), *Handbook of Industrial Organization*, Amsterdam: Elsevier Science Publishers, pp. 136–78.

4. Recent trends in infrastructure-based sectors

After the generic reflections in the preceding chapters about strategic behaviour in general, we will zoom in on the network-based industries in this chapter. We will do so by first setting out the characteristic features of network-based industries. We will focus on the features that present an opportunity for, or give rise to, strategic behaviour. We will then describe the change processes that manifest themselves in these sectors, again in so far as they are related to strategic behaviour.

4.1 CHARACTERISTICS OF NETWORK-BASED INDUSTRIES

Network-based industries are not ordinary industries. They are special. The core of this special status lies in the great and often irreplaceable importance of utility services for the well-being of citizens and for the functioning of the economy and in the fact that an infrastructure or network forms part of the production chain. In more detail, the following characteristics are typical of network-based industries:

- Many utility services facilitate other economic activities. Many of them are even necessary for conducting other economic activities. A reliable energy supply is indispensable for industrial activities; a good transport infrastructure is a necessary condition for trading activities. In other words, network-based industries have positive external effects on the economy as a whole. Strategic behaviour that would endanger the functioning of these industries poses a threat to the economy as a whole.
- Utility services are essential for running a comfortable and hygienically responsible household. Clean drinking water, telephony, television and a sewer connection form part of the standard equipment of homes. The quality of these facilities should always be safeguarded at the same, very high level. Citizens are therefore sensitive to the suboptimal functioning of these industries.

- The importance of the utility service requires universal coverage. In a geographically defined service area, the service should be universally available to a uniform technical standard with sufficient quality for the consumers. Different prices can sometimes be charged to different consumer groups, leading to divergent profitability levels for these various groups. Commercially thinking providers might thus be tempted to reconsider the supply of unprofitable services.
- The great importance of the utility service for consumers and the consequent desirability for everybody to actually buy the service make it necessary for the service to be affordable for all consumers. For a number of utility services, passing on the full costs would lead to such high tariffs that the sales of the facility would remain below critical levels. This is a reason to support the facility financially from public funds, which makes it possible to charge consumers a lower tariff and brings the facility within the budget of more people (this is called *marit good* nature of the utility service). For example, many public-transport services are subsidized. Passing on the full costs of building and operating the rail infrastructure would make fares so expensive that few people would use public transport. This is societally undesirable. The merit-good nature of many utility services also causes many of them to have a universal tariff, irrespective of the actual costs incurred to deliver the service to an address. The mail is an example of this. Irrespective of the distance between the addressee and the sender of the letter, the mail company charges one rate. A rate system in which rates, cost prices and value for consumers are not identical offers room and opportunities for strategic behaviour.
- Because of the great importance of the service, the government imposes demanding requirements on the quality of the service and its continuity. An example of this is the quality of drinking water. A strategically operating provider can exploit this, too. In many cases, the output of utility services demands infrastructural facilities, the building of which entails high costs. Besides, many of the investments are *sunk costs*: they are very specific and cannot be used for purposes other than the output of the utility service (Guthrie, 2006). The costs tend to be so high and so specific that the building of more infrastructural networks is considered societally irresponsible. The electricity network is an example of this. Building several parallel transport networks or distribution networks is far too expensive. The high building costs combined with the sunk nature of the investment also present an opportunity for strategic behaviour. On the one hand, having made his investment, the investor in infrastructure is vulnerable to the behaviour of service providers

(business opportunism) and regulators (regulatory opportunism). Once the investment has been made, they can put pressure on the infrastructure operator by telling him that they are only willing to pay low tariffs for the use of the infrastructure. This behaviour is highly likely to succeed because the investor/operator has no alternative application possibilities for operating the infrastructure. On the other hand, the infrastructure operator is a monopolist with the attendant possibilities for exploiting this comfortable position.

- An additional reason to settle for only one network is that utility companies have considerable economies of scale and scope. In other words, the marginal costs of an extra service over the network or an extra connection to the network are very low. The marginal proceeds easily exceed the marginal costs. To put it more strongly, the new service and new connection increase the value of the other connections and other services. The higher the number of connections on the network, the higher the value of each telephone connection. This so-called Matthew effect ('winner takes all') (network effects) makes infrastructure operators aggressive in their acquisition behaviour (Varian and Shapiro, 1998).

The conclusion is that network-based industries have a number of special characteristics that cause or present an opportunity for strategic behaviour.

4.2 CHANGE PROCESSES IN INFRASTRUCTURE-BASED SECTORS

In network-based industries, a number of drastic change processes are manifesting themselves, such as convergence, liberalization, hiving-off/privatization and re-regulation.[1] The change processes are strongly related and often, but not always, occur simultaneously. We will briefly discuss these processes below and focus on the opportunity they create for strategic behaviour.

4.2.1 Convergence and Divergence

In the telecom sector, convergence is a dominant trend. In the transport sector, a cautious shift towards divergence is visible.

Convergence is technical in the first place. Infrastructures that used to be *dedicated* to a product or service are finding more applications, and mono-functional infrastructures are becoming multifunctional. The once different infrastructures are going to resemble each other increasingly from a functional perspective. The electricity cable and the television cable can also be used for telephony or the Internet. The manifestations of technical convergence differ. We speak of convergence when the same technical infrastructure can also generate other products or services, but even when a second infrastructure is built in or beside existing infrastructures. An example of the latter form of convergence is the building of a fibre-optic cable through a sewer or through the gas or water mains. Expectations are that technical developments will promote further convergence.

In addition, organizational convergence has taken place in recent years, some of which was due to this technical convergence. Companies that used to offer only one product or service are seeing commercial opportunities for offering several products or services. In recent years, this has led to the rise of the '*multi-utilities*'.

Another change is that companies always want to sell a customer more than one service at once. In *triple play*, a company sells the customer telephony, the Internet and TV in one transaction.

Divergence occurs in other sectors, although less than convergence in telecoms. On roads, types of traffic can be separated and the various types of transport can be given their own *dedicated lanes*. This leads to separate bicycle tracks, separate bus lanes and separate lanes for trucks. Some divergence is found in rail transport. There are more and more dedicated tracks for freight transport and for high-speed trains. These trains have an infrastructure that differs from that of ordinary trains.

Convergence causes the bundling of once separate markets. For example, until recently telephony and television were fully separate markets. The companies that were active in these two markets had nothing to do with each other. They had different owners and did not compete with each other. The two sectors each had their own regulations. The two sectors also had their own specialized infrastructure. Convergence has bundled these sectors. The once dedicated infrastructures can now be used for both services. TV images can be transported over the telephone line and voice can be transported over the TV cable. The consequence of this convergence is that the cable companies offer telephone services and the telecom companies try to sell television images. As a result, once monopolistic markets are opening up to competitors.

A side effect is uncertainty about the scope of rules. Do the rules that used to apply to TV and the TV cable also apply to telecoms now? Do the telecom rules apply to the TV sector? And what is the scope of the regulator's powers? Is the telecom regulator now also responsible for what happens on the market for TV images or is it not?

Convergence brings together formerly separate markets, giving rise to numerous uncertainties. Companies that until recently were 'locked up' in a sector suddenly see opportunities to spread their wings and conquer new markets. The vagueness of the rules in force will soon lead to a debate on whether this market conquest is good and is taking place fairly. In other words, to what extent is there strategic behaviour?

4.2.2   Liberalization

A second group of change processes comprises the changes that are mainly legal and economic. In this connection, liberalization, hiving-off and deregulation are often mentioned in one breath. However, a sharp distinction should be made between these three processes.

Liberalization focuses on opening up the market to new entrants, who can then compete for the favours of the consumer (Ehrhart and Burdon, 1999). Where only one organization used to be active, several organizations operate after liberalization. The competition arising between the providers should eventually result in more efficiency, a stronger customer-orientation and lower prices.

Until recently, these sectors were organized as monopolies. One company owned all the links of the production chain. Therefore, there was a vertically integrated monopolist. The fact that particular technical facilities have the nature of a natural monopoly,[2] in many cases the infrastructure, justified the monopolistic nature of these links, because it would be far too expensive to duplicate these infrastructures. A second requirement was 'technical integrity'. This requirement implied that all the links of the production chain had to be united in one hand for technical reasons. The combination of the natural monopoly with the vertical integration caused a monopolist to own all the links of the production chain.

In the second half of the twentieth century, many economists observed that the productivity and the innovation of these sectors lagged behind that of other industries. They attributed this to the absence of competition. They also argued that it was no longer necessary to order these sectors in a way that differed from other sectors institutionally. The remedy they suggested was the introduction of competition in these sectors. They thus broke the tradition prescribing that these sectors should be ordered as vertically integrated monopolies. Three main reasons are often given as to why competition could be introduced in these sectors.

The first is the unbundling of the links in the production chain. It proved to be quite possible to have the various links of the production chain operated by different companies (Kessides, 2004). Contrary to what many had expected, unbundling the links did not prejudice the quality of the service provided. A separation made in many sectors in many countries is that between the infrastructure and the service. As a result, a company other than the one operating the services over the infrastructure began to operate the infrastructure. On the level of service provision, competition proved easy to organize. Nevertheless, this did not yet affect the monopoly on the level of the infrastructure.

The second reason is convergence (see above), which has brought competition, also on the level of infrastructures, particularly in the telecom sector.

The third reason is the introduction of the concept of the *contestable market* (Baumol et al. 1982). This involves competition *for* the infrastructure. When there is competition *for* the infrastructure, a network owner periodically organizes a process in which a number of parties bid for the exclusive right to operate the infrastructure for a certain period. The idea is that, although the winner of this process is the monopolist for this period, their competitors are breathing down their neck, ready to take over this exclusive right in the next round. This keeps the winner on the alert, ensuring a better performance than in a permanent monopoly.

These changes provide ample opportunity for strategic behaviour. They posed a threat to a number of parties, particularly the incumbents, who looked set to lose their comfortable position. Even more parties might have felt threatened by these changes, such as those involved in the 'public interests' looked after by these companies. They might think that in a situation of competition the competing companies would no longer look after these interests adequately. Parties that feel threatened by such changes might easily be tempted to delay the changes or deflect them in a less radical direction.

These changes might tempt not only vested parties to behave strategically. Also companies that see opportunities for themselves can regard these changes as a reason to enter the arena and join 'the fight'. These entrants and potential entrants, too, may therefore be expected to show strategic behaviour.

4.2.3 Hiving-off/Privatization

Hiving-off involves widening the distance between government and 'the utility company' and has several degrees. The lightest variants imply internal hiving-off. The utility companies are given some operational freedom. They can also be hived off externally. The former government agencies are given a private legal format, the shares of which are owned by public bodies (that is a government-owned private limited company or a government-owned public limited company). Recent decades have seen a marked shift from utility companies as government agencies to government companies.

One step further is privatization: the sale of the utility companies to private enterprises, in many cases foreign enterprises. Freeing up the market, in combination with the breakthrough of new technologies, forces the utility companies to make substantial investments. Currently, governments are not easily inclined to bear the related risks. It is generally expected that this is different for private enterprises that see plenty of new market opportunities here.

Hiving-off, particularly privatization, can be seen as a catalyst for strategic behaviour. We should by no means assume that state-owned firms would not behave strategically and that private parties would. That would be an inadmissible simplification, contrary to reality, which shows that state-owned firms also behave strategically. However, the advantages gained by a public company with its strategic behaviour have diffuse effects. They eventually benefit the public shareholder and thus the public funds. This is different as regards private parties. Rather than having diffuse effects, the advantages are concentrated with the private shareholder, who will therefore feel a strong incentive to display this behaviour. This catalysing effect of private ownership on strategic behaviour is more or less compensated for. Since the advantages of strategic behaviour of public companies eventually benefit public funds, this behaviour will be accepted and legitimated sooner than similar behaviour of private parties. These private parties will not be granted this latitude. They will face strict rules and/or a strict regulator, which decreases the possibilities for strategic behaviour. On the one hand, privatization catalyses strategic behaviour. On the other hand, it creates the arrangements that counter this behaviour.

4.2.4   Re-regulation

A free market and hived-off companies are easily associated with deregulation. This association occurs because liberalization and hiving-off on the one hand, and deregulation on the other hand have a common denominator: less government. Deregulation aims at reducing statutory constraints that the government imposes on infrastructure-based sectors.

The idea behind deregulation is that companies are given more room to actually take the wishes of the market into account. The question is, however, whether hiving-off, liberalization and deregulation are such a logical trio. Liberalization and hiving-off tend to require more regulation. A large number of new rules prove to be necessary to actually get competition off the ground. In addition, hiving-off is accompanied by new rules, if only because it is not self-evident that the privatized utility company is willing to define its utility function. In short, liberalization and privatization are, on second thoughts, not a logical combination with deregulation at all. This has already been observed in the literature, and the phenomenon has been referred to as the re-regulation paradox (Bergman et al., 1998). Thinking in terms of re-regulation rather than deregulation is more fruitful (Vogel, 1996; Hulsink and Wubben, 2003).

This paradoxical nature of re-regulation offers possibilities for strategic behaviour. Many parties are uncertain about the desirability of regulations and about the nature and intensity of the desired regulations. This offers scope for parties to influence the introduction of rules, because parties that realize that their interest is at issue in the institutional changes will try to serve their interest by influencing the rule, particularly its content and timing. All this might lead to a delay of regulations and possibly suboptimal regulations.

4.3 A PARADIGM SHIFT

Remarkably, the processes of convergence, liberalization, hiving-off and re-regulation are developing in many infrastructure-based sectors at the same time. This justifies the proposition that the changes are systematic and related. The above-mentioned changes concern almost all activities in the production chain: the relation with the consumers, the way of funding, ownership, the perspective of the technology and the relation with governments. All in all, this is reason enough to speak of a *regime change* or, to put it more strongly, a paradigm change (Hunt and Shuttleworth, 1996; Kwoka, 1996; Bauer, 1998). Below, we will describe the classic paradigm and the modern paradigm. Both paradigms combine the variables described above (see Figure 4.1).

4.3.1 Classic Paradigm

Characteristic of the classic paradigm is the full integration of activities in the production chain. This integration is justified by the fact that particular technical facilities have the character of a natural monopoly. Infrastructures are marked, among other features, by sustainability, technical integrity, indivisibility (or their network character), high investment risks, advantages of scale and the absence of regular market incentives. This is why it is economically unacceptable to duplicate this infrastructure. This justifies a monopoly, one that covers the entire production chain.

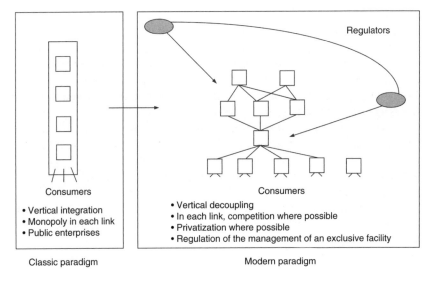

Source: Parker and Saal, 2005.

Figure 4.1   The classic paradigm and the modern paradigm

The US has opted for regulated private monopolies. Europe has opted for public monopolies.

4.3.2   Modern Paradigm

According to the modern paradigm, the thinking in monopolies should be opposed and room should be found for competition. As we set out above, the idea is that some of the traditional characteristics of infrastructures do not apply, or apply far less, in the present era. Besides, the idea of competition *for* the infrastructure was introduced.

In addition, the modern paradigm explores the possibilities for organizing competition *on* the infrastructure. Although the infrastructure itself cannot be duplicated, there are possibilities of having companies that need the infrastructure for their services compete with each other. The heart of the matter is that more service operators use the infrastructure at the same time and side by side and compete with each other for the favour of the consumer.

The key feature of the modern paradigm is the unbundling of activities and roles in the production chain and the introduction of competition where possible: natural monopolies should be unbundled of activities that can be offered in competition, and conflicting roles, such as that of owner and that of regulator, should not end up in the same organization. According to the modern paradigm, the facilities should be privately owned where possible.

Unbundling, competition and private effort should eventually guarantee in particular an improvement in efficiency and transparency in infrastructure-based sectors (Joskow, 1998; Crew and Kleindorfer, 1999). Where there is an exclusive position in the production chain, adequate regulation should prevent abuse of this position.

The recent changes in the sectors are considerable for all the organizations involved. The companies that used to operate as vertically integrated, monopolistic public companies in the old paradigm, more or less decoupled from their consumers and suppliers, now have to compete with newcomers on the market. Other companies see an opportunity to extend the *scale* and/or *scope* of their activities and enter the formerly closed market. Governments also see their position in the arena changed. The role of the parent ministry is changing. In many cases, the legislator calls a regulator into being that operates at a relatively great distance from the parent ministry.

The ministry is starting to look for a new role. The role of politicians is also changing. At first sight, the dominant movement points towards greater aloofness on the part of the politicians, but it repeatedly appears that the politicians still wish to intervene when major problems arise in the newly formed markets.

4.4 EFFECTS OF INSTITUTIONAL CHANGES

- *Efficiency*. The institutional changes were launched to improve the performance of the sectors. Economists generally define 'improved performance' as higher efficiency. Two kinds of efficiency are important, that is static and dynamic ones (Motta, 2004). Allocative efficiency means that price and quantity produced are such that they reflect the wishes of consumers. How has this worked out in practice? However difficult it may have been, a great deal of empirical research has been conducted in recent years that tries to answer this question. These studies have, in turn, been summarized in a number of general studies.[3] Although the empirical studies differ strongly from each other (different economic sectors, variety of countries/continents, different periods, divergent methodologies), a number of conclusions are possible. The dominant picture is that in a large number of cases, but not always, privatization and liberalization have led to better-performing companies. In particular the introduction of competition has positive effects, but privatization, either in combination with the introduction of competition or otherwise, generally also has positive effects. The next question is: who benefits from this higher efficiency? Do these benefits manifest themselves in lower prices for consumers, in pay rises for employees, in more investments, in pay rises for management or in a higher value of the shares of the enterprise? Although sloppily launched change processes lead to a higher efficiency, they may result in disappointments, for example because management and the stock-exchange value of the enterprise benefit one-sidedly from the efficiency drive. This explains why some privatization operations are regarded as failures, despite a rise in allocative efficiency.

- *Dynamic efficiency.* Allocative efficiency is a static concept. What also matters in the daily course of business is dynamics, that is technological development. Technological development can realize great advances in quality improvement. The effect of the institutional changes on dynamic efficiency is not unambiguous. On the one hand, competition and privatization also stimulate dynamic efficiency. The reason is that it may enable a company to build up a major advantage over its competitors, which is attractive, of course. On the other hand, it is doubtful whether a company that is involved in a fierce competition battle will be given the time and room to work on substantial technological innovations requiring large investments and a long return time. Probably, subtle combinations of competition and monopoly are optimal. On the one hand, such a situation creates scope for investment, but the enterprise on the other hand feels the incentive to take action (Scherer and Ross, 1990).

- *Public values.* Efficiency is not the only criterion for the functioning of network-based industries. Network-based industries constitute a special category of companies, for example because public values are at issue in their operations. One judgment merely by efficiency would be too one-sided for these companies.

Hardly any overarching studies have been conducted into the consequences of the institutional changes for performance with regard to public values. One of the public values that plays a part in all sectors is the reliability of supply of the service. De Bruijne concludes in a survey that the relation between these institutional changes and performance as regards reliability is not unambiguous (De Bruijne, 2006). The hypothesis obvious to many is that the institutional changes are likely to decrease reliability. In general terms, this hypothesis has not yet come true.

The conclusion is that, in terms of outcomes, the effects of the institutional changes are ambiguous both as regards efficiency and as regards public values. This is hardly surprising, given the multitude of variables that are at issue in these institutional changes. Convergence, liberalization, privatization and re-regulation together encompass the room for change, which means that the number of potential changes is very large and that no institutional change is identical to any other. Besides, these changes are launched in starting situations that tend to differ. Sectors happen to differ and countries are also structured in different ways. In short, every starting situation is different, every change is unique and the combination of starting situation and change makes a situation even more unique. Unsurprisingly, the outcomes differ.

To avoid problems in establishing the outcomes, in this book we choose another way to establish the consequences of institutional changes. We examine what strategic behaviour is to be expected after, and as a consequence of, the changes launched. We will *not* evaluate the consequences of strategic behaviour for the outcomes in terms of efficiency, the allocation of potential benefits of higher productive efficiency and performance as to public values.

4.5 ENTRIES FOR STRATEGIC BEHAVIOUR IN NETWORK-BASED INDUSTRIES

In Chapter 3 a number of sources conducive to strategic behaviour were presented. As we have seen above, the network-based industries have undergone a paradigm shift providing players in the emerging oligopolistic markets with more specific types of opportunities for operating strategically. We have decided to call these opportunities in the network-based industries 'entries'. These entries can help us to identify the entrance doors actors have at their disposal for deploying strategic behaviour. Below the following entries will be presented:

1. strategic use of rules: legal rules and contracts;
2. strategic utilization of intertwined relations with government agencies and other actors;
3. strategic use of control over so-called 'bottleneck facilities' and other crucial technical facilities and standards;
4. strategic use of the essential and indispensable nature of infrastructure utilities;
5. strategic use of the factor 'time' through delays and accelerations in decision and production processes;

6. strategic use of financial resources to buy off rivals, thus restricting competition.

These six entries for strategic behaviour will now be discussed one by one.

4.5.1   Strategic Use of Rules: Legal Rules and Contracts

More often than not the meaning of language is ambiguous, because linguistic phrases have been consciously or unconsciously formulated to allow for various interpretations. In case of conflict or disagreement players tend to refer to formal legal documents, such as public regulations, informal organizational rules and standards and contracts. On many occasions the chosen wordings make it possible for actors to adopt a take on their meaning which benefits them most, even when the intention behind the original formulations clearly was a different one. This selective, warped and self-interested interpretation of language in important documents can be done both proactively in order to strengthen one's own position or weaken that of one's opponent, and in self-defence against complaints of abuse of one's power position.

4.5.2   Strategic Utilization of Intertwined Relations with Government Agencies and other Actors

In many cases hiving off capacity management of infrastructure and the services around it does not immediately lead to a situation where the organizational and personal networks of regulators and incumbents or infrastructure managers and service providers are completely separated. Rather the opposite, it remains functionally and politically quite advantageous for old monopolists to foster these connections and make tactical use of them. During the transition some specialists have come to work for the one side, while others have found employment on the other side. Who would give up such excellent and valuable possibilities to effectively lobby for one's own interests? In this way, old friends in other organizations can still be instrumental in serving in one's own interests, while new players do not have such good access to these organizations, since they do not know the relevant people equally well. Applying this 'intertwinement benefit' naturally involves 'quid pro quo' relations in the long run, which implies that the favours are to be returned at some future point. On the other hand, it is also true that maintaining such relationships make players vulnerable to accusations of unfair competition or even abuse of power from rivals or the outside world.

4.5.3 Strategic Use of Control over so-called 'Bottleneck Facilities' and other Crucial Technical Facilities and Standards

Since many network-based facilities are costly to construct and simply unaffordable for newcomers to the market, single infrastructure connections and networks are used by several suppliers at the same time. And yet, one player, usually the former monopolist, is in charge of the technical facilities. Having control over those bottleneck facilities has an enormous impact on access to and use of them, because special technical equipment is needed to provide the services. Newcomers, however, have neither the knowledge nor the financial resources to buy or develop this by themselves. By blocking or complicating access to these facilities by means of intricate devices or tricks or influencing their quality negatively, the attractiveness of providing services can be substantially reduced for competitors. And it is often not obvious for rivals or outsiders what the reasons for these complications are, thus making it very hard to provide evidence of power abuse or illegal actions.

4.5.4 Strategic Use of the Essential and Indispensable Nature of Infrastructure Utilities

As said before, the social and economic dependence on network-based infrastructures is enormous. This gives players that own or control these facilities an influential means to put pressure on regulators. If the regulator threatens to make institutional, price-related or operational interventions harming the interests of the incumbent, only the latter has the relevant knowledge and information to decrease infrastructure performance artificially and influence the position of the regulator. To justify this fall in service quality the former monopolist will invariably point at the measures taken by the regulator and keep it under pressure through complaints aired by the dissatisfied end user. No other actor is capable of demonstrating the precise reasons for the quality failure or the veracity of the claims made by the former monopolist, which makes strategic use of the situation very appealing. On the other hand, due to the indispensable nature of the utility, the incumbent is always obliged to deliver, while newcomers can selectively choose to provide those services that offer the highest profit potential.

4.5.5 Strategic Use of the Factor 'Time'

Actions that promote or discourage full competition, implementation of legislation and respecting agreements that have been reached for the delivery of technical facilities can be both speeded up and delayed. Timing can be a crucial factor for the profitability of a particular service, the technology of which requires frequent updates, and also decisive for the survival chances of newcomers to the market. Dominant firms in an imperfect market can fruitfully make use of this phenomenon by stretching out legal procedures for as long as possible, delivering equipment with considerable delay or withholding crucial information until the moment when an adequate response to it is hardly possible any more. Toying with 'time' is a promising strategy. Information asymmetry does not allow weaker players to establish to what extent the delays were really necessary, how much the dominant player did to prevent them from occurring and how much truth there is in the arguments it uses in its defence.

4.5.6 Strategic Use of Financial Resources

Dominant players in markets for network-based industries usually have many more financial resources at their disposal than newcomers do. They can obviously make much larger investments in better infrastructures or high quality services than these newcomers can, but this is not always sufficient to protect their dominant positions. In cases where small players realize technological or other innovations that can shake up the market or revolutionize the products or services that are sold, these financial resources can also be utilized to buy up those smaller players. Or alternatively, the money can be used to pacify them by buying off the technological threat and preventing them from deploying this new technology against their interest. Since owners and/or shareholders of these smaller firms are normally not completely insensitive to the enormous amount involved in such transactions, this strategy is often used with remarkable success.

NOTES

1. By the term 'hiving-off', we refer to the various levels of reduced government control (also see section 4.2.3).
2. An industry is said to be a natural monopoly (also called technical monopoly) if only one firm is able to survive in the long run, even in the absence of legal regulations or predatory measures by the monopolist. This is the result of high fixed costs of entering an industry which causes long-run average costs to decline as output expands.
3. For example: Profiton (1993); Megginson and Netter (2001); Letza et al. (2004); Donahue (1989) and Parker and Saal (2005).

REFERENCES

Bauer, J.M. (1998), 'The role and evolution of public utility regulation, tasks of regulation in an era of partial competition', paper presented at 40th NARUC

Annual Regulatory Studies Program at Michigan State University, Michigan: East Lansing.

Baumol, W.J., J.C. Panzar and R.D. Willig (1982), *Contestable Markets and the Theory of Industrial Structure*, New York: Harcourt Brace Jovanovitch.

Bergman, L., C. Doyle, J. Gual, L. Hultkrantz, D. Neven, L.H. Röller and L. Waverman (1998), *Europe's Network Industries: Conflicting Priorities*, London: Centre for Economic Policy Research.

Bruijne, M. de (2006), *Networked Reliability, Institutional Fragmentation and the Reliability of Service Provision in Critical Infrastructures*, Delft: Delft University of Technology.

Crew, M.A. and P.R. Kleindorfer (1999), 'Regulatory governance and competitive entry', in M.A. Crew (ed.), *Regulation under Increasing Competition*, Boston, MA: Kluwer Academic Publishers, pp. 1–25.

Donahue, J. (1989), *The Privatization Decision*, New York: Basic Books, pp. 57–78.

Ehrhart, D. and R. Burdon (1999), 'Free entry in infrastructures', Policy Research Working Paper, WPS 2093, Washington, DC: The World Bank.

Guthrie, G. (2006), 'Regulating infrastructure: the impact on risk and investment', *Journal of Economic Literature*, **44**(4), 925–72.

Hulsink, W. and E.F.M. Wubben (2003), 'Introduction', in E.F.M. Wubben and W. Hulsink (eds), *On Creating Competition and Strategic Restructuring: Regulatory Reform in Public Utilities*, Cheltenham, UK and Northampton, MA, USA: Edward Elgar, pp. 1–26.

Hunt, S. and G. Shuttleworth (1996), *Competition and Choice in Electricity*, Chichester: John Wiley and Sons.

Joskow, P.L. (1998), 'Restructuring, competition and regulatory reform in the US electricity sector', in H. Chao and H.G. Huntington (eds), *Designing Competitive Electricity Markets*, Dordrecht: Kluwer Academic Publishers, pp. 3–29.

Kessides, I.N. (2004), *Reforming Infrastructure, Privatization, Regulation, and Competition, A World Bank Policy Research Report*, Washington, DC: The World Bank.

Kwoka, J.E. (1996), *Power Structure. Ownership, Integration, and Competition in the US Electricity Industry*, Boston, MA: Kluwer Academic Publishers.

Letza, S.R., C. Smallman and X. Sun (2004), 'Reframing privatization. Deconstructing the myth of efficiency', *Policy Sciences*, **37**(2), 159–83.

Megginson, W. and J. Netter (2001), 'From state to market: a survey of empirical studies on privatization', *Journal of Economic Literature*, **39**(2), 321–89.

Motta, M. (2004), *Competition Policy: Theory and Practice*, Cambridge: Cambridge University Press.

Parker, D. and D.S. Saal (eds) (2005), *International Handbook on Privatization*, Cheltenham, UK and Northampton, MA, USA: Edward Elgar.

Profiton, C. (1993), 'Economic deregulation: days of reckoning for microeconomists', *Journal of Economic Literature*, **31**(3), 1263–89.

Scherer, F.M. and D. Ross (1990), *Industrial Market Structure and Economic Performance*, Boston, MA: Houghton Mifflin Company.

Varian, H.R. and C. Shapiro (1998), *Information Rules*, Cambridge, MA: Harvard University Press.

Vogel, S.K. (1996), *Freer Markets, More Rules, Regulatory Reform in Advanced Industrial Countries*, Ithaca, NY: Cornell University Press.

5. The EU–US 2007 Open Skies Treaty[1]

5.1 BACKGROUND: THE BILATERALS

For many years, the transatlantic air traffic between Europe and the USA has been made possible by bilateral treaties which various European countries have entered into individually with the Americans. Some EU member states have signed a treaty with scope for market forces, whereas other member states have tried to resist market forces in the aviation sector and have signed restrictive treaties.

These bilateral aviation treaties have become a common topic of discussion in recent years. The European Commission is fiercely opposed to them, arguing that they stand in the way of a level playing field in Europe. The EC is therefore demanding that they be terminated and replaced by one single treaty that confers equal rights on all airlines in the Community. In 2002, the Commission's standpoint was endorsed by the European Court of Justice, when it ruled on an action taken against a number of member states for infringement of Community law (Art. 226 EC Treaty).[2] In the same ruling, the Court confirmed the Commission's powers in the matter. When the EC obtained a mandate to negotiate with the USA, also on behalf of the member states, the legal problems seemed to have been solved. The rights and obligations of the EC and the member states were crystal clear.

However, legal coordination does not necessarily spell the end of recalcitrant practices. The aviation sector is complex and dynamic. To begin with, the airlines have considerable economic interests in transatlantic air transport. Secondly, the interests of the air carriers are inscrutably entwined with the interests of member states. And last but not least, the possibilities for individual states to secure their interests and thus the interests of national airlines are subject to the vagaries of international politics and economic power struggles.

This chapter discusses the evolution of the first-stage EU–US aviation agreement, which was signed on 30 April 2007, at an EU–US summit in Washington. The European Commission opened negotiations with the USA in October 2003 with the aim of formulating one Open Skies Treaty to replace all the bilateral treaties that the member states had signed separately with the Americans. The negotiations were arduous and continued for several years. Even though a first-stage agreement has been reached, future developments regarding a second-stage agreement remain highly uncertain and unpredictable.

5.2   AIR SERVICE AGREEMENTS

The steady development of aviation in the 1930s and 1940s created a need for a forum where countries could agree on flight routes, frequencies, arrival and departure times and interconnections. On 7 December 1944, the Convention on International Civil Aviation (the Chicago Convention) was established. The Chicago Convention sets out regulations on airspace, aircraft registration and safety, and specifies the air travel rights of the signatories. It has been revised several times since its inception. The Chicago Convention paved the way for the establishment of the International Civil Aviation Organization (ICAO) on 4 April 1947, a permanent body that serves the interests of the aviation sector at the global level.

The conference which led to the Chicago Convention and the subsequent establishment of the ICAO achieved another important result: the first version of Freedoms of the Air – a standardized set of separate air rights. Freedoms of the Air eased negotiations between states as it prevented misconceptions of the other party's intentions. The convention managed to draw up a multilateral agreement which accorded the first two freedoms, known as the International Air Service Transit Agreement (or the Two Freedoms Agreement), for all signatories. Though it was agreed that the third, fourth and fifth freedoms would be negotiated between the states, the International Air Transport Agreement (or the Five Freedoms Agreement), encompassing the first five freedoms, was also opened for signatories. Several other 'freedoms' have since been added, but they are not officially recognized under international treaty (Diederiks-Verschoor, 1983 [2006]).

The first freedom is the right to overfly a country without landing. The second is the right to stop in a country for refuelling or maintenance on the way to another country without transferring passengers or cargo. The third is the right to carry passengers or cargo from one's own country to another, while the fourth is the right to carry passengers or cargo from another country to one's own. Rights under the third and fourth freedom are nearly always granted simultaneously in bilateral agreements between countries. The fifth freedom is the right to carry passengers from one's own country to a second country, and then to a third country. Another important freedom in the light of this chapter is the eighth freedom, which is the right to carry passengers or cargo within the borders of a foreign country, more commonly referred to as cabotage.

As the Chicago Convention sets out only a few basic principles of international aviation law, the details need to be fleshed out in bilateral treaties, known as Air Service Agreements (ASAs), which regulate the supply of air transport services. As a result, countless ASAs are currently in force that, literally, guide the air traffic on a global scale. The content of these ASAs can vary widely. Freedoms of the Air can be embedded in the treaty in line with the wishes of the parties. Some ASAs protect markets, while others allow scope for competition (the latter category is relatively small). The states try to allocate the transport rights granted to their airlines on the basis of equal exchange of economic benefits, that is quid pro quo. The key role played by ASAs in commercial civil aviation is illustrated by the fact that, at this moment, each EU member state has, on average, 60 to 70 ASAs with other countries.[3]

At the end of the 1970s, the US Government decided that it would no longer intervene in the aviation sector. It launched an extensive deregulation programme designed to give the market space to develop. Countless anti-competition regulations were scrapped. This dramatic change ended a period of intensive government participation, largely via the Civil Aviation Board (CAB). For example, airlines had to charge CAB-approved fares and fly CAB-approved routes. Even the frequency and the type of aircraft had to be CAB-approved. After being more or less straitjacketed, US airlines were now free to compete. As a result, they were able to develop business acumen at an early stage, which – as became clear later – gave them a head start over their European rivals.

In the early 1980s, after the wave of deregulation in the USA, competition in the aviation sector was also added to the European agenda, as a result of the obligations that the signatories to the EC Treaty had assumed with regard to the realization of a single transport market. In 1986, it was decided that the European aviation market would be liberalized in phases.

The single European market has been in existence since 1 April 1997. Each airline with an EU licence is free to operate national and international routes within the Community. Under Regulation 2407/92, issued by the Council of Ministers on 23 July 1992, the member states are obliged to grant an operating licence to each European airline that meets the fixed criteria.[4] Pricing is addressed by Regulation 2409/92, also issued by the Council of Ministers on 23 July 1992.[5] The thrust of this regulation is that market forces must determine the rates for air transport services provided within the Community.

Table 5.1   Differences between bilateral and Open Skies Agreements

Type of agreement	Service provider	Service frequency	Fares	Extended traffic right
Traditional bilateral agreement	Restrictions on which airlines can operate	Restrictions on which markets airlines may serve Restrictions on the number of flights that can be flown	Restrictions on pricing	Restrictions on operations to and from additional countries
Open Skies Agreement	No restrictions	No restrictions	No restrictions	No restrictions

Source: www.gao.gov.

Strictly speaking, there are two types of bilateral Air Service Agreements between EU member states and the USA: the traditional restrictive bilaterals and the free, modern Open Skies Agreements. The traditional bilaterals establish a tightly regulated market in which the power of the airline industry is heavily curtailed by, for example, stipulated prices and flight frequencies for each route. The Open Skies Agreements, which establish a market with scope for competition, have become increasingly popular in recent years. The degree of liberalization varies from one agreement to another. Table 5.1 shows the main differences between a traditional bilateral agreement and an Open Skies Agreement.

5.3   BILATERALS UNDERMINE SINGLE EU AVIATION MARKET

With the establishment of the internal market in 1997, the European Commission felt that bilateral Air Service Agreements between member states and third countries were no longer desirable. The multifarious conditions were not only creating a tangled web of rules and regulations; they were also – and most importantly – causing inequality among EC airlines. One particularly sharp thorn in the flesh of the EC was treaties that allow only national airlines to offer transport services between two countries, thereby excluding foreign competition. The term 'national airlines' is understood as airlines which are owned and controlled by subjects of the two states who are signatory to the treaty. The Commission takes the view that advantages like these ('nationality clauses') can seriously undermine the market.[6] It means that:

- EC airlines which are majority-owned by parties from outside the member state have no access to international routes to and from that state;
- EC airlines which are officially registered in one member state and have a base in another member state cannot utilize their EC Treaty rights to operate international routes from both states;
- mergers and takeovers whereby EC airlines become involved with international networks are virtually impossible;
- it is extremely difficult to develop Community airlines with multi-hub systems, such as those operated by US airlines.

Article 307 of the EC Treaty regulates the relationship between EU law and agreements between member states and third parties. The starting point is that the EC Treaty leaves intact any agreement that was entered into before the EC Treaty came into force, unless the agreement is irreconcilable with the EC Treaty. In the latter case, the member state is obliged to use all appropriate means to solve the problem as soon as possible.

As the member states were unwilling to terminate these lucrative bilaterals, the Commission had no choice but to initiate actions for infringement of Community law by member states under Article 226 of the EC Treaty. In 1998, the Commission took out court proceedings against eight member states that had entered into bilateral agreements with the US.

5.4   THE EUROPEAN COURT OF JUSTICE INTERVENES

In a decision of November 2002, the European Court of Justice ruled unequivocally that the nationality conditions in the agreements constitute an infringement of the freedom of establishment principle as set out in Article 43 of the EC Treaty.[7]

The Court found that the eight agreements in question contain elements that deprive Community air carriers of their rights under the Treaty, the nationality clauses in the agreements being a clear violation of the right of establishment enshrined in Article 43. Therefore, although the Court could not have invalidated the agreements under international law, they still constitute an infringement of Community law under which member states have a responsibility towards the beneficiaries of the right of establishment. The agreements that were challenged have strict clauses covering ownership and control, which ensure that only airlines that are owned and controlled by nationals of the two parties to the agreement can benefit from the granted traffic rights. As was discussed in section 5.3, this means that Community carriers that are majority-owned by interests from outside their home member state are shut out of international routes to and from that country. Moreover, Community carriers that are officially registered in one member state and have a base in another cannot exercise their rights under the Treaty to fly international routes from both locations. These clauses therefore prevent any mergers and acquisitions involving Community carriers with international networks. They also prevent the development of Community carriers with multiple hub systems, similar to those operated by American carriers.

Under Community law, such discrimination must now be considered illegal, and all Community carriers, as long as they have a base in a member state, must be able to fly international routes from there, regardless of where their principal place of business is in the Community or where the owners come from in the Community. The beneficiaries of an international air transport agreement at Community level are 'Community carriers'. This is the sole definition of airlines within the Community as laid down in EC Directive 2407/92 of 23 July 1992, on the licensing of air carriers[8] and EC 2408/92 of 23 July 1992, on Community carrier access to intra-Community air routes.

In the same decision, the Court ruled that the EC has exclusive powers regarding rates, computerized reservation systems and slots, but not regarding landing rights. As a result of this, the member states are more or less compelled to give a mandate to the Commission to start negotiations with all the third countries that are party to existing aviation agreements in order to establish new bilateral treaties on landing rights and other matters between the countries in question and the EC as a whole. As the negotiations are bound to produce mixed results, the new agreements will have to be ratified by all national parliaments.

5.5 START OF NEGOTIATIONS ON 1 OCTOBER 2003[9]

After receiving a mandate from the Council of Ministers in June 2003, the European Commission opened negotiations in October of the same year on the creation of an Open Aviation Area between the EU and US. This would create a single market for air transport between the EU and the US in which investment could flow freely and which would allow European and US airlines to provide unrestricted air services, also in the domestic markets of both parties. Significant legislative changes would be required in the US to achieve the mandate in full, especially when it came to removing the legal restrictions on foreign ownership and control of US airlines and on cabotage – all extremely politically sensitive issues in the US. Hence, the mandate explicitly recognizes the possibility of implementing a phased agreement, but with proper mechanisms to ensure progression to subsequent phases.

The first round of talks was held in Washington DC on 1 and 2 October 2003. It was already clear at this early stage that the path to an agreement would be long and arduous. Though progress was made on questions like ground handling and computerized reservation systems, the talks became deadlocked on the question of ownership rules. The main sticking points were:

- granting rights to EU carriers to offer services in the US (cabotage);
- the EU demand that the US scrap the 'Fly American' rule for US government employees and armed forces;
- the level of foreign investment. (Goeteyn and Soames, 2005)

The EC's trump card in the negotiations was access to London Heathrow, the EU's busiest airport for transatlantic flights (Goeteyn and Soames, 2005). At that time, under the Bermuda 2 Agreement, only four airlines were licensed to fly between Heathrow and the US: Virgin Atlantic and British Airways (BA) from the UK and United Airlines and American Airlines from the US (BBC News, 2003).

The negotiations were resumed in Washington from 17 to 20 February 2004. At that moment, the US proposal offered unlimited fifth freedom rights in the EU for all American passenger and cargo airlines, but it denied European airlines access to the US domestic market (TCM, 2004). In a speech on 6 April 2004, the US Transport Secretary, Norman Mineta, repeated in no uncertain terms that cabotage was a no-go area for European carriers in the US and that it was most unlikely that the US would accept a foreign investment level higher than 49 per cent (Goeteyn and Soames, 2005).

5.6   PROPOSAL REJECTED ON 10 AND 11 JUNE 2004

The negotiations suffered another heavy blow when the EU Transport Council rejected a proposal on 10 and 11 June 2004. The Transport Council, notably Britain, argued that the US had not made enough concessions. At that moment, after almost a year of negotiations between the European Commission and the United States, a draft agreement lay on the table. This agreement managed to reconcile the EU–US deal with

Community Law by removing all discrimination between EU airlines, thus affording them equal opportunities to fly on any transatlantic route between the EU and the US. However, the Transport Council was not happy with the concessions and continued to maintain that the EU airlines should get better access to the American domestic market (European Commission, 2004; Gow, 2005).

The proposal that was rejected in June 2004 included, for the first time, US recognition of the concept of the 'EU carrier' – a gesture that the US saw as more than generous. In general, bilateral Air Service Agreements, including Open Skies Agreements, give the airlines of each party the right to operate air services from any point in one country to any point in the other country. This 'nationality clause' prevented EU air carriers from doing what every US carrier was able to do, that is, fly from any point in the United States to any point in the EU, apart from a few exceptions such as Heathrow. It is the nationality clause that the European Court of Justice deemed incompatible with the EC Treaty. According to the US, recognition of the concept of EU carrier would generate a great many benefits for the European airlines, as they would no longer be subject to nationality restrictions. Hence, from that moment on, every EU carrier could fly from any city in the EU to the United States. By offering to recognize the concept of the 'EU carrier', the US cashed in on the legal situation in Europe which had arisen as a result of an announcement by the European Court of Justice that nationality clauses in the bilateral treaties were incompatible with the EC Treaty. The offer was not as generous as it appeared, given the pressure that the Commission was exerting on the member states to terminate the bilaterals and the self-interest of the US. In exchange for recognition of the EU carrier concept, the US wanted to retain the rights under existing ASAs and to extend them to EU countries with which it had (as yet) no bilateral agreement (United States Embassy in London, 2005). The British felt that increased US access to Heathrow was too high a price, particularly as the Americans were not prepared to open the US domestic market (White, 2005).

A move by the European Commission on 20 July 2004 significantly stepped up the pressure on the EU and the US to reach an Open Skies Agreement. On that date, the Commission formally called upon eight EU member states to terminate their bilateral aviation agreements with the US in response to the ruling by the European Court of Justice in November 2002. According to the Commission, this action would not have any direct consequences for the airlines, as these bilateral agreements were subject to 12 months' notice and left enough time for the US and the EU to arrive at an open skies deal. But the US and the airlines were not so sure that the EC's action would have no adverse effects. The Secretary General of the Association of European

Airlines (AEA) said: 'Once termination of the agreements becomes effective, airlines will have no legal certainty; capacity planning and pricing will be subject to governmental ad hoc approval.' (Euractiv, 2004).

On 21 and 22 March 2005, the EU Transport Commissioner Jacques Barrot was due to visit Washington to relaunch the open skies negotiations. Following its action in July 2004, and prior to this visit, the EC instructed twelve EU member states to terminate their bilateral agreements with the US (Euractiv, 2005). The pressure on the US and the EU to reach agreement was raised again in a joint letter sent by the associations of EU and US airports (ACI Europe and ACI North America) to the EU and US administrations, urging EU Commissioner Jacques Barrot, and US Transport Secretary, Norman Y. Mineta, to make progress on EU–US air service negotiations. The ACIs wrote that an agreement would deliver huge economic benefits for both the airports and the communities they serve by increasing business, tourism, investment and jobs (ACI Europe, 2005).

5.7   RE-OPENING ON 17 OCTOBER 2005

The negotiations were re-opened in Brussels on 17 October 2005 (United States Embassy in London, 2005). Three days earlier, on 14 October, the US Deputy Secretary of State for Transport at the Bureau of Economic and Business Affairs, John Byerly, delivered a conference speech in which he made a number of statements about the status of the open skies negotiations. He stressed the need for progress by referring to the uncertain legal position of the EU member states: 'The negotiations this fall are the last clear chance to achieve an historic breakthrough in transatlantic aviation before storm clouds gather on the European legal horizon in 2006.' He repeated that the US was still prepared to accept the concept of the EU carrier. Perhaps more interesting were his comments on the issue of ownership and control:

> The possible expansion of opportunities for foreign participation in the US airline industry is, from my perspective, an issue that we Americans must examine based on whether it makes sense for us, balancing the clear advantages of increased access to capital and business know-how against concerns about safety, security, and the essential role that US carriers play in the national defense. [. . .] The Administration is aware of the keen interest of European parties in this issue. What is important, however, is to emphasize that this issue is being considered by the Administration on its own merits and cannot be linked to air services negotiations. (Byerly, 2005)

What Byerly did, in effect, was to exclude ownership and control from the negotiations on an EU–US open skies agreement.

On 3 November 2005, in the run-up to the next round of negotiations scheduled for 14–18 November 2005, in Washington, the US Department of Transportation (US DOT) submitted proposals on the deregulation of foreign ownership of US-domiciled airlines. DOT proposed easing the restrictions on overseas investment in US airlines, giving foreign investors more input in marketing, routing and fleet planning (Crawly, 2005). The proposal did not ease restrictions on foreign ownership – foreigners would not be allowed to own more than 25 per cent of the shares in a United States carrier – but the interpretation of the rules of control would be relaxed. As long as American citizens remained in charge of safety and other key aspects of airline operations, foreigners would be allowed control (Sunday Times, 2005).

This proposal ran into a barrage of criticism in both the US and the EU. Some felt that it went too far while others felt that it did not go far enough. The US trade unions argued that it gave too much scope for foreign control over the domestic airline industry and that such a proposal should be approved by Congress and not introduced via a change in the regulations. The proposal also proved highly controversial among British airlines. BA and Virgin complained that it did not go far enough and took the view that a true Open Skies Agreement would abandon all ownership and control restrictions. BMI, a British rival of BA and Virgin, responded by saying that BA and Virgin were simply protecting their own privileged positions (Sunday Times, 2005).

5.8   TENTATIVE AGREEMENT OF 18 NOVEMBER 2005

The next round of negotiations went ahead as planned on 14–18 November 2005. On 18 November, the negotiators announced that a tentative agreement had been reached. The deal, which still needed approval by the EU Council of Transport Ministers, was conditional on the outcome of the rulemaking process initiated by US DOT to expand opportunities for foreign citizens to invest and participate in the management of US air carriers (Euractiv, 2005).

If approved, the tentative agreement of 18 November 2005 would authorize every EU and US airline:

- to fly between every city in the EU and every city in the US;
- to operate without restrictions on the number of flights, the aircraft type, or the routes, including unlimited rights to fly beyond the EU and US to points in third countries;
- to set fares freely in accordance with market demand;

- to enter into cooperative agreements with other airlines, including code-sharing and leasing.

The agreement, if approved, would come into force at the end of October 2006. It was hailed as the first step towards opening markets and enhancing cooperation. The EU and the US had agreed to begin a second round of negotiations within 60 days of implementation of the Agreement (United States Mission to the European Union, 2005).

The tentative agreement met with fierce criticism from many quarters. Various airlines and trade unions in the US feared the impact of an increase in foreign competition and threatened to take legal action to block it. The US Congress also raised objections, particularly against the DOT proposal to give foreign investors greater control without seeking official approval. Some members of Congress expressed concern that giving foreign nationals more power in the managerial decisions of airlines could pose a risk to national defence and security. The tentative agreement also met with criticism from the four carriers that were licensed to fly between Heathrow and the United States. The agreement meant that the lucrative market between Heathrow and the US would be opened up to dozens of carriers. BA pointed out that the agreement would not give EU carriers cabotage rights for the US domestic market. Moreover, EU carriers would still be denied access to the segment of the US market controlled by the Fly America programme. Fly America holds no less than one fifth of the US market.

The tentative agreement of 18 November 2005, did, however, get support from France as it would get rid of the nationality clause (see above) which denied European airlines US landing rights if they merged. The nationality clause had already led to fragmentation and inefficiency in the European industry. At that time, France desperately wanted US approval for the merger between Air France and KLM and for alliances with North West and Delta. Most of the other EU member states also supported the agreement, so the UK found itself increasingly out on a limb by insisting that opening up Heathrow to all US and EU airlines had to be accompanied by genuine liberalization. The future of the negotiations now depended on what Washington decided about foreign ownership of US carriers (Daily Tribune, 2005; United States Mission to the European Union, 2006a; Webster, 2005; White, 2005).

On 3 May 2006, the US DOT issued a revised proposal, largely in response to the criticism from Congress. In the original DOT proposal, foreign investors would be allowed to enter into deals with US airlines, which would empower them to take operational decisions on, for instance, carrier rates and routes. In the revised proposal, US citizens with voting stock in an airline or a seat on the board would be able to veto any decision made by non-US stockholders or their representatives. The revised proposal would also lend weight to the demand that US citizens have full control over all policies and decisions relating to safety, security and national defence. Under the existing regulations, foreign investors could exert no influence on any of the operations of a US airline in which they invested. According to the revised proposal, the majority US investors could delegate some commercial decisions to foreign investors, such as which routes to fly and which aircraft to buy and sell. It also allowed foreign investors to hold up to 49 per cent of the equity in a US airline even though they could control no more than 25 per cent of the voting rights (United States Mission to the European Union, 2006b and 2006c; Euractiv, 2006).

The US Congress had 60 days to consider the revised DOT proposal. At first, there was strong criticism from Democrats and Republicans alike. The greatest fear was that US safety, security, or national defence might be compromised. Some senators also expressed concern that foreign investors might decide to halt low-profit services to rural areas of the US, such as Montana. But, even if the proposal did get through Congress, the question of EU approval was still far from certain. Daniel Calleja, Director at the EC Transport Directorate, said that he could not prejudge the decision of the EU transport ministers and pointed out that they would approve the deal if the new rule was clear, meaningful, and legally safe. One crucial element in the Council's decision was whether the European companies were actually given more scope to invest in US airlines (United States Mission to the European Union, 2006c; Euractiv, 2006). However, in December 2006, US DOT decided to withdraw its proposal regarding the American policy on the control of airlines under pressure from some members of Congress, who threatened to block its implementation. These members of Congress argued that increased foreign influence over US airlines could pose a threat to national security (United States Mission to the European Union, 2007). As EU approval for the tentative agreement depended on US concessions regarding foreign control of US airlines, the negotiations had to start again.

5.9   A FIRST-STAGE AGREEMENT

Eventually, the negotiations resulted in a first-stage aviation agreement drafted on 2 March 2007, by EU and US negotiators. The draft was unanimously approved by the EU Transport Council on 22 March 2007. It did not require the approval of the American Congress. The EU–US aviation agreement was signed on 30 April 2007, at an EU–US summit in Washington. It took effect on 30 March 2008. The deadline for the start of the second stage of the negotiations was 30 May 2008 (European Union, press and public diplomacy delegation of the European Commission, 2007; International Herald Tribune, 2007a).

Under this agreement, Britain will have to open the lucrative route between Heathrow and the United States to other airlines besides the four that are currently licensed to fly it (Euractiv, 2007). Moreover, any EU-based airline will be allowed to fly from any city in the EU to any city in the US, and vice versa. However, though US airlines will gain free access to EU airports, EU carriers will not be allowed free access to domestic routes in the US (BBC News, 2007).

Ownership of US airlines will remain restricted. The US has insisted on precluding any foreign company from owning more than 25 per cent of the voting rights in a US airline (BBC News, 2007). US investors can invest in EU airlines if they are majority-owned by Europeans (International Herald Tribune, 2007a). The agreement includes a 'suspension clause' that commits the United States to opening up more of its domestic market and relaxing its rules on foreign investment and ownership by mid-2010 (Euractiv, 2007). The European Commission has threatened to cancel the deal if the United States does not make more concessions on foreign operators of domestic routes and foreign ownership by 2010 (International Herald Tribune, 2007b).

Originally, the agreement was to become effective in October 2007, but this was postponed until March 2008 at the insistence of the UK government. This gave Heathrow more time to finish building a new terminal, which would give it more capacity, and gave BA extra time to prepare itself for tougher competition in transatlantic aviation (Euractiv, 2007).

The current EU–US first-stage agreement is seen as largely favouring the United States. EU carriers in general will probably benefit from it, but BA and Virgin Atlantic will face much heavier competition. A lot will depend on future negotiations between the EU and the US and the American position on opening the US market to Europe. It will probably be harder to win concessions in this area, as any attempts in this direction will generate fierce political opposition in Washington (International Herald Tribune, 2007b). Indeed, BA Chief Executive Willie Walsh said that the EU had been 'naive to believe the US will deliver on the next stage of liberalization without sanctions' (BBC News, 2007). He also said: 'With the EU having given away their most valuable negotiating asset – Heathrow – the UK government must stand by its pledge to withdraw traffic rights if the US does not deliver further liberalisation by 2010.' (BBC News, 2007).

On 14 March 2007, the European Parliament passed a resolution calling on the Transport Council to approve the draft agreement. The wording of the resolution suggests that the Parliament would also have preferred more concessions from the US:

Parliament emphasises that a new EU–US aviation agreement should be balanced in terms of market access, considering also such issues as cabotage, right of establishment, ownership and de facto control and state aid. MEPs, therefore, prefer the inclusion of cabotage in the agreement, as without cabotage an agreement will tend to be in favour of US carriers, who are allowed flights between points in different EU Member states, whereas EU carriers are not allowed flights between points in the US. MEPs regret that no progress has been made on cabotage and that the possibility for EU carriers to exercise effective control over a US airline is still limited, even with the extended ownership clauses. (European Parliament, 2007)

5.10   STRATEGIC BEHAVIOUR

Tables 5.2, 5.3, 5.4 and 5.5 present a detailed overview of all kinds of strategic behaviour as we found them. In describing our empirical findings, we have focused on entries for and forms of strategic behaviour as we introduced them in Chapters 3 and 4. Each table focuses on a particular actor: United States, European Commission, the government of the United Kingdom, British Airways, and Virgin Atlantic. The Open Skies case study presents a clear pattern of using networks. The dominant picture is strategic utilization of intertwined relations with government agencies and other actors. In the aviation sector, we see an immense mixing of interests of airlines with those of states.

Table 5.2   United States

Entry	Strategic behaviour: type and description
Indispensable nature + rules and contracts	*Divide and rule + carrot and stick.* US conclude bilaterals with EU member states.
Indispensable nature	*Use of rhetoric, occasional arguments.* US refuse to grant cabotage rights using the arguments of national security and lacking reciprocity.
Intertwined relations	*Rhetoric, occasional arguments.* US negotiators disconnect issue of foreign ownership and control from EU–US negotiations about an Open Skies Treaty. They also use those they represent as an 'excuse'.
Rules and contracts + indispensable nature	*Making a small compromise seem big, occasional arguments, naming and framing.* US recognize the EU carrier.

Table 5.3 European Commission

Entry	Strategic behaviour: type and description
Rules and contracts	*Threatening + strategic use of litigation.* European Commission initiates actions for infringement of Community law by member states under Article 226 of the EC Treaty.
Rules and contracts	*Threatening + strategic use of rule-making/litigation.* European Commission obtains exclusive power to conclude air traffic agreements.
Factor 'time'	*Quid pro quo / package deal + threatening.* EU negotiators link approval for Open Skies Treaty with US proposals on foreign ownership and control.
Indispensable nature	*Rhetoric, occasional arguments.* EU negotiators argue that US already has de facto cabotage rights in the EU.

Table 5.4 Government of United Kingdom

Entry	Strategic behaviour: type and description
Factor 'time'	*Rhetoric, occasional arguments.* UK government pretends that it only wants a 'truly open skies' agreement and presents this as the reason why the British are not yet satisfied with the result of the negotiations (e.g., in June 2004).

Table 5.5 British Airways and Virgin Atlantic

Entry	Strategic behaviour: type and description
Factor 'time'	*Rhetoric, occasional arguments.* BA and Virgin Atlantic reject US proposals, because they do not truly open up markets.
Rules and contracts + indispensable nature	*Collusion.* BA tries to obtain antitrust immunity from the US, in order to establish strategic alliances with US carriers.

NOTES

1. Also see Kars and Stout 2006a and 2006b, 2008.
2. Cases C-466/98, C-467/98, C-468/98, C-469/98, C-471/98, C-472/98, C-475/98 and

C-476/98 versus United Kingdom, Denmark, Sweden, Finland, Belgium, Luxemburg, Austria, Germany.
3. Communication from the Commission 19 November 2002, COM (2002) 649 final, p. 4.
4. Official Journal of the European Union 1992, L 240/1.
5. Official Journal of the European Union 1992, L 240/15.
6. Communication from the Commission 26 February 2003, COM (2003) 94 final, 2003/0044 (COD), p. 3.
7. Cases C-466/98, C-467/98, C-468/98, C-469/98, C-471/98, C-472/98, C-475/98 and C-476/98 versus United Kingdom, Denmark, Sweden, Finland, Belgium, Luxemburg, Austria, Germany. In a decision of 24 April 2007 the European Court of Justice ruled on similar grounds that the open skies deal between the US and the Netherlands was in violation of EU law (Case C-523/04).
8. Official Journal of the European Union 1992, L 240/1.
9. For a discussion of the negotiations on an EU–US open skies treaty, see also: Button (1998), (2002); Staniland (1996); Stober (2003).

REFERENCES

ACI Europe (2005), 'European, US airports call for urgent progress on open skies negotiations', *ACI Europe Press Release*, 21 March.
BBC News (2003), 'EU–US in "open skies" talks', *BBC News*, 1 October, http://news.bbc.co.uk/2/hi/business/3156854.stm, accessed 22 December 2005.
BBC News (2007), 'EU backing for "open skies" deal', *BBC News*, 22 March, http://news.bbc.co.uk/2/hi/business/6477969.stm, accessed 2 May 2007.
Button, K.J. (1998), 'Opening US skies to global airline competition', *Trade Policy Analysis*, 24 November 1998, (5), 1–17, Center for Trade Policy Studies.
Button, K.J. (2002), 'Toward truly open skies', *Regulation*, **25**(3), 12–16.
Byerly, J.R. (2005), 'Liberalizing transatlantic aviation: the case for stability, expansion, and vision', Speech, USA-BIAS conference, Washington, DC, 14 October, www.state.gov//e/eb/rls/rm/2005/55129.htm, accessed 22 December 2005.
Crawley, J. (2005), 'Update 3-US–EU reach tentative deal on "open skies" pact', *Reuters*, 18 November, http://today.reuters.com, accessed 21 December 2005.
Daily Tribune (2005), 'Emulate open skies negotiators of US-EU, Filipino execs urged', *Daily Tribune*, www.tribune.et.ph/metro/20051212.met03.html, accessed 22 December 2005.
Diederiks-Verschoor, I.H.Ph. (1983), *An Introduction to Air Law*, reprinted in I.P.H. Diederiks-Verschoor (2006), *An Introduction to Air Law*, Alphen aan den Rijn: Kluwer Law International.
Euractiv (2004), 'Commission pressures US and Member states to agree "open skies" deal', *European Union Information Website*, 22 July, www.euractiv.com/Article?tcmuri=tcm:29-128683-16&type=News, accessed 31 March 2005.
Euractiv (2005), 'EU members told to scrap US bilateral airline deals', *European Union Information Website*, 17 March, www.euractiv.com/Article?tcmuri=tcm:29-136887-16&type=News, accessed 21 December 2005.
Euractiv (2006), 'EU renew push for "open skies" deal', *European Union Information Website*, 12 May, www.euractiv.com, accessed 12 June 2006.
Euractiv (2007), 'UK wins delay in EU–US "open skies" pact', *European Union*

Information Website, 28 March, www.euractiv.com/en/transport/uk-wins-delay-eu-us-open-skies-pact/article-162699, accessed 2 May 2007.

European Commission (2004), 'Commission takes action to enforce "open skies" Court rulings', *European Commission Press Release*, 20 July, Reference IP/04/967.

European Parliament (2007), *Open skies EU–US agreement – MEPs call for it to be endorsed*, 14 March, www.europarl.europa.eu/news/expert/infopress_page/062-4174-071-03-11-910-20070314IPR04173-12-03-2007-2007-true/default_en.htm, accessed 2 May 2007.

European Union, press and public diplomacy delegation of the European Commission (2007), 'Open skies: Jacques Barrot in Washington to sign historic aviation deal at the EU–US transatlantic summit', *News Release*, No. 44/07, 30 April, www.eurunion.org/News/press/2007/2007044.htm, accessed 2 May 2007.

Goeteyn, G. and T. Soames (2005), 'Towards airline consolidation in the EU?', *Aviation Law Committee Newsletter*, April, pp. 15–27.

Gow, D. (2005), 'EU and US resume talks on open sky aviation deal', *The Guardian*, 18 October, www.guardian.co.uk/print/0,3858,5311727-110878,00.html, accessed 22 December 2005.

International Herald Tribune (2007a), 'US and Europe sign "Open Skies" deal', *International Herald Tribune*, 30 April, www.iht.com/bin/print.php?id=5508563, accessed 2 May 2007.

International Herald Tribune (2007b), 'EU/US: open skies talks face challenging second round', *International Herald Tribune*, 26 March, www.iht.com/bin/print.php?id=5026657, accessed 2 May 2007.

Kars, M. and H. Stout (2006a), 'Open skies and hidden agendas. The case of the Open Skies Treaty from the perspective of strategic behaviour', paper prepared for the ECPR Standing Group on the European Union, Third Pan-European Conference on EU Politics, 21–23 September 2006, Istanbul, Turkey. Panel: The European Union and International Economic Cooperation.

Kars, M. and H. Stout (2006b), 'Open skies and hidden agendas. The case of the Open Skies Treaty in a multi-level governance perspective', paper prepared for a two-day expert seminar on Multilevel Regulation (The Interrelation between Regulatory Activities of the European Union and other International Organizations and its Effect on the State – Legal, Political and Philosophical Dimensions of Legitimacy, Accountability and the Rule of Law), organized by CONNEX (Connecting Excellence on European Governance), in close cooperation with the Hague Institute for the Internationalisation of Law (HiiL), The Hague, the Netherlands, 26–27 June 2006.

Kars, M. and H. Stout (2008), 'The transatlantic common aviation area: Competing legal orders and state self-interest', in A. Follesdal, R. Wessel and J. Wouters (eds), *Multilevel Regulation and the EU. The Interplay between Global, European and National Normative Processes*, Leiden and Boston, MA: Martinus Nijhoff Publishers, pp. 185–212.

Staniland, M. (1996), 'Open skies – fewer planes? Public policy and corporate strategy in EU–US aviation relations', *European Policy Paper Series*, (3).

Stober, A. (2003), 'Who soars in open skies? A review of the impacts of anti-trust immunity, and international market deregulation on global alliances, consumers, and policy makers', *Journal of Air Transportation*, **8**(1), 111–33.

Sunday Times (2005), 'EU steps in to end open skies impasse', *Sunday Times*,

6 November, www.timesonline.co.uk/printFriendly/0,,1-528-1858944-528,00. html, accessed 22 December 2005.

TCM (2004), 'BA chief advises EC on open skies negotiations', *TCM archives breaking news, 2004*, http://archives.tcm.ie/breakingnews/2004/02/12/story 133944.asp, accessed 22 December 2005.

United States Embassy in London (2005), 'US enters talks with EU on liberal aviation service pact', 17 October, www.usembassy.org.uk/euro308.html, accessed 22 December 2005.

United States Mission to the European Union (2005), 'United States, European Union reach tentative air transport pact', 21 November, http://useu.usmission. gov/Article.asp?ID=4CBDF9E6-D97A-4F1D-9F3F-C81F0C00FFD6,accessed 1 March 2006.

United States Mission to the European Union (2006a), 'Airline foreign control rule might be delayed, US official says', 25 April, http://useu.usmission.gov/ Article.asp?ID=CE1729F4-EFBB-451F-ABA7-163A2766A059, accessed 13 June 2006.

United States Mission to the European Union (2006b), 'US revised proposed rule on airlines might delay EU deal', 4 May, http://useu.usmission.gov/Article. asp?ID=5EEBAFDA-5644-4713-838D-531E98241C2A, accessed 13 June 2006.

United States Mission to the European Union (2006c), 'Official defends proposal on foreign investment in US airlines', 9 May, http://useu.usmission.gov/ Article.asp?ID=AD0FB082-37AE-486F-A779-DC64BCE55088, accessed 13 June 2006.

United States Mission to the European Union (2007), 'US, EU to look at options to finalize open skies deal', 17 January, http://usinfo.state.gov/xarchives/display. html?p=washfile-english&y=2007&m=January&x=20070117150349saikceinaw z8.289737e-02, accessed 2 May 2007.

Webster, B. (2005), 'Clouds gather over the future of "open skies"', *Times Online*, http://business.timesonline.co.uk/printFriendly/0,,2020-9082-1895152-9082,00. html, accessed 21 December 2005.

White, A. (2005), 'British Airways Exec slams EU–US talks', *Airport Business Online*, 29 November, www.airportbusiness.com/article/printer.jsp?id=4430, accessed 22 December 2005.

6. Enron

Mark de Bruijne

6.1   INTRODUCTION

In the wake of the accounting scandal that doomed Enron (cf. McLean and Elkind, 2003; Fox, 2003), Enron has gained notoriety for its strategic behaviour during arguably one of the more bizarre episodes ever to occur in a liberalized and deregulated energy market anywhere: California's 'electricity crisis' during 2000–2001. Although suspicions about gaming and market manipulation by Enron's West Coast electricity traders arose the very moment California's markets went out of control, it was only until after the bankruptcy of Enron that documents and tape recordings emerged which provided unique evidence of the ways in which Enron traders had sought to 'game' California's markets. Mysterious code names attached to these strategies such as 'Fat Boy', 'Get Shorty' or 'Ricochet' lent credibility to what some considered a 'smoking gun'. From documents and previous research an interesting picture emerges of the behaviour of an energy trading company that was to become synonymous with all that was evil: Enron.

6.2   SETTING THE STAGE: CALIFORNIA'S ELECTRICITY MARKET DESIGN

The trading strategies that Enron traders employed during California's electricity crisis were predominantly market-specific, meaning that they could only be employed under the rules and circumstances that were present in California's electricity industry at the turn of the new Millennium.[1] These market conditions will be shortly outlined, starting with the main players.

6.2.1   The Players

California's electricity restructuring programme at that time represented the boldest and most advanced state of deregulation in the US. California's plan outlined in legislation bill number AB1890 envisioned that competition and market incentives would take over the then-existing regulatory

Table 6.1   Changes in California's electricity industry structure as a result of restructuring

	Before restructuring	After restructuring
	California's regulated electricity industry	*California's restructured electricity industry*
Generation	State regulator: CPUC Mostly owned by the vertically integrated utilities Generators deal with utilities	Federal regulator: FERC Mostly owned by independent merchant generators Prices set on PX Generators deal directly or via *scheduling coordinators* with distributors
Transmission	State regulator: CPUC Owned and operated by the vertically integrated utilities	New state regulator: EOB Owned by utilities, but operated by ISO
Distribution	State regulator: CPUC Owned and operated by the vertically integrated utilities Retail prices set by regulator	State regulator: CPUC Owned and operated by former utilities (Temporary) frozen retail rates set by PX

Source: De Bruijne (2006, Table 4-1, p. 110).

structure that governed the electricity industry. The change resulted in a fundamentally changed and fairly complex industry structure – a novel mixture of private and public organizations – that were involved in the provision of electricity within a competitive and fully unbundled electricity production chain (see Table 6.1).

Electricity generation would become the business of competitive, independent electricity generators. The three Investor Owned Utilities (IOUs), which had dominated California's electricity industry until then as de facto vertically integrated monopolists, were forced to divest most of their in-state power plants and sell them to independent 'merchant' power producers. The IOUs remained the owners of the high-voltage transmission grid (and their distribution grid as well) in their service area and were transformed into utility distribution companies (Besant-Jones and Tenenbaum, 2001, p. 3).

Operational control of the utility-owned high-voltage transmission grid was transferred to the California Independent System Operator (CAISO or ISO), a hybrid not-for-profit public-benefit corporation (ISO, 2002).

The ISO became responsible for balancing load and generation through-out the grid so as to guarantee reliable and high-quality electricity pro-vision using nothing but markets, hence its motto: 'Reliability through Markets' (Alaywan, 2000, p. 70).

A new intermediary group was to enter the electricity industry: the electricity traders, commonly known as scheduling coordinators (SCs). Enron was but one of many other companies that set up 'trading desks' to engage in this lucrative market, which at that time was thought to present the future in the energy business. The task of the SCs was to match electricity supply and demand in a market setting and submit them to the grid operator, the ISO, which calculated whether the transactions met the capabilities of the high-voltage transmission grid.

Finally, a last new institution, the California Power Exchange (the PX or Cal-PX), a hybrid private non-profit organization, was to function as California's main SC and the primary wholesale electricity market where supply would meet demand.

By creating the PX and the ISO, the restructuring essentially federal-ized California's grid. Responsibility for electricity generation pricing and some grid management authorities – for example reviewing and approv-ing tariffs and inter-state access – were removed from the state level at the California Public Utility Commission (CPUC) to the federal level, the Federal Energy Regulatory Commission (FERC). The changes were made to stimulate wholesale inter-state electricity trading and formed part of the wider FERC efforts to 'deregulate' the electricity industry.

6.2.2 The Markets

Apart from the players, the way in which the markets were designed proved vital. In essence, California's market design envisioned a number of markets in which prices were set on an hourly basis.

The California Power Exchange (PX) consisted of two sequential markets which allowed for trading in power: a day-ahead market and an hour-ahead market. Buyers requested the amount of electricity they antic-ipated for each hour of the next day and stipulated the prices they were willing to pay. At the same time, sellers stated the amount of energy they could produce and the prices they required for each of those hours. Once the PX had received all of the demand and supply bids, it matched them, thereby acting and functioning as a large scheduling coordinator. The highest priced supply bid necessary for meeting demand during any given hour would set the single market clearing price to be paid by all buyers to all sellers for energy purchased for that hour (CSA, 2001, p. 9).

Apart from the PX, the CAISO operations were designed to avoid the

ISO 'imposing deals upon the market participants, and to function without performing traditional unit commitment unless necessary for reliability purposes' (Alaywan, 2000, p. 71). Markets would take over this role and provide various services needed to operate the high-voltage electricity grid reliably (CSA, 2001, p. 16). Consequently, the ISO used a so-called spot-market or 'real-time' market to buy power at the last moment to maintain system stability. Furthermore, the ISO would ensure the reliable operation of the electricity system through an 'ancillary services market' to procure reserve power and a day-ahead and hour-ahead 'congestion market' (adjustment bid markets), which were designed to relieve congestion (i.e. capacity shortages) on the transmission lines. If power flows exceeded the available capacity of the grid, the prices for so-called 'congestion relieving bids' over other 'paths' in the grid would increase. Finally, when the ISO needed more energy than what was bid in the ancillary services market and real-time imbalance market, the ISO could make 'out-of-market' (OOM) purchases to buy power.

6.3 THE CALIFORNIA ELECTRICITY CRISIS

With the beginning of operations of the PX and the ISO in March 1998, California opened its competitive electricity wholesale industry. The markets and organizations were developed and created from scratch in little more than nine months, and many problems were yet to be solved at the time operations began (Joskow, 2000b, p. 18; Blumstein et al., 2002, p. 25; Alaywan, 2000). Apart from these initial start-up problems, the market seemed to be working mostly as designed and planned for the first two years (Joskow, 2000a, p. 166). In fact, California's electricity market was considered largely successful in 1998 and 1999 (Cicchetti et al., 2004, p. 2).

Nonetheless, the ISO and PX repeatedly warned the CPUC and FERC from August 1998 onwards of serious flaws in California's rules and market structure, mentioning strategic behaviour among the factors plaguing market development, the IOUs' obligation to use short-term markets, and the lack of demand elasticity in the electricity market (Kahn and Lynch, 2000; CSA, 2001; Cicchetti et al., 2004). To remedy the problems, the ISO and the PX sought to change the market rules and called for new investment in generation. However, their alarms came too late and were effectively ignored by both regulators.

The first months of 2000 brought a series of disturbing events, which some have considered a 'perfect storm', and which resulted in electricity shortages (Cicchetti et al., 2004; Brennan, 2001). With temperatures rising in the spring of 2000, California's electricity market started to run into trouble. Electricity wholesale prices exploded and reached $750 per MWh in the ISO's markets on 23 occasions in May (Blumstein et al., 2002, p. 27). That same month, residents of San Francisco experienced a black-out as a result of transmission constraints. Electricity became increasingly scarce on the markets. On 22 May, the ISO had to purchase over 9100 MW of 'out-of-market' (OOM) energy at an average price of $723 per MW, to maintain reserves for reliability purposes (Hughes, 2000, p. 7). During the previous months, these alarms and the subsequent measures had proven effective and helped to restore prices to normal levels. But this time, electricity wholesale prices did not drop and stayed at extraordinarily high levels for the rest of the summer as demand increased and temperatures peaked.

Throughout the summer, wholesale electricity prices in California were nearly 500 per cent higher than during the same months in 1998 and 1999 (Joskow and Kahn, 2002, p. 1). Regulatory investigations by the CPUC and FERC concluded that California's market was seriously flawed, and that evidence showed that this could lead to unjust and unreasonable rates in the PX markets. Nevertheless, no evidence for misconduct by electricity trading companies could be found. However, even during times of reduced electricity demand and lower temperatures in the autumn and winter of 2000, electricity wholesale prices remained well above average, as large amounts of generating capacity were out of service (Joskow, 2001a). Wholesale electricity prices fell briefly in October 2000, only to peak again at unprecedented heights in November and December 2000 as natural gas prices exploded as well. Between May and December 2000, the average electricity prices traded in the PX were '[b]etween 2 and 13 times higher than in the same months of the previous year' (GAO, 2001, p. 3). By December 2000, the monthly *average* wholesale electricity price had risen to $250 per MWh (see Table 6.2).

As part of California's electricity restructuring programme, the utilities were not allowed to pass on the increased electricity prices to consumers. Consequently, the creditworthiness of the utilities declined rapidly as they were forced to pay unusually high prices to purchase electricity, while they could only sell it at a fixed price, losing as much as $50 million *per day* (Joskow, 2001a, p. 38; Weare, 2003, p. 44).

A number of federal emergency orders by the Secretary of Energy were barely sufficient to keep California's lights on in December and January, requiring electricity suppliers to continue the forward delivery of electricity to utilities in California, even though there were no assurances that they would be paid. However, in January, the new Bush administration decided no longer to use federal authority to force generators to keep supplying electricity to the utilities, which were fast heading for bankruptcy as a result of the extreme electricity prices. Consequently, electricity scarcity increased, prices rose even further and rolling blackouts became inevitable.

*Table 6.2   California PX day-ahead prices ($/MWh: weighted
               averages 7 × 24)*

Month	1998	1999	2000[1]	2000[2]	2001
January	–	21.6	27.7	31.8	272.0
February	–	19.6	24.1	18.8	304.4
March	–	24.0	23.3	29.3	249.0
April	23.3	24.7	20.0	27.4	265.9
May	12.5	24.7	18.5	50.4	239.5
June	13.3	25.8	18.8	132.4	159.8
July	35.6	31.5	28.0	115.3	137.8
August	43.4	34.7	40.9	175.2	120.1
September	37.0	35.2	45.3	119.6	126.8
October	27.3	49.0	32.2	103.2	69.4
November	26.5	38.3	31.6	179.4	74.8
December	30.0	30.2	30.7	385.6	69.6
Average	30.0	30.0	28.5	115.0	174.0

Note: 1 initial CEC estimate for PX day-ahead prices; 2 actual prices found by
Joskow (2001a).

Source: De Bruijne (2006, Table 4-3, p. 120).

On a number of days, the ISO had to resort to rotating blackouts in order
to maintain system reliability.

Under increasing public pressure, California's legislature, the CPUC
and Governor Gray Davis decided to involve the state in the electricity
crisis. As a stop-gap measure to relieve California's electricity shortages,
Davis ordered the state to purchase the electricity the utilities needed,
starting from 17 January 2001. However, throughout the first quarter of
2001, electricity supplies remained tight, and prices remained high.

On 31 January 2001, the electricity crisis caused the PX to suspend its
trading operations (CSA, 2001, p. 40). The market operator was forced
into bankruptcy on 9 March. Another victim of the electricity prices was
PG&E, the largest utility in the US, which had to file for bankruptcy.

As the summer of 2001 approached, serious trouble was again feared.
To prevent a second series of rolling blackouts in the summer of 2001,
the State of California entered into large-scale long-term contracts with
electricity providers and FERC issued new orders effectively prohibiting
certain types of bid curves often attributed to strategic or gaming behaviour. During the summer, electricity supply shortages did not occur on the
scale initially predicted. California's total energy consumption during the
summer months fell significantly in 2001, and so did the extreme prices

Table 6.3   Total costs of California's electricity market (US$)

Year	Total energy costs	Total energy costs +A/S	Average energy costs + A/S
1998 (9mths)	$4,913 mln	$5,551 mln	$32.80
1999	$7,028 mln	$7,432 mln	$32.66
2000	$25,373 mln	$27,083 mln	$114.01
2001	$25,410 mln	$26,756 mln	$117.86
2002	$9,900 mln	$10,065 mln	$43.38
2003	$10,626 mln	$10,826 mln	$52.70
2004	$11,665 mln	$11,849 mln	$49.41

Note: A/S: ancillary services.

Source: ISO (2005, Table 2.3, p. 2–9).

and volatility in California's electricity markets. It was time to assess the damage. Annual total power expenditures had roughly quadrupled as a result of the power crisis (see Table 6.3).

6.4   THE BEHAVIOUR OF ENRON'S WEST COAST POWER TRADERS

From the above description, it can be concluded that California's market design was extremely complex. Because of its complexity and a number of more or less obvious design flaws, many experts assumed that gaming and strategic behaviour had been taking place: '[g]aming was predicted, expected, and observed. Buyers and sellers attempted to game the system' (Cicchetti et al., 2004, p. 138). From the beginning of the crisis in May 2000, rumours circulated and accusations were made about price-gouging power marketers who profited from California's energy woes. 'Many observers suspected that energy traders were gaming the system a little – by, say, withholding power they could deliver in the morning until the prices rose further in the afternoon – but also figured that however sneaky or unfair these manoeuvres were, they were legal tactics exploiting a poor market system' (Fox, 2003, p. 199).

However, faced with power prices topping over $1000 per MWh in the summer of 2000, California state senators, the CPUC and Governor Gray Davis called for an investigation into potential price manipulation. Although Enron ranked among the obvious 'victims' of accusations about market manipulation from the start, undisputed evidence could not be found. The enormous profits which the new power trading companies boasted in this period did nothing to reduce the rumours and accusations, yet research conducted by FERC, during the electricity crisis, could not identify market manipulation. Instead, FERC (2000) criticized California's market design for the abnormal price explosions on the PX.

Only after the crisis was over did evidence of gaming behaviour in California's electricity markets become available. As a result of the bankruptcy of Enron in December 2001 (cf. McLean and Elkind, 2003; Fox, 2003), additional information was supplied to FERC and California authorities, which included a number of detailed memorandums that described in detail a number of trading strategies that electricity traders used to game the markets (FERC, 2002, 2003 and 2007). However, far more damaging to the public image of Enron's behaviour on California's market was the discovery of a series of audio recordings, on which Enron traders could be heard joking and making fun of the problems California faced.[2] Based upon these documents and tapes and subsequent investigations, FERC staff were able to reconstruct how Enron traders had acted in California's electricity market (see FERC, 2003).

Enron's traders operated from a building housing Enron's Oregon utility affiliate: Portland General. At the height of its success, the Western trading desk consisted of about 100 traders. Enron traders were known to be highly aggressive and prided themselves on being able to make use of any opportunity to earn money (see McLean and Elkind, 2003). Already before becoming operational, Enron's West Coast Traders had prepared thoroughly for California's new electricity market. This included trying to figure out exactly how California's electricity market would work. In 1998, Enron traders met with representatives of Perot Systems, a company that had helped to build California's electricity market systems, '[w]hich had inside information', and according to FERC (2007, p. 34) 'utilized the information [. . .] to locate vulnerabilities in the system' that the traders could use to their advantage. The 'stacked' markets and the complexity of the rules and regulations that guided them proved a natural playground for traders to devise ways to sell their electricity at the highest costs. It did not take long for the West Coast electricity traders to find out that California's electricity market design was indeed plagued by problems and loopholes, some of which the ISO and PX would later identify.

The generic idea among the electricity traders was that California's electricity market was just badly designed and did not resemble the pure markets in which many traders genuinely believed. Consequently, the prevailing attitude was: 'If they're going to put in place such a stupid system, it makes sense to try to game it' (McLean and Elkind, 2003, p. 267). By withholding electricity or ingeniously transporting electricity, power traders found out that they could earn fees without having to engage in physical transmission of power. Furthermore, they found that by engaging in various tactics, they could create (artificial) scarcity in the markets and could influence electricity prices and thus increase their earnings. All through 1999, Enron traders studied the market rules and perfected their tactics by engaging in various experiments.

One of these 'experiments' that was later identified concerned the over-scheduling of the 'Silverpeak' transmission line. The strategy sought to abuse weaknesses in the computer systems that supported California's deregulated market design (FERC, 2007). On 25 May 1999, Tim Belden, the manager of Enron's West Coast power trading desk, scheduled 2900 MW of power which he aimed to sell to California via the PX. The snag was that he proposed to use the 15 MW-rated 'Silverpeak' transmission line between southern California and Nevada to deliver it. Because this schedule called for 2900 MW to go across a line with only 15 MW of available capacity, it triggered CAISO's congestion management procedures (cf. McLean and Elkind, 2003, pp. 268–69; FERC, 2003, p. VI-26):

> This single announcement confused grid operators, caused a false congestion on the automated system that manages the state's transmission lines, allowed [the trader, MdB] to offer a series of counterbids to relieve the congestion, and raised the price of electricity by more than 70% across California. Californians paid about $5 million in added electricity charges that day, and Enron, which shared the profits with some of the local electricity operators, paid a penalty of $25,000 for its failed bid to the power grid. (Ekbia, 2004, p. 1)

The ISO quickly identified Enron's behaviour, filed a complaint, and received Enron's assurance that it would not engage in these schedules any more. However, the experiment had proved the viability of a concept that would become infamous as 'Death Star'.[3]

In various investigations that followed Enron's bankruptcy, a large number of Enron trading strategies were identified and analysed (see Table 6.4).[4] The strategies were designed to accomplish different goals and could be categorized in a number of ways.[5] DeCesaris et al. (2005) identify three categories of strategic behaviour based upon the different markets in which they sought to gain some advantages:

- strategic behaviour in electricity market trading;
- strategic behaviour in the congestion relief market;
- strategic behaviour in the ancillary services market.

The material showed how Enron traders systematically and willingly engaged in the creation and implementation of these strategies. 'When a trader found a formula that worked, he would send an e-mail around the office' (McLean and Elkind, 2003, p. 270).

Table 6.4   Overview of Enron strategies described in various investigations

	Strategy	Description
Energy market trading	'Export of Californian power'	Sell energy outside of California to avoid price caps
	'Ricochet' (Megawatt Laundering)	'Sell' energy outside of California to avoid price caps and increase scarcity, only to 're-import' the energy at higher prices
	'Fat Boy' ('inc-ing' Load)	Falsely overschedule load in hour-ahead and day-ahead markets to profit from higher real-time electricity prices
	'Thin Man'	Falsely underschedule load in hour-ahead and day-ahead markets to profit from lower real-time electricity prices
Congestion relief	'Load Shift'	Schedule large demands for power to change prices and then buy or sell in the targeted market to take advantage of the price differential
	'Death Star' (Circular schedules)	Circular schedules that fake transmission use in directions counter to ones where congestion is sure to arise to collect congestion revenues
	'Wheel Out'	Scheduling power over transmission lines that are taken out-of-service to collect congestion revenues
	'Non-firm Export'	Scheduling of export of non-firm power by a market participant that does not intend to or is incapable of providing the power but aims to receive congestion payment for cutting the schedule
	'Scheduling to Collect Congestion Charges'	Scheduling of power by a market participant designed solely to cause and subsequently remove congestion, aiming to receive congestion payments for cutting the schedule
Ancillary services	'Get Shorty'	Paper trading of ancillary services
	'Selling Non-firm as Firm'	Sell power as backed up by operating reserves, while in fact it is not
	'Double Selling'	Selling ancillary services twice in different markets

Source: Based on DeCesaris et al., 2005, Table 1: Overview of California Trading Strategies, p. 164; Woychik, 2006a; and FERC, 2007.

As time wore on, the strategies of the traders increased in complexity and also involved the cooperation of different partners. For these reasons, a specific handbook was made. 'An Enron Services Handbook contains a list of California market conditions with instructions for the Enron

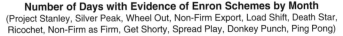

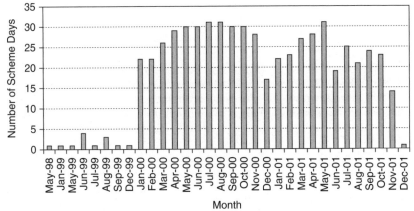

Source: www.snopud.com/Content/External/Documents/enron/020305/ChartDaysw
Schemes.doc, October 24, 2007.

Figure 6.1   Frequency of Enron's trading schemes

Employee concerning whom to call and what steps the partner should
follow to take advantage of a particular market situation' (FERC, 2003,
p. VI-40; Woychik, 2006a, p. 51).

Enron was eventually accused of being engaged in illegal trading
schemes on a daily basis (see Figure 6.1), and FERC claims that Enron
gamed the Californian market 'at least 597 days between May 1998 and
December 2001' (FERC, 2007, p. 34).

The various strategies and how they worked will be briefly explained.

6.5   STRATEGIC BEHAVIOUR IN ELECTRICITY MARKET TRADING

California's PX market was fairly complex. Enron traders used a variety
of strategies to 'play' these markets.

6.5.1   'Export of Californian Power'

This strategy resembled a normal arbitraging strategy. For example, on 1
August 2000 day-ahead prices on California's PX averaged $95 per MWh

while prices for electricity in Arizona 'exceeded $500 per MWh' (DeCesaris et al., 2005, p. 164). This strategy basically resulted in 'pure' market behaviour where electricity traders sold power where prices were highest. This could take place as prices differed across the region. However, the effects on the different power markets were disastrous in the sense that vital power resources were often moved out-of-state.

The increased shortage of resources, however, did not result in increased prices in California to reflect this scarcity and stimulate electricity suppliers to sell electricity to California. When California's power crisis persisted in the summer and fall of 2000, regulatory officials decided to lower the so-called 'price caps', effectively setting maximum power prices in the PX. Enron traders, however, used the same tactic to circumvent these price caps by simply exporting the power they had sold cheaply in California and sell it against far higher prices in other Western states that faced similar electricity shortages but did not have a price cap in place (FERC, 2003, p. VI-15). For example, on 5 December Enron was able to buy wholesale power in California at the $250 per MWh price cap and sell it in Oregon at $1200 per MWh (Fox, 2003, p. 209).

6.5.2 'Ricochet'

This strategy led Enron traders to schedule large power exports on a day-ahead or hour-ahead basis only to 're-import' this power in the 'real-time' market or via an 'out-of-market' deal with the ISO in order to evade price caps, which were only set in the PX markets and did not pertain to imports. Ricochet therefore aimed to profit from differences between day-ahead and real-time markets. Enron would buy power on the day-ahead market and sell it to an out-of-state trader. The next day, Enron would buy the energy back and sell it into the real-time market against higher prices. The overall effect of this strategy was to increase the scarcity of electricity and drive up the electricity prices without helping supply or demand. 'Since the strategy involves sending the power out of state in order to disguise the source, it has also been referred to as "megawatt laundering"' (DeCesaris et al., 2005, p. 165).

In reality, the power never left California. For example, on 22 May 2000 an Enron trader purchased electricity at $75 per MWh from CAISO in the day-ahead market. Then Enron set up the export and subsequent import of the electricity on paper to mask its origin and subsequently sold the electricity back to the CAISO under emergency conditions in an OOM deal, 'netting a profit of more than $222 per MWh' (Woychik, 2006b, p. 8).

Enron's strategy depended on the cooperation of non-public utility operators of electricity systems that connected with the ISO, including the City of Los Angeles Department of Water and Power (LADWP), the Bonneville Power Administration (BPA), Avista, and Enron's public utility affiliate (Portland General) (FERC, 2003, p. VI-17). Enron traders struck deals with these parties to disguise the source of the power and shared the extra revenues generated by the deals. 'Transcripts of Portland traders and transmission personnel include detailed instructions by Enron personnel on how the various participants (Portland and Avista) were to record transactions and how to report the various parts of the transactions consistent with NERC requirements and the Commission's regulations' (FERC, 2003, p. VI-17/18).

Although the strategy looked promising, in reality 'out-of-state markets rarely exceeded the price cap until November 2000, so Ricochet was not a major strategy for in-state generators during the Summer of 2000' (DeCesaris et al., 2005, p. 166). However, although FERC in initial research found no evidence of Ricochet tactics, the CAISO reports found evidence of the practice in 2003. Subsequent research showed that Enron engaged in Ricochet tactics from 1999. For example, a Ricochet transaction on 12 December 2000 shows how Enron profited by $650 per MWh from this practice (FERC, 2007, p. 47).

6.5.3 'Fat Boy'

'Fat Boy' was designed as a strategy to evade the requirement for all SCs to submit balanced schedules, meaning that supply must equal demand. As a result, Enron traders were able to withhold power from the day-ahead market and sell this power in real-time against higher prices. Enron traders employed this strategy 'whenever the ISO's load forecasts were smaller than their own and they believed that real-time prices would be favourable', in order to be paid for the excess generation against higher prices in real-time (DeCesaris et al., 2005, p. 167). Enron traders would schedule excess purchases of power in the day-ahead and hour-ahead markets to achieve these goals. 'Fat Boy' thus created large amounts of power in the grid, for which there was no load scheduled; so-called 'uninstructed energy'. According to the market rules, the ISO needed to pay the real-time market-clearing price for these 'uninstructed deviations'.

The strategy was well known among electricity traders and useful. In fact, many analyses show that the strategy itself was designed by the power traders as an answer to counter the strategic behaviour of the IOUs, who consistently underspecified their load in the day-ahead and hour-ahead markets in the hope of buying cheaper electricity in the real-time market. The irony was that this strategy thereby more than once helped California avert black-outs as the electricity that was withheld 'improved system reliability' by reducing supply shortfalls in real-time (cf. FERC, 2003; DeCesaris et al., 2005).

In another way, Enron traders also engaged in the scheduling of excess power when they believed that too much power would be produced. Then Enron would decide the next day not to buy that electricity after all, earning a real-time market payment for giving up power it never needed to begin with. This was known as 'inc-ing' (short for increasing) the load (Fox, 2003, p. 208).

Prior to September 2000, California's market rules had few incentives in place to curb this behaviour as this overgeneration was paid the same as real-time instructed generation. Consequently, during 2000, Enron routinely overscheduled 500–1000 MW (ISO, 2003a, p. 2), and used both its own assets as well as those of its partners, such as the Cities of Glendale and Redding (FERC, 2003).

6.5.4 'Thin Man'

'Thin Man' sought to achieve the direct opposite of 'Fat Boy' and was used by Enron traders to lower electricity prices by underscheduling load if day-ahead and hour-ahead prices were considered too high and then buy electricity in real-time (Woychik, 2006a, p. 51). Enron traders falsely underscheduled load by coordinating the assets of various partners to create the impression of low load, with the aim of explicitly reducing market prices (FERC, 2003, p. VI-16).

6.6 STRATEGIES DESIGNED FOR THE CONGESTION RELIEF MARKET

A number of tactics were devised to take advantage of the fact that California's electricity market used so-called congestion payments to provide market incentives to energy traders to help manage the electricity grid.

The idea was that energy traders who scheduled power flows that lifted or reduced congestion in the transmission system would be paid. One of the peculiarities of California's electricity markets was that congestion was optimized per participant based upon the need to provide balanced schedules. This created ample opportunities for market players to create congestion and get paid for relieving it.

Enron traders devised a number of strategies that sought to take advantage of these payments, which were not based on actual flows, but on planned flows. Enron's strategies were

> designed to generate payments for relieving transmission congestion by 'fooling' the CAISO's computerized congestion management program. These trading strategies generally involved scheduling transmission in the opposite direction of congestion, and thereby getting paid for the counterflow. They are all premised on imaginary transactions that are nonetheless eligible for congestion payments from the CAISO. (FERC, 2003, p. VI-26)

6.6.1 'Load Shift'

This was a strategy in which Enron traders attempted to drive congestion market prices higher. Enron traders submitted false load schedules, which deliberately created congestion on specific transmission lines to increase the value of Enron's transmission rights and profit from the creation and subsequent relief of artificial congestion (DeCesaris et al., 2005, p. 174).

Enron employed this strategy mainly on two vital transmission lines for which it held transmission rights: Path 15 and Path 26, which basically form the links between the north and south of California.

For example, Enron purchased 62 per cent of the capacity of 'Path 26', one of the vital North–South connections in California. Enron traders systematically overscheduled the load in the southern area it intended to serve with hundreds or sometimes thousands of MWs of load and understated the load in northern California that it served with a corresponding amount. That way, Enron increased the congestion on Path 26, and without having to provide power to either of the markets, it created 'phantom loads' and was paid for congestion relief when it chose not to serve this power in real-time. In reality, Enron never intended to serve this power anyway and could therefore earn congestion payments for trades it never intended to carry out.

In its report, FERC staff (2003, p. VI-12) concluded: 'This Enron trading strategy is particularly complicated and its success was dependent, in part, on the independent bidding behaviour of other entities.' Furthermore, the strategy was difficult to retrace, given the complexity of Enron's portfolio. Despite these problems, investigators found that Enron engaged in 'Load Shift' frequently. Of the 332 days studied by FERC, Enron traders used 'Load Shift' on 273 days. Traders even developed a computer model for dealing with the complex calculations to figure out how much load they needed to schedule to create artificial congestion (FERC, 2007, p. 45).

However, perhaps because of their dependence on the bidding strategies of other market parties, the ISO researchers (2003a, p. 18) calculated that the 'Load Shift' strategy had not been particularly successful. Estimations of profits range between $1.4–3.2 million.

6.6.2 'Death Star'

One of the best known and notorious strategies originally started out under a different name. The strategy was invented by Mr Forney, Enron's Real Time Trading Desk manager and originally christened the 'Forney Loop' or 'Forney Perpetual Loop' (DOJ, 2003). The strategy called 'Death Star' was used to route power in California's electricity grid deliberately around known choke points with little transmission capacity to collect congestion fees. Although 'Death Star' indeed did relieve congestion, the tactic was merely used to collect the fees, and never to provide the real power to the places where it was needed.

The first experiment in which a 'Death Star' type strategy was applied was the so-called 'Silverpeak' experiment described earlier (FERC, 2002). As we have seen, Enron was quickly reprimanded for employing this obvious ploy by the ISO.

The traders responded by devising increasingly sophisticated strategies that involved other parties. Possibilities were to use the transmission grids of parts of California's grid that were not owned by the ISO and/or to coop-erate with trading partners to 'disguise' Enron's involvement and share the profits. The cooperation of these trading partners – among them non-investor-owned Californian utilities, such as the Northern California Power Agency, LADWP, the City of Redding, the Modesto Irrigation District and Enron's Oregon-based utility affiliate Portland General Electric Company – was vital for the success of these strategies. These partners owned trans-mission facilities that interconnected with the ISO's system but fell outside the control of the ISO, which was crucial for camouflaging and avoiding detection of the loop schedules by the ISO (FERC, 2003, p. VI-27).

Enron traders started exploiting this strategy frequently from 2 January 2000 and the strategy was developed in a number of variants such as: 'Red Congo', 'NCPA Cong Catcher', 'Big Foot'[6], 'Small Death Star', 'Black Widow', 'Big Tuna', and 'the LOOP', 'which all had the fundamental purpose of creating simultaneous off-setting schedules where no energy would actually enter or be taken off the system' (De Cesaris et al., 2005, p. 169; FERC, 2007, p. 35).

The strategies all involved two or more schedules, which together formed a 'loop' so that in reality no electricity was transported. The loop was scheduled to run in a direction opposite well-known congested transmission paths so that congestion relief payments would be collected. FERC even reported instances where 'partners' were unaware of being part of this strategy (FERC, 2003, p. VI-27).

To provide an idea of the complexity of these schedules and appreciate the amount of coordination necessary to devise these 'loop schedules' the following example of a 'Forney perpetual loop' is provided (cf. FERC, 2002, p. 108). Enron would schedule to export non-firm energy from Palo Verde in Arizona, through California, and across the Oregon border. There Avista, a partner electricity trader, would buy the energy from Enron and then sell the energy to Portland (Enron's Oregon utility), which would transfer the electricity across Portland's system and sell the energy to Enron. Enron, in turn, would schedule the energy in Oregon back to the border with California. LADWP would subsequently schedule the energy from the California–Oregon border to Palo Verde in Arizona, where finally, the energy would be scheduled to return to California. In effect, the schedules resulted in zero energy flows.

In the period January 2000–June 2001 Enron's traders engaged in these strategies on at least 585 occasions, earning a total of $2.1 million from potential circular schedules or 'Death Star' strategies (FERC, 2007, p. 35).

6.6.3 'Wheel-Out'

The 'Wheel-Out' strategy aimed to schedule energy across a transmission line that was known to be out-of-service in order to create artificial congestion and receive congestion relief payments to relieve this congestion. Due to a software flaw in the ISO system 'the key to the strategy is that when the schedules are submitted, the traders know that the line capacity is zero and thus are certain that the schedules will be cut in real-time' (DeCesaris et al., 2005, p. 170).

Consequently, Enron received congestion relief payments, without ever having transmitted any energy. Although the ISO knew the flaw existed and wanted to change the congestion management programme to remedy this flaw, the PX rejected the proposal, arguing that its software could not cope with the proposed change. Enron admitted to have engaged in 'Wheel-Out' at least 11 times from 4 February 2000 and earned $225 075 (FERC, 2007, p. 49).

6.6.4 'Non-Firm Export'

This strategy involved the scheduling of non-firm energy exports in the day-ahead market by Enron traders to earn congestion fees without ever having the intention of exporting this energy. This meant that Enron scheduled the energy flow opposite a well-known congested transmission path. After having been paid the congestion relief payment, the schedule would be cut. In the discovered memo, Enron was said to have scheduled 'non-firm energy from SP15 to an area outside of California. After two hours a congestion relief payment is received because the energy flow is scheduled opposite a congested line. Then, the trader cuts the non-firm energy, and the congestion is resumed on the other line.'

The ISO found evidence that Enron had used this strategy on three days between 14 July and 20 July 2000 and 23 instances where no power was transmitted and no congestion was relieved, earning $54 414 (ISO, 2003a, p. 7; FERC, 2007, p. 48). The ISO reacted to this behaviour through a Market Notice in which this behaviour was banned.

6.6.5 'Scheduling Energy to Collect Congestion Charges'

When the amount of power scheduled for delivery in California's grid exceeded the capacity of the transmission lines, the ISO would pay traders 'congestion relief fees' to either reduce the power they were selling into the state's system or to transmit power in the opposite direction. Enron would schedule power deliveries it never intended to make in order to make it appear as if the grid would get congested in certain areas; the ISO would then ask energy traders to reverse deliveries on these congested lines and pay traders like Enron 'congestion relief fees'. Because congestion relief fees could be very high, it could make sense for Enron traders to sell electricity at a loss in order to create the appearance of congestion, only to reverse the trade later to earn the congestion relief payment. The penalties Enron traders thus incurred for not having transmitted the power they had scheduled initially in some instances outweighed the profits gained by the congestion relief payments. The practice was quickly discovered by the ISO and prohibited from 21 July 2000 (ISO, 2003b, p. 26). The ISO found no evidence of the use of these strategies since this date.

6.7 STRATEGIC BEHAVIOUR DESIGNED FOR THE ANCILLARY SERVICES MARKET

In the ancillary services market, the ISO obtained a variety of services that it needed for maintaining the reliability of service provision, such as immediate, 'spinning' reserve power capacity. Basically, ancillary services consisted of electricity trades that boasted a number of stringent conditions which would help the ISO maintain grid stability, such as the absolute guarantee that some electricity would be provided under any condition or within a certain amount of time. Hence, ancillary services were traded under premium prices. Enron traders used a variety of strategies to profit from the opportunities that the market seemed to provide.

6.7.1 'Get Shorty'

'Get Shorty' involved the provision of ancillary services in the day-ahead market, and only acquiring these ancillary services at lower prices in the hour-ahead or real-time market (Fox, 2003, p. 209; DeCesaris et al., 2005, p. 172).

This strategy strongly resembled a legitimate form of arbitrage in the market which was acknowledged in the ISO tariffs. This was based on the principle that energy traders could take advantage of the price differences between the different ancillary services markets. What made this strategy different from the buyback strategy was that Enron traders who used the 'Get Shorty' tactic 'never possessed the reserve energy and had no intention of ever supplying it' (DeCesaris et al., 2005, p. 172). Instead, Enron traders would then cut the offer for ancillary services, and subsequently provided ancillary services in the real-time market.

Enron traders were required to identify the source of the ancillary services to the ISO (that is the specific power plant that would provide the emergency power). However, because they had not yet acquired the energy, Enron traders submitted false information to the ISO (FERC, 2003, p. VI-31). On 10 July 2000, an Enron email was sent to the traders in which the shorting of ancillary services market as an ongoing strategic ploy was explicitly mentioned: 'First, congratulations on earning so much money on shorting the ancillary services market last month. That is textbook . . . Once again, amazing job on the [ancillary services] plays over the last few weeks' (Woychik, 2006b, p. 10).

In hindsight, the ISO had difficulties tracing back this behaviour and establishing the amount of profits gained from the strategy. Nevertheless, Enron traders were accused of engaging in this strategy constantly and more recent information confirmed that Enron engaged in these transactions with other power traders and that explicit agreements were set up to share the profits. Enron admitted to being engaged in these trades 949 times from 13 April to 25 August 2000 and earned almost $4 million (FERC, 2007, p. 40). In reality, the number might be higher.[7]

6.7.2 'Selling Non-Firm Energy as Firm Energy'

This strategy involved the deliberate selling or reselling of non-firm energy (energy that is not backed-up by emergency generation to ensure its delivery) to the ISO while claiming it was firm energy. Enron often bought electricity out-of-state and then imported it to California. For example, the ISO bought firm energy from Enron which turned out to be non-firm and cut, leaving the ISO left with no energy even though it had been sold as firm energy. Subsequent research has found it difficult to establish this type of behaviour.

6.7.3 'Double Selling'

Enron used the strategy at least once to sell ancillary services in the day-ahead market, but resold the same energy in the day-ahead or real-time markets (FERC, 2007, p. 49).

6.8   THE CONSEQUENCES OF ENRON'S STRATEGIC BEHAVIOUR

What was the result of the behaviour of Enron's traders? And how should this behaviour be characterized? Was it blatant misconduct, as many critics of Enron have presented it, or was it clever trading tactics? Two important characteristics of strategic behaviour emerge when we try to grapple with the questions.

6.8.1   Strategic Behaviour is Intangible

First of all, establishing the scale and scope of strategic behaviour and gaming at Enron has been found to be difficult. Various extensive investigations into gaming strategies at Enron led to a partial reconstruction of the behaviour that West Coast traders had engaged in.

Consequently, the true extent and nature of the behaviour of Enron's traders in California's electricity market cannot be easily established. Some have argued that the '[m]arket manipulation accusations, while troublesome, were mostly related to individual traders seeking to game the rules or to cheat' (Cicchetti et al., 2004, p. 135).

The information in the famous Enron-memos[8] (Rivera Brooks et al., 2002), the audio tapes and the subsequent FERC investigations and statements of accused power traders lend credibility to the more critical claim that gaming behaviour by Enron was not about 'rogue' traders, but a deliberate corporate strategy designed to play the markets (cf. FERC, 2003, 2005 and 2007).

However, it could also be argued that Enron did have a vested interest in making California's deregulated market – the first and most far-reaching deregulation undertaken up to that point in the US – work. In fact, in an Enron memo, staff were reminded that '[i]f Enron doesn't do well in California, Enron will have a difficult time convincing anyone outside California that they are capable of and committed to providing power services' (McLean and Elkind, 2003, p. 267). Consequently, Enron senior management immediately ordered the cessation of the tactics of West coast traders on 10 December 2000, after being informed about these practices through the infamous memo (ibid, p. 274).

6.8.2   Strategic Behaviour is not Illegal by Definition

Second, to clearly distinguish legitimate strategic behaviour from illegal behaviour has proven anything but straightforward. The list of behaviour of Enron's traders shows a myriad of strategies, '[s]ome of which seem less than kosher and some of which are just clever' (Taylor and VanDoren, 2002, p. 4).

Although the behaviour of Enron traders may look suspicious or incriminating on paper, it should be noted that some behaviour was anything but abnormal in the electricity business for a number of reasons. Although Enron's traders took advantage of the rules, they did not always actually break them. In the energy trading world 'talking your book' – lying about your position in order to get the market to move your way – was common practice (McLean and Elkind, 2003, p. 275).

In fact some have argued that (some of) the strategies were not abusive at all, but were simply the behaviour of a power trader looking for arbitrage opportunities which in turn enhances economic efficiency (DeCesaris et al., 2005; Taylor and VanDoren, 2002; Falk, 2002). Rather than condemning these activities, these critics have noted that Enron's strategies often increased 'market efficiency', stability and provided proper market incentives delivering power when it was apparently needed. Similarly, FERC staff (2003, p. VI-16/17) maintained that California power exports, although they affected California's power prices and increased scarcity in California, were considered entirely acceptable behaviour: 'A merchant generator who exported power out of California in search of a better price or the opportunity to sell in forward (rather than spot) markets was behaving in a rational economic manner'. If at all, critics and regulators invariably criticized California's 'flawed', 'ill-conceived' and 'over-regulated' markets as main culprits for the behaviour shown by market parties (FERC, 2000; Falk, 2002; DeCesaris et al., 2005); mere 'clever exploitations of overly complex rules by companies that do not account for the impact of their decisions on prices and customers' (FERC, 2003, p. VI-3).

Some strategies could be employed in a wide variety of forms, while others were considered largely unsuccessful and unprofitable (for example 'Load Shift', 'Scheduling Energy to Collect Congestion Charges') according to the FERC and CAISO staff investigations (cf. DeCesaris et al., 2005, p. 169). Others were only successfully used on a few occasions. 'Non-Firm Export' was only successfully employed by Enron on three days in June and July 2000, earning Enron a mere $54 000, before being identified by the ISO and becoming a prohibited trading strategy (DeCesaris et al., 2005, p. 171).

Furthermore, Enron was by no means the only electricity trading company to resort to these behaviours. Almost immediately after the discovery of the Enron memos, FERC requested all West Coast power traders to admit or deny having been engaged in Enron-type trading strategies and filed data requests from more than 130 electricity trading companies, including municipal and governmental agencies in California and public utilities (FERC, 2003, p. VI-3). Company responses and subsequent analyses by the ISO showed that other power companies engaged in strategic behaviour as well. In total FERC has accused over 60 power companies that were engaged in market manipulation in Western energy markets in 2000–2001, either unilaterally or in tandem. Many electricity trading companies (for example Xcel Energy, Mirant Energy, Williams Cos., Reliant Energy) settled and admitted that their traders schemed and withheld production capacity to markets to 'game' California's market (cf. Fox, 2003, p. 210). The ISO (2003a) and FERC (2003, p. VI-28) concluded that some other companies had earnings from the strategies outlined here many times larger than Enron.

And finally, it should be acknowledged that to a considerable extent Enron traders could have engaged regularly in these transactions only with the help of third parties, be they clients or other power trading companies. Evidence provided by Enron indicated that traders from other companies willingly cooperated in several of the trading strategies (FERC, 2003, p. VI-2). Enron for example engaged in 'parking and lending agreements with the Public Service Company of New Mexico to facilitate its gaming practices' (FERC, 2007, p. 51).

According to FERC, however, Enron fielded these practices to a far greater extent and level of sophistication than any other power trading company (FERC, 2007, p. 41). FERC investigators claim Enron deliberately set out to control the assets of partners and customers for whom it provided services, such as the running of the plants[9] to increase Enron's trading flexibility and influence on the energy markets and to engage in various types of gaming.[10] These deliberate strategies were known as 'partnership plays' and these types of relationships existed with over 30 customers (Woychik, 2006a).

However, where does that leave us with regard to the effects of Enron's trading behaviour? From what has been argued above, one can only concur that it is impossible to gauge the 'indirect and cumulative impact of these strategies on overall market prices and outcomes' (McLean and Elkind, 2003, p. 274).[11] The complexity and sheer number of power trades by Enron, the large number of strategies and variations and its use of and collaboration with many other companies were so complex that the ISO and FERC found it difficult to assess the effects of the behaviour of Enron (FERC, 2003, p. VI-3; ISO, 2003b, p. 3). These difficulties were compounded by the widespread gaming practices fielded by many other actors in the West Coast power markets, which included the ISO and the utilities (cf. Broder, 2002; Fox, 2003; DeCesaris et al., 2005), generation companies and other power trading firms (FERC, 2002; 2003).

The total revenues that Enron gained directly from these strategies were relatively modest, several millions of dollars. The behaviour was but one tactic used by Enron traders to increase revenues in California's electricity market. Enron's main earnings resulted from another, legitimate tactic; it speculated on rising electricity prices in power trading by taking a long position in the various markets (Barboza, 2002). According to FERC, Enron was able to engage successfully in speculation due to the availability of unique knowledge on market conditions through Enron Online – Enron's real-time energy trading tool – causing market volatility and distorted prices (FERC, 2003). In the Summer of 2000, Enron's West Coast trading desk made a profit of $200 million, roughly quadrupling the results the desk had made for all of 1999 (Keila and Skillicorn, 2005, p. 196; McLean and Elkind, 2003, p. 273). At the height of the crisis on 4 December 2000, Enron traders earned $485 million on a single day, only to lose $550 million several days later. Enron's net profits for December were $440 million. 'Several Enron trading officials said that to justify their risk-taking, they told the company's executives and directors that, like a casino, Enron had a "house advantage" in the energy markets' resulting from their large influence in the energy markets through Enron Online (Barboza, 2002; FERC, 2003). Some have argued that Enron alone 'booked unusually large and secret reserves for its trading profits during the California energy crisis. The company put as much as $1.5 billion into undisclosed reserves, hiding massive profits while denying accusations that it generated excessive profits by price-gauging Californians' (Barboza, 2002; Fox, 2003, p. 220). FERC estimated from the raw data taken from Enron's databases that Enron's cumulative profits in the Western electricity markets approached $1.8 billion in 2000–2001 (FERC, 2002, p. 92) (see Figure 6.2).

This of course brings us to the question regarding whether Enron's practices had any impact on California's electricity shortages. In a report,

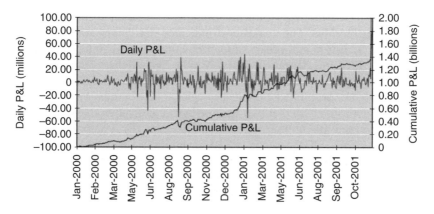

Source: FERC (2002), Figure 11: Daily and Cumulative P&L for the Western Electricity Trading Desk, p. 93.

Figure 6.2 Enron's West coast profits and losses (P&L)

the ISO concluded that 'while Enron strategies could have financial impacts on the markets, they did not contribute to the outages during the winter of 2000–2001' (FERC, 2003, p. VI-12; Rivera Brooks et al., 2002). Most experts agree that California's electricity market was flawed to such an extent that even if parties had not behaved illegally, electricity shortages would have occurred. California's electricity crisis was not caused by Enron, nor was Enron the sole party that had acted strategically during the electricity crisis (e.g. Broder, 2002; Fox, 2003; DeCesaris et al., 2005).

Furthermore, not only was it energy traders who were engaging in strategic behaviour. As was stated before, it was widely known that the IOUs were systematically underscheduling their load in the PX day-ahead market to reduce costs (DeCesaris et al., 2005, p. 166). The California ISO even knew of the behaviour of energy trading companies. The ISO 'was aware of the overscheduling of load and even acted to encourage it at times by creating fictitious load points' (FERC, 2003, p. VI-25), thereby engaging in strategic behaviour to counter the strategies employed by market participants (Cicchetti et al., 2004, pp. 138/144–5).

6.8.3 FERC's Ruling

Despite the evidence that California's market was at best only relatively modestly affected by the behaviour displayed by Enron's power traders, FERC moved hard against the practices that were designed by and practised by Enron's West coast power traders. On 26 March 2003, FERC

(2003) reported finding significant evidence of market manipulation in the energy markets. The final report indicated that 'many trading strategies used by Enron and other companies violated anti-gaming provisions in the CAISO and PX tariffs'. On 1 March 2005 after investigating over 3000 hours of Enron trader conversations, FERC staff claimed that Enron participated in prohibited gaming strategies. The Commission found that Enron 'advocated a market that was inefficient and vulnerable to manipulation and then sought out to detect weaknesses in the system that it could exploit' (FERC, 2007, p. 33). FERC eventually ruled that Enron did manipulate the market (FERC, 2007, p. 51) and that some of its trading strategies posed a threat to system reliability and market efficiency. In its most recent initial ruling, FERC ordered that the total amount of unjust profits by Enron made by its Western markets desk had to be disgorged, amounting to an estimated $1.6 billion (FERC, 2007, p. 63).

6.9 STRATEGIC BEHAVIOUR

In hindsight, the strategic behaviour that Enron's West Coast power traders (and those of the other power companies) displayed in California's electricity market may be explained by analysing the factors that triggered their emergence. First of all, it should be noted that Enron's West Coast electricity traders and those of other companies could not have engaged in this behaviour if California's market design and the rules guiding the various markets had been more carefully designed and did not represent such a radical change from electricity (market) operations in the past. Electricity experts have claimed that California's deregulation, which sought to reduce government involvement in the electricity industry, was botched (Brennan, 2001; CSA, 2001; Joskow, 2001a; Cichetti et al., 2004; DeCesaris et al., 2005; Kahn and Lynch, 2000). The system of incentives that was put in place in California's electricity market design was seriously flawed and provided the wrong incentives to market participants.

However, in the various strategic ploys that were designed, Enron's electricity traders used the flawed market rules to their advantage and (ab)used the fact that they were trading a vital commodity that cannot be stored or produced at a moment's notice and the provision of which demands an enormously complicated technical system. Many of the strategies in some way were intended to take advantage of the technical constraints that specifically apply to the electricity market and the unique product characteristics of electricity (see Table 6.5). For example, Enron's congestion relief strategies sought to game the scarce yet vital high-voltage transmission capacity on a number of connections in California's electricity grid.

Table 6.5 Enron

Entry	Strategic behaviour: type and description
Rules and contracts + Bottleneck facilities+ indispensable nature (+ factor 'time')	*Congestion relief strategies.* Enron traders used the scarce yet vital transmission capacity to increase earnings in a variety of ways.
Rules and contracts + indispensable nature + factor 'time'	*Energy market trading strategies.* Enron traders used time to increase the earnings from the vital function that electricity provides.
Rules and contracts + bottleneck facilities + indispensable nature	*Ancillary services strategies.* Enron traders used vital and scarce services that were designed to ensure grid stability.

Similarly, Enron's market trading strategies were largely based on the crucial advantage that the sequential markets provided them to increase the earnings of the vital commodity that electricity is. And finally, Enron's ancillary service strategies similarly sought to (ab)use some of the vital characteristics of ancillary power. Ancillary services performed a vital role in the overall reliable management of California's electricity system.

Enron's traders crossed the line between illegal and strategic behaviour in search of ways to 'game' California's market. However, with this chapter, we hope to convey the message that Enron was by no means the only culprit, nor was it the biggest culprit of all. FERC's recent ruling means that roughly 10 per cent of the excess energy costs that resulted from California's electricity crisis are being recouped (Weare, 2003, p. 3). This may serve as a sobering thought for those that think that California's electricity crisis has been resolved.

NOTES

1. See for detailed accounts of California's electricity markets and electricity crisis: Joskow (2001a); Kahn and Lynch (2000); CSA (2001); Brennan (2001); Cicchetti et al. (2004); De Bruijne (2006).
2. A number of files and audio recordings can be found at: http://ag.ca.gov/antitrust/energy/content/enron.php; and http://www.snopud.com/?p=2647, accessed 25 October, 2007.
3. See sub-section 6.6.2.
4. Some strategies have not been properly identified. Although the FERC found evidence that Enron traders engaged in other strategies, insufficient evidence could be found to reconstruct their precise meaning (FERC, 2007, p. 49). These included: 'Big Tuna', 'Donkey Punch', 'Little Tuna', 'Ping Pong', 'Russian Roulette', 'Sidewinder',

and 'Spread Play'. Some games are believed to have been variations or combinations of the identified strategies (cf. Woychik, 2006a, p. 15). These included: 'Project Stanley', 'Silver Peak', 'Spread Plan', 'Donkey Punch', and 'Ping Pong'. Schemes that are referenced in documents other than the Enron memorandums include 'Black Widow', 'Red Congo', 'Big Tuna' and the 'Forney perpetual loop'. These are all considered variations of 'Non-firm', 'Wheel-Out' and 'Death Star' strategies (FERC, 2003, p. VI-26).

5. For example, FERC (2003) has identified three generic roles which the strategies sought to achieve: price manipulation, price maximization and trading strategies based on false information. Woychik (2006a) classified the goals of the strategies as: avoidance of price caps set in the PX, the triggering of ISO emergency conditions, or the triggering of so-called OOM calls and the withholding of power. For example, the following strategies could be used to stimulate the ISO to make OOM deals: 'Partnership Plays', 'Ricochet', 'Perpetual Loop', 'Wheel Out', 'Load Shift', and 'Fat-Boy' (Woychik, 2006a, p. 53, footnote 69).

6. See FERC (2003), p. VI-38.

7. However, Enron was by no means the largest perpetrator of this strategy. FERC estimated that the five biggest perpetrators of the 'Get Shorty' strategy earned $57 million. Some evidence suggests, however, that Enron coordinated many of the strategic actions of these entities (FERC, 2003, p. VI-32).

8. These memos can be found at: http://www.ferc.gov/industries/electric/indus-act/wec. asp, accessed 9 April 2008.

9. Among the customers to whom Enron offered power trading or operational services were smaller utilities, public utility districts, municipalities, qualifying facilities, and cogeneration facilities.

10. For example, the FERC controlled and operated El Paso's assets during certain periods and more or less controlled 'decision-making authority over sales of electric energy' (FERC, 2007, p. 51). In return, Enron engaged in equity type agreements to share the profits when engaged in certain games (FERC, 2003, p. VI-37/38).

11. Cf. DeCesaris et al. (2005, footnote 1).

REFERENCES

Alaywan, Z. (2000), 'Evolution of the California Independent System Operator Markets', *The Electricity Journal*, **13**(6), 70–83.

Barboza, D. (2002), 'Despite denial, Enron papers show big profit on price bets', *New York Times*, 13 December.

Besant-Jones, J. and B. Tenenbaum (2001), 'The California power crisis: lessons for developing countries', Energy & Mining Sector Board Discussion Paper Series, Paper No. 1, Washington, DC: The World Bank.

Blumstein, C., L.S. Friedman and R. Green (2002), 'The history of electricity restructuring in California', *Journal of Industry, Competition and Trade*, **2**(1–2), 9–38.

Brennan, T.J. (2001), *The California Electricity Experience, 2000–01: Education or Diversion?*, Washington, DC: Resources for the Future.

Broder, J.M. (2002), 'California power failures linked to energy companies', *New York Times*, 18 September.

California State Auditor (CSA) (2001), 'Energy deregulation: the benefits of competition were undermined by structural flaws in the market, unsuccessful oversight, and uncontrollable competitive forces', Bureau of State Audits, 2000-134.1R, Sacramento.

Cicchetti, J., J.A. Dubin and C.M. Long (2004), *The California Electricity Crisis: What, Why, and What's Next*, Boston, MA: Springer Science.

De Bruijne, M.L.C. (2006), 'Networked reliability, institutional fragmentation and the reliability of service provision in critical infrastructures', Dissertation, Delft University of Technology.

DeCesaris, M., G. Leonard and J.D. Zona (2005), 'Energy trading strategies in California', in M.A. Crew and M. Spiegel (eds), *Obtaining the Best from Regulation and Competition*, Topics in Regulatory Economics and Policy, Volume 47, New York: Kluwer Academic Publishers, pp. 161–78.

DOJ (2003), *Press release*, 4 December, www.usdoj.gov/tax/usaopress/2003/txdv032003_12_04_forney.html, accessed 24 October 2007.

Ekbia, H.R. (2004), 'How IT mediates organizations: Enron and the California Electricity crisis', *Journal of Digital Information*, **5**(4), http://journals.tdl.org/jodi/rt/printerFriendly/jodi-157/144, accessed 23 November 2007.

Falk, J. (2002), 'Substituting outrage for thought: the Enron "smoking gun" memos', *The Electricity Journal*, **15**(7), 13–22.

FERC (2000), 'Market order proposing remedies for California wholesale electric structure', Docket No. EL00-95-000, Washington, DC.

FERC (2002), 'Initial report on company-specific separate proceedings and generic reevaluations; published natural gas prices and Enron trading strategies, fact-finding investigation of potential manipulation of electric and natural gas prices', Docket No. PA02-2-000, Washington, DC.

FERC (2003), 'Final report on price manipulation in Western markets, fact-finding investigation of potential manipulation of electric and natural gas prices', Docket No. PA02-2-000, Washington, DC.

FERC (2005), 'The commission's response to the California electricity crisis and timeline for distribution of refunds', Report submitted to Congress, Washington, DC.

FERC (2007), 'Initial decision', Docket No. EL03-180-000, Washington, DC.

Fox, L. (2003), *Enron, The Rise and Fall*, Hoboken, NJ: John Wiley & Sons, Inc.

General Accounting Office (GAO) (2001), 'Energy markets, results and studies assessing high electricity prices in California', Report to Congressional Requesters, GAO-01-857, Washington, DC.

Hughes, J.P. (2000), 'California's summer 2000 power crisis', Report for Elcon members, Washington, DC: Elcon.

ISO (2002), 'California ISOpen', 2001 Annual Report, Folsom.

ISO (2003a), 'Analysis of trading and scheduling strategies described in Enron memos', Department of Market Analysis, California ISO, 4 October, Folsom.

ISO (2003b), 'Supplemental analysis of trading and scheduling strategies described in Enron memos, Department of Market Analysis', California ISO, June, Folsom.

ISO (2005), '2004 Annual report on market issues and performance', April, Folsom.

Joskow, P.L. (2000a), 'Deregulation and regulatory reform in the US electric power sector', in S. Peltzman and C. Winston (eds), *Deregulation of Network Industries: What's Next?*, Washington, DC: AEI-Brookings Joint Center for Regulatory Studies, pp. 113–88.

Joskow, P.L. (2000b), 'Deregulation and regulatory reform in the US electric power sector', paper prepared for the Brookings-AEI Conference on Deregulation in Network Industries, 9–10 December, revised discussion draft, 17 February,

MIT Center for Energy and Environmental Policy Research, Cambridge, MA, http://web.mit.edu/ceepr/www/2000-003.pdf, accessed 21 August 2005.

Joskow, P.L. (2001), 'California's electricity crisis', NBER Working Paper 8442, National Bureau of Economic Research, Cambridge, MA.

Joskow, P.L. and E. Kahn (2002), 'A quantitative analysis of pricing behavior in California's wholesale electricity market during Summer 2000', *The Energy Journal*, **23**, 1–35.

Kahn, M. and L. Lynch (2000), 'California's electricity options and challenges, report to Governor Gray Davis', Sacramento: California Electricity Oversight Board and the California Public Utilities Commission.

Keila, P.S. and D.B. Skillicorn (2005), 'Structure in the Enron email dataset', *Computational & Mathematical Organization Theory*, **11**(3), 183–99.

McLean, B. and P. Elkind (2003), *The Smartest Guys in the Room, The Amazing Rise and Scandalous Fall of Enron*, New York: Portfolio.

Rivera Brooks, N., T.S. Mulligan and T. Reiterman (2002), 'Memo shows Enron role in power crisis energy', *New York Times/The Los Angeles Times*, 7 May.

Taylor, J. and P. VanDoren (2002), 'Did Enron pillage California?', CATO Institute Briefing Papers, No. 72, Washington, DC: Cato Institute, www.cato.org/pub_display.php?pub_id=1511, accessed 26 November 2007.

Weare, C. (2003), *The California Electricity Crisis: Causes and Policy Options*, San Francisco, CA: Public Policy Institute of California.

Woychik, E.C. (2006a), 'How Enron et al gamed the electricity market: an empirical assessment', research paper, School of Management, Cleveland: Case Western Reserve University, www.weatherhead.case.edu/edm/archive/papers.cfm?topic=25, accessed 25 November 2007.

Woychik, E.C. (2006b), 'Appendix 2, Data sources and summary statistics', research paper, School of Management, Cleveland: Case Western Reserve University, www.weatherhead.case.edu/edm/archive/papers.cfm?topic=25, accessed 25 November 2007.

7. American Telephone and Telegraph Company

7.1 BACKGROUND: THE BELL SYSTEM

Since its foundation in 1885, the American Telephone and Telegraph Company (AT&T Corporation) had been owned by the American Bell Telephone Company, also called Bell System. Right from the start, AT&T had been an active player. It tried to strengthen its market position particularly by taking over smaller independent telephone companies. Other links in the chain also attracted AT&T's interest. An important takeover was that of Western Electric Manufacturing Company by Bell System in 1882. Western Electric manufactured telegraph and telephone equipment and components.[1]

The takeover of Western Electric brought AT&T an important trump card, which it managed to play smartly. AT&T forbade its subscribers to use their own equipment. Instead, they were forced to rent telephones and, if necessary, other peripherals from AT&T, which, in turn, only offered products manufactured by Western Electric. Many phones made by Western Electric carried the following disclaimer permanently moulded into their housings: 'Bell System property. Not for sale'. Telephones were also labelled with a sticker marking the Bell Operating Company that owned the telephone. AT&T leased out the phones at a fixed rate per month. In this way, AT&T collected an amount in rent many times higher than the production costs, while the advantage for AT&T increased the longer the rental agreement lasted. The prohibition to use phones of producers other than Western Electric had to be taken seriously. AT&T had inspectors monitor compliance with the prohibition by checking household line voltage levels to establish if consumers used non-leased phones (Adams and Butler, 1999; Smith, 1985).

The renting out brought AT&T and Western Electric an extra income worth millions of dollars, while at the same time strengthening Western Electric's market position. This allowed Western Electric to become one of the prime manufacturers of telecommunication equipment in the United States and Canada. As Western Electric was able to sell phones at all times, it had no incentives for change and innovation. The fixed range of products hardly changed over the years. Subscribers could only choose from a limited number of types of phones. Occasionally, AT&T gave old, returned phones a new housing and recirculated them. Subscribers that insisted on using a phone of a make other than Western Electric could do so by transferring its ownership to AT&T and then renting the phone from AT&T at a monthly rate increased by a 're-wiring' fee (Adams and Butler, 1999).

Not until much later, in the 1980s, when more and more subscribers used phones of other makes, did AT&T change its policy in the sense that subscribers were allowed to choose a phone's housing. However, even in that situation AT&T did not entirely sacrifice its monopoly. The mechanical components remained the property of AT&T, for which the subscriber had to pay a monthly amount in rent (Adams and Butler, 1999; Smith, 1985).

7.2 KINGSBURY COMMITMENT 1913

Around the previous turn of the century, there were more than 6000 telephony providers (AT&T, 2007). Each provider had its own network and since the free market blocked interconnection and there was no legal obligation to allow interconnection, the United States presented the picture of numerous fragmented local and long-distance telephone networks. The fragmentation played into the hands of AT&T because it was able to pay its way while its competitors could not, because AT&T had by far the biggest long-distance network, which, besides, was in excellent technical condition. Repeatedly, AT&T turned down requests for interconnection from its competitors. AT&T did well out of its uncooperative attitude: several competitors went bust. In a vast country like the United States, users were simply not interested in subscribing to a small company, which could only provide telephone services within the local community. They were mainly interested in the possibility of making long-distance calls (Massey, 1997).

At the beginning of the last century, the Bell System gained so much market power that the federal administration began to be concerned about the future. It is not a coincidence that the administration had not taken an interest in telephony until then. There was a slowly growing awareness that the telephone offered great promises for the country's economic and social development. An unbalanced development of the telephony market might therefore have far-reaching consequences. The direct reason for the Justice Department to clamp down on AT&T was the large number of complaints of competitors about abuse of economic power and market distortion. In addition, however, those who felt that the government should take over the Bell System were gaining political strength in 1913 (Massey, 1997).

Driven by the fear of facing a large-scale investigation into its business operations, AT&T decided to make the best of a bad job. During the negotiations with the Department of Justice after the case had been taken to court, AT&T made the necessary compromise. In the Kingsbury Commitment, actually a letter from AT&T's Vice-President Nathan Kingsbury of 9 December 1913, AT&T agreed with the Attorney General to provide long-distance services to independent exchanges under certain conditions and to refrain from acquisitions if the Interstate Commerce Commission (ICC), the predecessor of the Federal Communications Commission (FCC), objected. The takeover prohibition was not absolute. AT&T was allowed to buy market shares in so far as this growth kept pace with the increase in subscribers. In practice, takeover prohibition hardly hampered AT&T. Between 1921 and 1934, the ICC approved 271 of AT&T's 274 purchase requests.

The Kingsbury Commitment did not settle all the differences between independents and Bell companies. Although AT&T agreed to connect its long-distance service to independent local carriers, it did not agree to interconnect its local services with other local providers (AT&T, 2007). This allowed AT&T to kill two birds with one stone. It would profit from the expected increase in long-distance traffic while at the same time heading off inconvenient competitors on the local market. The reason was that AT&T had the most profitable urban markets through Bell Operating Companies such as the New York Telephone Company, the Pacific Telephone and Telegraph Company and the Southwestern Bell Telephone Company. These companies would not benefit in any way from interconnection of their network with networks of other local companies (Smith, 1985).

The Kingsbury Commitment perpetuated rather than broke the hegemony of the Bell System, popularly known as 'Ma' Bell. The Bell System dominated the most profitable markets. Its competitors could whistle for them and had to be satisfied with what the Bell System left to them: less profitable outlying areas and vast stretches of rural America (Massey, 1997).

However, in 1929 AT&T indicated through Arthur Page, its first vice-president of public relations, that it advocated regulation:

> The public, acting through its legislators, has a right to expect and demand good service at reasonable prices from business. It has the power to take any action it pleases to insure this. [. . .] The regulatory bodies as well as legislators have a responsibility [. . .] to see that business does serve the public well [. . .] and that the commissions do not force a disintegration of responsibility that renders healthy industries and the best service to the nation possible. (Massey, 1997)

7.3   WESTERN ELECTRIC NOT DIVESTED AFTER ALL?

The mutually profitable cooperation between AT&T and Western Electric (see above) was first tackled in 1949. The US Department of Justice sued Western Electric and AT&T, charging that they had monopolized the manufacture and sale of telephones and equipment (Civil Action No. 17-49). What the Justice Department sought was the divestiture by AT&T of Western Electric, the termination of the exclusive relationship Western Electric enjoyed with AT&T, and the total separation of telephone manufacturing from the provision of telephone service and research (US District Court, D.D.C., 11 August 1982, at 135).

In 1956, the court approved a consent decree. A consent decree is a judicial decree expressing a voluntary agreement between parties to a suit, especially an agreement by a defendant to cease activities alleged by the administration to be illegal in return for an end to the charges. The Justice Department did not get what it originally envisaged. The 1956 decree did not include the divestiture of Western Electric. Instead, an injunction was issued which barred AT&T from engaging in any business other than the provision of common carrier communication services, and required Western Electric and AT&T to license their patents to anyone who wanted them upon the payment of appropriate royalties. This offered competing manufacturers a limited possibility of selling their products to AT&T subscribers (US District Court, D.D.C., 11 August 1982, at 138).

In 1959, the antitrust subcommittee of the House Judiciary Committee held hearings on the 1956 consent decree. The Subcommittee's investigations revealed that AT&T was very active behind the scenes in trying to get the administration to suspend its 1949 suit. AT&T continued its attempts to end the litigation as soon as the Eisenhower administration took office. As a result of AT&T's continuing lobbying of the Defense Department, the Secretary of Defense wrote a letter to the Attorney General asking him to end the 1949 litigation without requiring AT&T's divestiture of Western Electric. The Subcommittee, in its 1959 report, concluded that the Attorney General manifested a willingness to have the Justice Department consider a token settlement and forgo a decree consistent with the public interest – an attitude denoting partiality toward the defendants incompatible with the duties of this public office. The Subcommittee also uncovered the fact that AT&T had actually prepared the letter that the Secretary of Defense sent to the Attorney General (US District Court, D.D.C., 11 August 1982, at 136–8; Triebwasser, 1998).

Besides, AT&T made certain efforts to boost its public image and get rid of the dated image of 'Ma' Bell. The most successful of these efforts was the change that AT&T implemented in its shares policy: in 1959, a share split took place and there was a sharp rise in dividend. This changed the image of the AT&T share (and the company itself) from a stable factor into a growth-oriented company. Vitality became the new value that AT&T wanted to put across (Massey, 1997).

7.4 THE 1956 HUSH-A-PHONE DECISION

The story goes that one day an AT&T lawyer happened to see the Hush-A-Phone in a shop window (Gordon, 1997). Hush-A-Phone was a simple aid in the form of a protective cover that could be placed on the receiver to muffle the sound of the voice, giving the speaker more privacy. The lawyer decided to halt the sale of, and the trade in, the Hush-A-Phone. In his opinion, the use of the application constituted a breach of the prohibition to connect alien equipment with AT&T's phones. Article 2.6.1 of the General Provisions read as follows:

> No equipment, apparatus, circuit or device not furnished by the telephone company shall be attached to or connected with the facilities furnished by the telephone company, whether physically, by induction or otherwise except as provided in 2.6.2 through 2.6.12 following. In case any such unauthorized attachment or connection is made, the telephone company shall have the right to remove or disconnect the same; or to suspend the service during the continuance of said attachment or connection; or to terminate the service. (US Court of Appeals, D.C.Cir., 8 November 1956)

AT&T was certain that it would win the case. The omens were good. Until then AT&T had successfully taken steps against companies who sold advertising trinkets (premiums) that slipped over or could be otherwise attached to their phones. These trinkets had phone numbers for the local coal company, funeral parlour, general store, and so on. Under Section 203(a) of the US Communications Act 1934, AT&T claimed the right to forbid attachment to the telephone of any device not furnished by the telephone company. The case turned out quite differently from what AT&T had expected (Gordon, 1997).

On appeal, the US Court of Appeals dismissed AT&T's argumentation. It allowed the Hush-A-Phone (and every other similar device) to be stuck to AT&T's phones.

> It would seem that, although the Commission [*FCC* – eds] has no such control in general, there is asserted a right to prevent the subscriber from achieving such tones by the aid of a device other than his own body. Thus, intervenors [*AT&T and US Independent Telephone Association* – eds] do not challenge the

subscriber's right to seek privacy. They say only that he should achieve it by cupping his hand between the transmitter and his mouth and speaking in a low voice into this makeshift muffler. This substitute, we note, is not less likely to impair intelligibility than the Hush-A-Phone itself, for the Commission has found that whenever an enclosure is placed around the mouth of a person an intensification of frequencies below approximately 500 cycles occurs, and if the intensification is too great, a distortion or blasting effect results in the transmitter. In both instances, the party at the other end of the line hears a comparatively muted and distorted tone because the subscriber has chosen to use his telephone in a way that minimizes the risk of being overheard. In neither case is anyone other than the two parties to the conversation affected. To say that a telephone subscriber may produce the result in question by cupping his hand and speaking into it, but may not do so by using a device which leaves his hand free to write or do whatever else he wishes, is neither just nor reasonable. The intervenors' tariffs, under the Commission's decision, are in unwarranted interference with the telephone subscriber's right reasonably to use his telephone in ways which are privately beneficial without being publicly detrimental. Prescribing what changes should be made in the tariffs to render them 'just, fair, and reasonable' and determining what orders may be required to prohibit violation of subscribers' rights there under are functions entrusted to the Commission. (US Court of Appeals, D.C.Cir., 8 November 1956, at 269)

The court's decision, which exonerated Hush-a-Phone Company and prohibited further interference by AT&T toward Hush-a-Phone users, stated that AT&T's prohibition of the device was not 'just, fair, and reasonable', as required under the Communications Act of 1934, as the device 'does not physically impair any of the facilities of the telephone companies', nor 'is anyone other than the two parties to the conversation affected' (US Court of Appeals, D.C.Cir., 8 November 1956, at 268–9). A decade later, this criterion was extended to the effect that a device for wireless communication could also be connected to the telephone.

7.5   THE 1968 CARTERFONE DECISION

In 1959, the Carter Electronics Corporation started the production of the Carterfone, a device for wireless communication at home that can be connected to the telephone. The Carterfone connects to a two-way radio at the base station serving a mobile radio system. When callers on the radio and on the telephone are both in contact with the base station operator, the handset of the operator's telephone is placed on a cradle in the Carterfone device. A voice control circuit in the Carterfone automatically switches on the radio transmitter when the telephone caller is speaking; when he stops speaking, the radio returns to a receiving condition. The Carterfone comes with a separate loudspeaker, allowing the base station operator to follow the call, to adjust the volume and hang up the telephone at his end when the call is finished (FCC Decision, 26 June 1968).

Of the 4500 Carterfones that were produced between 1959 and 1966, some 3500 were sold to dealers and distributors across the US and abroad (FCC Decision, 26 June 1968). Although the market showed an interest, Thomas Carter, the owner of Carter Electronics Corporation, saw his chances of profit threatened by a use prohibition that AT&T imposed on its subscribers. Following a complaint by Carter, the FCC dealt with the matter. When asked, AT&T substantiated the use prohibition by referring to its public responsibility and the public interest:

> Since the telephone companies have the responsibility to establish, operate and improve the telephone system, they must have absolute control over the quality, installation, and maintenance of all parts of the system in order effectively to carry out that responsibility. Installation of unauthorized equipment, according to the telephone companies, would have at least two negative results. First, it would divide the responsibility for assuring that each part of the system is able to function effectively and, second, it would retard development of the system since the independent equipment supplier would tend to resist changes which would render his equipment obsolete. (FCC Decision, 26 June 1968, at 424)

The FCC deemed none of these arguments to be convincing, because why would a prohibition on non-harmful interconnection be necessary in order to permit the telephone company to carry out its system responsibilities? The FCC concluded as follows: it allowed the Carterfone and other devices to be connected directly to the AT&T network, as long as they did not cause damage to the system.

> Even if not compelled by the Hush-A-Phone decision, our conclusion here is that a customer desiring to use an interconnecting device to improve the utility to him of both the telephone system and a private radio system should be able to do so, so long as the interconnection does not adversely affect the telephone company's operations or the telephone system's utility for others. (FCC Decision, 26 June 1968, at 424)

The FCC judged that the Carterfone did not adversely affect the operation of the telephone network. Connection was therefore permitted (FCC Decision, 26 June 1968).

Henceforth, this ruling became the prime rule in deciding on the permissibility of the use of alien equipment or peripheral equipment. This ruling created the possibility of selling devices that could connect to the phone system and opened up the market to numerous products, including answering machines, fax machines, cordless phones, computer modems and the early, dial-up Internet. AT&T nevertheless managed to turn this loss into a modest success: it was allowed to make a protecting technical device obligatory. AT&T leased out these 'protective couplers' for about ten dollars a month per line. In exchange, AT&T paid for any repairs to the couplers. However, when repairs were needed, AT&T was not very quick to react . . .

> From my own experience, these [protective couplers – eds] were very unreliable. They often left phone lines dead because they were defective, or the card cage they went into was defective. The Phone Company didn't care, and didn't really try to fix them very hard. They figured eventually the subscriber would get tired of dealing with the problems and go back to renting from them. I guess they were wrong. (Sandman, 2007)

This situation continued until 1976, when the FCC began to allow connection of registered equipment without protective couplers.

7.6   THE BEGINNING OF THE END

The 1968 Carterfone decision encouraged new companies to enter the telecommunications industry. In August 1968, William G. McGowan established Microwave Communications of America Incorporated (MICOM), which changed its name to MCI Communications five years later. MICOM had plans to set up a microwave relay system that would run through 40 states. In 1969, MICOM received permission from the FCC to set up a microwave service between St Louis and Chicago. The FCC issued a final ruling, MCI's licensing request, on 14 August 1969. By a decision of 4–3, MCI was licensed for operation. This decision also gave MCI the right to interconnect with the Bell System network to enable MCI to provide its proposed services. Unsurprisingly, this ruling was quickly appealed by AT&T, and after a denial of the appeal by the commission AT&T filed a suit with the US Court of Appeals to have the ruling overturned. A favourable result for AT&T was not forthcoming (FundingUniverse, 1999).

Following this approval, MICOM began to form subsidiary corporations and file applications with the FCC to create microwave relays between other city pairs. Between July 1969 and February 1971, 15 new regional carriers were created allowing for interconnection between a number of major cities in the United States, and MICOM purchased an equity position in Interdata, an independent regional carrier that planned to build a microwave relay chain between New York City and Washington, DC (Cantelon, 1993, pp. 250–56).

For McGowan it was clear that AT&T's monopoly had to be broken to make MICOM a major player on the national telecom market. This is why McGowan launched its own offensive, intensively lobbying Congress, the

FCC and the courts. In 1971, it was even decided to appoint Kenneth Cox, former FCC commissioner, senior vice-president in charge of lobbying the FCC. This proved a success (FundingUniverse, 1999).

In 1971, the FCC opened up the entire private-line market to all entrants with its Specialized Common Carrier Decision (FCC Decision, 3 June 1971). The Decision permitted private leased lines to interconnect to the network. In its own words, the Decision affirmed the right of corporations 'to offer only specialized services'. However, the question was: what exactly is a specialized service? Since carriers were only supposed to connect to the AT&T system, the FCC did not state anything about allowing anyone to compete with AT&T by offering a basic phone service. The Decision enabled the bypassing of the public network by large long-distance users. AT&T feared MCI and other specialized carriers could 'cream skim' the best routes by providing cheaper services than AT&T on high-density routes.

Meanwhile, AT&T did whatever it could to thwart MCI. MCI ordered interconnections from the local exchange carriers, which in most cases was a Bell System Operating Company, owned by AT&T. The relationship between MCI and the Bell Operating companies was not that of a typical supplier and customer, as the local operating companies were generally reluctant to do business with a company that its parent was attempting to put out of business. And since the FCC ruling did not indicate at what costs or how soon lines had to be delivered, there were good possibilities for AT&T to delay MCI's access to the market.

However, MCI saw an important future in store for the satellite, mainly because of the possibilities that the satellite offered of steering clear of the expensive AT&T network. Besides, satellites offered a cheap and effective way to reach remote areas without having to build a microwave tower every 30 or 60 miles. MCI and Lockheed Missiles & Space Company formed a joint venture called the MCI Lockheed Satellite Corporation. The plan was to build a $168 million satellite communications system. MCI Lockheed indeed was one of the first companies to request FCC authorization for domestic satellite-based communications. In 1973, MCI ran into financial difficulties, which it was not to overcome until 1975 (Cantelon, 1993, pp. 250–56).

To make matters worse, AT&T decided to pull the plug on interconnection, which meant that MCI could not use the existing network to offer its services. Ultimately, this was the kind of monopolistic behaviour that was the basis for AT&T's defeat in the antitrust suits brought against it, but that was six to seven years in the future. In the meantime, all that MCI could see was that it had a great deal of cash going out (the loss in working capital was a million dollars per month at the time), but very little coming in. During the following seven years, MCI survived mostly by winning court decisions. The joke is that in its early years, MCI had more lawyers than land lines or that it was 'A law firm with an antenna on the roof'. The first victories came in 1977 and 1978, when MCI bypassed the FCC and won the right essentially to offer common carrier services (Cantelon, 1993, pp. 250–56).

To resolve the financial difficulties, MCI started Execunet, a service nearly identical to AT&T's regular, very profitable long-distance service, in 1975. AT&T immediately protested to the FCC. It decided in AT&T's favour and forbade MCI to offer Execunet service any longer (FCC Decision, 1976 , 60 FCC 2nd, 65). In 1977, the US Court of Appeals of the District of Columbia issued its Execunet decision, which opened the long-distance market to full competition by reversing FCC decisions limiting MCI and other specialized carriers to private line services (US Court of Appeals, D.C.Cir, 28 July 1977). In effect, the original ambiguity of the Specialized Common Carrier Services decision had finally come back to haunt the FCC. The federal court allowed MCI and other firms to provide switched long-distance services. The court argued that if Execunet was a specialized service similar to a regular long-distance service, that was too bad. Once the FCC had come out in favour of competition and innovative services, it could not dictate the validity of specific offerings.

> In so holding we have not had to consider, and have not considered, whether competition like that posed by Execunet is in the public interest. That will be the question for the Commission to decide should it elect to continue these proceedings. In that eventuality the Commission must be ever mindful that, just as it is not free to create competition for competition's sake, it is not free to propagate monopoly for monopoly's sake. The ultimate test of industry structure in the communications common carrier field must be the public interest, not the private financial interests of those who have until now enjoyed the fruits of de facto monopoly. (US Court of Appeals, D.C.Cir., 28 July 1977, at 380)

In subsequent decisions (Execunet II, 1978 and Execunet III, 1981; Byrnes, 1999, pp. 31–105) the court ruled that AT&T and its local telephone companies must permit the other long-distance carriers to interconnect to their local networks to start and complete their calls (adapted from Cantelon, 1993, pp. 250–56; FundingUniverse, 1999).

7.7   THE END OF THE OLD AT&T

The end of AT&T was heralded by two lawsuits that AT&T lost in 1980: the private lawsuit of MCI and the antitrust suit filed by the US Department of Justice.

The 1980 case of MCI v. AT&T began in 1974, when MCI filed a suit for damages in the US District Court for Northern Illinois on the grounds that AT&T had violated the Sherman Antitrust Act of 1890. The direct reason for the suit was the conduct of Illinois Bell, which disconnected MCI circuits for what MCI believed was no other reason than to restrain trade. The jury awarded MCI damages of $600 million, which under federal law had to be trebled to $1.8 billion, making it the largest monetary award in US History until then (US Court of Appeals, 7th Cir., 12 January 1983, at 1092–1093). However, in 1985 this amount was lowered to $113 million on appeal (FundingUniverse, 1999). MCI's private lawsuit had only been about monetary damages and concerned the past. Only the Government could ensure that AT&T would behave in compliance with the regulations in the future.

The Justice Department, too, regarded Bell System's behaviour as possible antitrust violations. In November 1974, the Justice Department therefore brought its own civil suit against AT&T, Western Electric, Bell Telephone Laboratories and the 22 Bell operating companies (Civil Action No. 74-1698; US District Court, D.D.C., 18 October 1978; US District Court, D.D.C., 11 August 1982). The premise behind the suit was fundamentally simple. The Justice Department alleged that AT&T monopolized the long-distance telephone business by exploiting its control of the local telephone companies to restrict competition from other telecommunications systems and carriers by creating obstructions to the interconnection with the local phone service. It further alleged that since Western Electric supplied substantially all the telecommunications equipment of the Bell System, AT&T restrained competition in this area. As a consequence of these practices, AT&T allegedly denied the benefits of a free and competitive market to purchasers of telecommunications service and equipment (US District Court, D.D.C., 18 October 1978, at 1318).

Initially, the Government sought the divestiture by AT&T of all Western Electric stock; the separation of the Long Lines Department of AT&T from the Bell Operating Companies; the divestiture and fragmentation of Western Electric sufficient to insure competition in the manufacture and sales of telecommunications equipment; and whatever relief against Bell Labs as the Court would deem appropriate (US District Court, D.D.C., 18 October 1978, at 1318). The tough demands of the US Department of Justice can be understood against the background of the criticism it attracted after the disappointing results of the 1956 consent decree, which, in fact, had hardly yielded anything. Also after 1956, AT&T was able to continue to build its empire relatively undisturbed.

While the action was pending, the Government changed its relief requests several times. Alarmed by what might be awaiting it, AT&T threw all its weapons into the fray. AT&T used all its political clout and social power to get the file dropped, but to no avail. The Defense Department was politically against AT&T, as was virtually the entire Reagan administration when it superseded the Ford regime. AT&T tried to dismiss the case as nothing more than a regulatory dispute that should be decided (exclusively) before the FCC (US District Court, D.D.C., 24 November 1976). When that did not work, they tried to subpoena any government document that mentioned the word 'telephone'. But that did not work either, mainly because the initial Judge, Joseph C. Waddy, refused the notion that the world's largest corporation was a victim to a tiny company or the regulatory framework which it had created for itself over a hundred years (CedarSteve, 2007).

Between 1974 and 1980, there were several abortive attempts by the Justice Department and the Bell System to settle the suit before going to trial. Since no settlement was reached, however, Judge Greene announced that the trial of the antitrust case would begin on 15 January 1981, in the Federal Courthouse in Washington, DC (US District Court, D.D.C., 11 August 1982, at 140).

After months of witness examinations and the studying of exhibits, AT&T asked the court to dismiss the case. It said the Justice Department did not have a leg to stand on. Judge Greene, however, did not intend to drop the suit, his response to the case made by the Justice Department being quite different. In a legal opinion of 11 September 1981 (US District Court, D.D.C., 20 August 1981), he stated:

> The Court concludes that the evidence sustains the allegation that defendants have used their local exchange monopolies to foreclose competition in the terminal equipment market [. . .] The Court finds that, as of now, sufficient evidence has been adduced to dictate the conclusion that AT&T has monopolized the intercity services market by frustrating the efforts of other companies to compete with it in that market on a fair and reasonable basis. (US District Court, D.D.C., 20 August 1981, at 1352 and 1357)

And:

> The motion to dismiss is denied. The testimony and the documentary evidence adduced by the Government demonstrate that the Bell System had violated the antitrust laws in a number of ways over a lengthy period of time. . . The burden is on defendants to refute the factual showings. (US District Court, D.D.C., 20 August 1981, at 1381)

Greene's preliminary opinion was 'a big, big blockbuster' that boosted the confidence of the Government (Bell, 2000). After a lengthy pushing and shoving of concepts, AT&T and the Justice Department reached a final Consent Decree in January 1982. In it, AT&T pledged the following: divesting 22 operating companies – about two-thirds of AT&T's assets – that provide local telephone service and exchange access around the United States. This implied that AT&T would mainly remain active in the area of the long-distance service, while at the same time it had to enter into competition with other long-distance carriers, such as MCI and Sprint. AT&T would remain, minus its local companies, and it would keep all of Western Electric and Bell Labs (US District Court, D.D.C., 11 August 1982, at 141–3 and 224–5). After making major alterations of his own, Judge Greene finally approved it on 11 August 1982 (US District Court, D.D.C., 11 August 1982, at 225). The settlement, less than nine pages long, became the Modification of Final Judgment, the title referring to the fact that it modified the Final Judgment or Consent Decree of 1956 (US District Court, D.D.C., 11 August 1982, at 226).

AT&T chairman C.L. Brown reacted to the Consent Decree as follows:

The consumers of America want three things: dependable local phone service at affordable rates; more competition in the marketplace [. . .] but certainly not excluding the Number One brand name, Bell; and more free enterprise and less government regulation where it isn't needed.

[. . .] In the end, we realize, of course, that our obligation is to conform to national policy, not make it.

[. . .] We truly believe the consent order is an alternative which meets the relevant tests of the public interest, and we look forward to getting out of court and getting back to business. (Brown, 1982)

The Consent Decree of 1982 was decisive for Bell System's future.

7.8   WESTERN ELECTRIC DIVESTED

On 1 January 1984, the break-up of AT&T was a fact. AT&T began with a newly designed organization; one the company hoped would be more suited to its new circumstances. Underneath the corporate offices were two subsidiaries. AT&T Communications Inc. focused on the regulated long-distance business. AT&T Technologies Inc. contained almost everything else, including Western Electric. Western Electric was split up into several subdivisions including units in Consumer Products and International Business (Hochheiser, 1989). Telephones made by Western Electric prior to the break-up continued to be manufactured and continued to be marked 'Western Electric'. However, Judge Greene prohibited the use of the name Bell, or the Bell logo. This is why the telephones were produced with the Bell logo absent, or the logo was 'hidden' by a metal filler inside all telephone housings. Most components, including new electronic integrated circuits, were marked with the famous 'WE' initials. Later on, Western Electric no longer marked housings or telephones with 'WE', but continued to mark the modular plugs of telephone cords with 'WE'. Western Electric came to a total end in 1995 when AT&T changed the name of AT&T Technologies into Lucent Technologies. The assets that were once part of one Western Electric are now in the hands of more than five companies (FundingUniverse, 2005).

7.9   STRATEGIC BEHAVIOUR

Tables 7.1, 7.2 and 7.3 present a detailed overview of all kinds of strategic behaviour as we found them. In describing our empirical findings, we have focused on entries for and forms of strategic behaviour as we introduced them in Chapters 3 and 4. Each table focuses on a particular actor: AT&T, entrants and judicial authorities. The AT&T case study presents a dominant picture of using bottleneck facilities as an entry for strategic behaviour. In chapter 10 we will analyze this strategic behaviour in a broader perspective.

Table 7.1   AT&T

Entry	Strategic behaviour: type and description
Financial resources	*Vertical foreclosure.* AT&T takes over Western Electric
Bottleneck facilities	*Vertical foreclosure.* AT&T refuses to connect its long-distance network with local independent carriers
Financial resources	*Cross subsidization + vertical foreclosure.* AT&T subsidizes local operations by transferring to them money earned from long-distance services
Factor 'time' + rules and contracts	*Strategic use of litigation.* AT&T waits and passively undergoes judicial screening
Rules and contracts	*Strategic use of litigation.* AT&T pursues various legal actions to derail the 1974 antitrust suit of the Justice Department
Intertwined relations	*Political lobbying.* AT&T manipulates the outcomes of judicial procedures (consent decree 1956) through political lobbying

Table 7.1   (continued)

Entry	Strategic behaviour: type and description
Indispensable nature	*Cherry picking.* RBOCs (Regional Bell Operating Companies) pick out profitable urban areas
Bottleneck facilities + rules and contracts	*Vertical foreclosure.* Customers are not allowed to use telephones and telephone equipment of competitors
Bottleneck facilities + rules and contracts	*Vertical foreclosure.* Customers are obliged to lease AT&T's equipment, no ownership possible
Bottleneck facilities + rules and contracts	*Vertical foreclosure.* Customers are allowed to use telephones of competitor on condition of leasing and back-leasing
Bottleneck facilities + rules and contracts	*Vertical foreclosure.* Introduction of 'Protective Coupler' that has to be leased by customers
Bottleneck facilities	*Vertical foreclosure.* Poor operation of 'Protective Coupler', poor service of AT&T
Bottleneck facilities	*Vertical foreclosure.* AT&T denies MCI interconnection
Rules and contracts + factor 'time'	*Strategic use of litigation.* AT&T tries to exhaust MCI financially

Table 7.2   *Entrants*

Entry	Strategic behaviour: type and description
Rules and contracts	*Puppy dog.* Independents (e.g. MCI) initiate various (civil) antitrust actions against AT&T
Rules and contracts	*Puppy dog.* Hush-A-Phone Co. tries to break AT&T's monopoly through court

Table 7.2 (continued)

Entry	Strategic behaviour: type and description
Rules and contracts	*Puppy dog.* Carter Electronics Corp. tries to break AT&T's monopoly through court
Indispensable nature	*Cherry picking / cream skimming.* Satellite use by MCI

Table 7.3 Judicial authorities

Entry	Strategic behaviour: type and description
Rules and contracts	*Threatening.* Justice Department puts pressure on AT&T by threatening antitrust suit.
Rules and contracts	*Threatening.* Judicial authorities require AT&T to ensure interconnection.
Rules and contracts	Court decision demanding divestiture of Western Electric

NOTE

1. Bell System later was to establish AT&T. AT&T soon acquired the position of Bell System's parent company. This happened against the background of a reorganization that Bell System thought necessary in 1899 to increase the company's strength. The direct reason for the reorganization was the expiry of Graham Bell's patent in 1894, as a result of which thousands of independent companies entered the telephony market (AT&T, 2007; Iardelli, 1964, pp. 8–9; Temin and Galambos, 1987).

REFERENCES

Adams, S.B. and O.R. Butler (1999), *Manufacturing the Future: A History of Western Electric*, New York: Cambridge University Press.

AT&T (2007), 'Milestones in AT&T History', www.corp.att.com/history/milestones.html, accessed 5 November 2007.

Bell, T. (2000), 'The decision to divest: incredible or inevitable?', *IEEE Spectrum*, **37**(6), 46–55.

Brown, C. (1982), 'Dear reader: we stopped the press. . .', *Bell Telephone Magazine*, **60**(5).

Byrnes, W.J. (1999), 'Telecommunications regulation: something old and something new', in M.D. Paglin (ed.), *The Communications Act: A Legislative History of the Major Amendments, 1934–1996*, Silver Spring, MD: Pike & Fischer, Inc., pp. 31–105.

Cantelon, P.L. (1993), *The History of MCI: 1968–1988, The Early Years*, Dallas, TX: Heritage Press.

CedarSteve (2007), 'Voice – the end of a monopoly', www.cedarsteve.com/tele comhistory4.htm, accessed 5 November 2007.

FCC Decision (26 June 1968), 13 FCC 2d, 420, *Carter v. AT&T*, Release Number: FCC 68–661.

FCC Decision (3 June 1971), 29 FCC 2d, 872, *Specialized Common Carrier Services*, First Report and Order, Docket 18920.

FCC Decision (1976), 60 FCC 2nd, 65, *AT&T v. MCI*.

FundingUniverse (1999), 'MCI WorldCom, Inc.', www.fundinguniverse.com/ company-histories/MCI-WorldCom-Inc_Company-History.html, accessed 5 November 2007.

FundingUniverse (2005), 'AT&T Corporation', www.fundinguniverse.com/ company-histories/ATamp;T-Corporation-Company-History.html, accessed 5 November 2007.

Gordon, J.S. (1997), 'The death of a monopoly', *American Heritage*, **48**(2), 168.

Hochheiser, S. (1989), 'The American Telephone and Telegraph Company (AT&T)', AT&T Archives, www.porticus.org/bell/pdf/tattc.pdf, accessed 5 November 2007.

Iardelli, A. (1964), *Western Electric and the Bell System. A Survey of Service*, New York: Western Electric Company Inc.

Massey, D. (1997), 'A capsule history of the Bell System. Compiled and edited from previously published material by Kenneth P. Todd, Jr.', www.porticus. org/bell/capsule_bell_system.html, accessed 5 November 2007.

Sandman, M. (2007), 'Telephone history, Mike Sandman Enterprises (MSE)', www.sandman.com/telhist.html, accessed 5 November 2007.

Smith, G.D. (1985), *The Anatomy of a Business Strategy: Bell, Western Electric and the Origins of the American Telephone Industry*, Baltimore, MD: Johns Hopkins University Press.

Temin, P. and L. Galambos (1987), *The Fall of the Bell System: A Study in Prices and Politics*, Cambridge: Cambridge University Press.

Triebwasser, M. (1998), 'The telephone industry', www.ims.ccsu.edu/Tele.htm, accessed 5 November 2007.

US Court of Appeals, 7th Cir. (12 January 1983), 708 F. 2d 1081, *MCI Communications Corp. v. AT&T*.

US Court of Appeals, D.C.Cir. (8 November 1956), 238 F. 2d 266, *Hush-A-Phone Corp. v. United States*.

US Court of Appeals, D.C.Cir. (28 July 1977), 561 F.2d 365, *MCI Telecommunications Corp. v. FCC, (Execunet I)*.

US District Court, D.D.C. (24 November 1976), 427 F. Supp. 57, *United States v. AT&T*.

US District Court, D.D.C. (18 October 1978), 461 F. Supp. 1314, *United States v. AT&T*.

US District Court, D.D.C. (20 August 1981), 524 F. Supp. 1336, *United States v. AT&T*.

US District Court, D.D.C. (11 August 1982), 552 F. Supp. 131, *United States v. AT&T*.

8. UMTS spectrum auctions in the EU

8.1 BACKGROUND: THIRD GENERATION SYSTEMS

Universal Mobile Telecommunication System (UMTS) is the European standard for third generation (3G) digital mobile communication systems, indicated by the International Telecommunication Union (ITU) as *International Telecommunication System*, IMT-2000. Where the second generation (2G) of systems, *Global System for Mobile Communications* (GSM), only involves voice traffic, UMTS also enables data traffic (wireless broadband multimedia services including the Internet and other services based on the Internet Protocol (I/P)).

The GSM network was introduced in the early 1990s. Although, at the end of the 1990s, the capacity of the GSM network in Europe still offered enough room to cope with the growth in users and use in the next few years, people nevertheless realized the risk of an overload in the near future. UMTS offered a solution. UMTS is faster than GSM, while the UMTS network also has more capacity than the GSM network. For the telecom operators, the changeover to UMTS meant making substantial investments. Not only did they have to build expensive new networks, but they also had to reach deep into their pockets to obtain the required frequency licences.

Within the UMTS frequency range designated by the ITU, it is for the respective governments to distribute the frequencies at a national level. For EU member states, there is the additional obligation to use the instrument of the licence to do so.[1] This ensues from Article 3 (1) of the Decision of 14 December 1998, pursuant to which the member states have to introduce a licence system to enable a coordinated and gradual introduction of UMTS services.[2] A member state may choose between various ways of distribution: in order of entry (*first come, first served*), by auction or with the help of a comparative test (*beauty contest*). In a comparative test, the government fixes advance criteria which the candidates have to satisfy to qualify for a licence. After comparing the candidates, the government allocates the licence to the candidate(s) it thinks best. In a comparative test, the government may ask the successful applicants to pay for the licence, but it is not obliged to do so.

A procedural precondition to the chosen way of distribution is that it should meet requirements arising from the proportionality principle. This implies that the method used should be transparent, proportional, objective and non-discriminatory.[3] This is prescribed by Article 10 (3) of the Licensing Directive.

In 2001 and 2002, all EU member states distributed their available UMTS frequencies. Most countries opted for an auction, with the licence going to the highest bidder. In some cases, this was a resounding success, as in the UK and Germany. Germany sold six licences for a total of 50.5 billion euros and the UK for just over 37 billion euros. Although, in these cases, the aim of the auction was to ensure efficient use of the spectrum and to create a competitive 3G market, there was every appearance that there was a more important aim, that is to generate revenue. Auctioning was not always a success, as in the Netherlands, where the proceeds worth 2.69 billion euros were simply disappointing. Or Belgium, which had to be satisfied with meagre proceeds worth 450 million euros. Spain and the Nordic Countries used a beauty contest instead of an auction (Van Damme, 2002).[4]

8.2   AUCTIONING AS A DISTRIBUTION METHOD

8.2.1   What is Auctioned and Who may Bid

Before there can be an auction, it must first be established how many lots will be auctioned and of what size. The question should also be answered as to who does so: the government or the market? Except for Austria and Germany, in all countries the government adopted the role of decision maker. It determined the number of lots and their size. In all countries, the available spectrum was 60 MHz, which was offered paired.[5] Technical requirements imply that this spectrum be split in blocks of 5 MHz while for a viable network at least 10 MHz is needed. It follows that market structures with three players (3×20), four players (4×15), five players (2×15 and 3×10) and six players (6×10) are possible (Van Damme, 2002).

All countries had a light qualification procedure before the auction, in which interested parties had to prove that they were capable of offering the 3G services. Countries differed in the extent to which new entrants received some preferential treatment. In the UK, five licences were auctioned. Each bidder could acquire at most one licence. The operators of existing 2G networks (Vodafone, BT Celnet, Orange and One2One) were not allowed to bid for licence A, a large licence. New entrants also had the right of roaming,[6] according to regulated rates, on existing 2G networks. In Germany, Austria, Belgium and Denmark, each bidder could acquire at most one licence. There were no specific rules relating to incumbent operators of 2G networks.[7] In the Netherlands, there were no rules restricting the bidding rights of operators of existing 2G networks. In Italy, in addition to having roaming rights, an entrant could buy additional spectrum at a reduced rate. The Greek system was very similar (Van Damme, 2002).

8.2.2   Structure of the Auction

There are several options for the auction design. The two main ways of setting up an auction are the ascending auction and the sealed-bid auction. The ascending auction is the type of auction that is normally used to sell arts and antiques. Such an auction opens with a low bid. The price then rises until no bidder is prepared to make a higher bid. The last and highest bidder pays the price he has bid. An important characteristic of this type of auction is that each bidder knows the level of the other bids at any point in time. As regards licences for mobile telephony, simultaneous ascending auctions tend to be used, which means that several licences are sold at the same time. In the second type of auction, the sealed-bid auction, each bidder makes a bid and the parties that have made the highest bids win the licences. In case of a first-price sealed-bid auction, the winners have to pay exactly the prices they tendered. This is also called a discriminatory auction, because different bidders may pay different prices, even for equivalent spectrum. In a second-price sealed-bid auction or Vickrey auction, the winner pays the amount of the second highest bid (Kruse, 2002; Klemperer, 2002; Bjuggren, 2003).

All countries except Denmark used a variant of the simultaneous multi-round ascending auction. Denmark wanted to stimulate entry and argued that an ascending auction would be less likely to attract new entrants than a sealed-bid discriminatory auction. At the same time, it was apparently considered undesirable for winners to pay different amounts for identical licences. As a compromise, a fourth-price sealed-bid auction was adopted; hence, all winners paid the lowest accepted price. Though the other countries used the same multi-round format, they differed in the way they dealt with transparency. The German, Austrian and Dutch governments were worried that transparency might make collusion easier. For this reason, bidders were not fully informed about all bids that were made. Bidders only knew the currently highest bids and currently highest bidders. The UK, by contrast, stressed free competition, which might be restrained by limiting information (Van Damme, 2002).

8.3 ANTI-COMPETITIVE BEHAVIOUR

Not all auctions proceeded smoothly. Bidding competitors accused each other of collusion, untruthfulness, deceit and unfair play. Insinuations, allegations and imputations frequently got publicity. Accusations of anti-competitive behaviour were made in Germany, Italy, Austria and the Netherlands. For instance, in Germany, France Telecom offered Debitel, a weak entrant, access to its network in case Debitel did not win a licence. In Italy, the unexpectedly early exit of Blu, a weak incumbent, made the case a suspect one. In Austria, Telekom Austria (TA), the largest player in the field, informed the market before the auction that it would be satisfied with just two of the blocks,[8] and that, if the others behaved similarly, it should be possible to get the frequencies on sensible terms. TA also made clear that it was willing to bid on three blocks if other bidders pursued such an aggressive strategy (Van Damme, 2002). In the Netherlands, newcomer Versatel invited other parties to negotiate about access to their GSM network and cooperation in the UMTS market. Versatel indicated that it was prepared to abandon its participation in the UMTS auction in exchange for this.

In the following four sections, we discuss a number of remarkable events from the practice of the UMTS auctions in Germany, Italy, Austria and the Netherlands.

8.4 GERMANY

The German UMTS auction took place in July and August 2000 and was a simultaneous ascending auction. The design of the German UMTS auction was rather complex. In the licence auction, 12 blocks of spectrum were offered, from which bidders could create licences of at least two or at most three blocks. Thus, the size of the licences and the number of licences were not fixed in advance. Four companies might acquire big three-block licences, or, for example, six companies might win smaller two-block licences. It had been determined in advance, however, that each bidder could acquire at most one licence. The number of licences could therefore range from zero to six. If all blocks were sold, a minimum of four licences could be acquired, which equalled the number of GSM incumbents in Germany. The idea behind this auction design was that the bidders would determine the number of winners (Kruse, 2002; Jehiel and Moldovanu, 2001; Van Damme, 2002). After this licence auction, another auction for additional capacity took place. The aim of this second auction was to allocate additional capacity among the bidders that were licensed at the first auction (Jehiel and Moldovanu, 2001; Seifert and Ehrhart, 2004).

According to Klemperer, the German auction design 'proved vulnerable to collusion and entry problems' (Klemperer, 2002). Only seven bidders participated in the German UMTS auction. Not a large number, certainly not if we remember that a maximum of six licences were on offer. The seven bidders were T-Mobile (a subsidiary of Deutsche Telekom, DT), Vodafone-Mannesmann, E-Plus (owned by the Dutch former monopolist KPN), VIAG Interkom (backed by British Telecom), MobilCom (backed by France Telecom), Group 3G (backed by Telefonica and Sonera), and Debitel (backed by Swisscom). The first four of these bidders were GSM incumbents (Schmid, 2000; Grimm et al., 2001).

A remarkable event during the German auction was that one bidder, MobilCom, made what seemed like a collusive offer to another bidder, Debitel, at an early stage of the auction. In an interview with the Financial Times, MobilCom stated that 'should [Debitel] fail to secure a licence [it could] become a "virtual network operator" using MobilCom's network while saving on the cost of the licence' (Klemperer, 2002). In reaction to these remarks, shares in Debitel rose by 12 per cent. MobilCom's statements could be regarded as an offer of a side payment by MobilCom to Debitel in order to persuade Debitel to quit the auction. The German government did not punish MobilCom for this action. The reason was probably that the government did not want to risk that excluding MobilCom would result in a premature end of the auction, with a corresponding low price level. Debitel did not immediately withdraw from the auction, but it does seem that MobilCom's statements made it more attractive for Debitel to quit the auction, because Debitel stopped bidding at a relatively low level (Klemperer, 2002; Van Damme, 2002).

After Debitel had withdrawn from the auction, the bidding accelerated (Schmid, 2000). Six firms were left, while, as we said, a maximum of six licences could be acquired. Among the six remaining firms were two dominant incumbents, T-Mobile (a subsidiary of DT) and Vodafone-Mannesmann, each of which held some 40 per cent of the German market for mobile telephony at the time (Grimm et al., 2001).

Klemperer states that DT and Vodafone-Mannesmann had two potential strategies ready at that moment. They could inflate the price to induce the weaker companies to withdraw from the auction. In this case, the proceeds for the German government would be high and it would create a market with a limited number of players. A second option was to lead all remaining firms to tacitly collude to reduce their demands to two blocks each. The auction would then be over relatively soon. In the second option, the proceeds for the government would be lower, but it would create a less concentrated market for mobile telephony (Klemperer, 2002).

There is every appearance that Vodafone-Mannesmann chose the second option, because the company ended a number of its bids with the digit 6. Supposedly, this digit was meant as a signal, by which Vodafone-Mannesmann wanted to indicate that it wanted to conclude the auction relatively soon with the six remaining bidders (Grimm et al., 2001). As regards the use of such signals in the German UMTS auction, the Financial Times wrote at the time that 'one operator has privately admitted' to this kind of behaviour (Klemperer, 2002).

Initially it seemed that Deutsche Telekom opted for the first strategy, that is, driving up prices. DT also seemed to use the potential signal function of the bids, because DT reacted to Mannesmann with bids ending in a 5, which seemed to suggest that DT was willing to bid even higher in order to reduce the number of licences to five (Jehiel and Moldovanu, 2001). DT thus continued to drive up the prices. However, Deutsche Telekom stopped driving up the prices even before the weaker companies could have decided to withdraw from the auction (Klemperer, 2002; Jehiel and Moldovanu, 2001).

Eventually, six licences were allocated, including four to the four incumbents. The proceeds of the auction were 50.5 billion euros (ITU, 2001). Given the result of the auction – relatively high proceeds and relatively large numbers of players in the market – it is suggested that Deutsche Telekom's strategy and aims during the auction were due to the fact that the German government still owned the greater part of the company at the time (Klemperer, 2002; Jehiel and Moldovanu, 2001).

A last interesting observation as regards the German UMTS auction concerns the consequences of the auction for KPN, the former Dutch telecommunication monopolist (owner of E-Plus, a German GSM incumbent) and Telefonica (as we pointed out above, Group 3G was backed by Telefonica and Sonera). According to Van Damme, the German UMTS auction could be regarded as a struggle between KPN and Telefonica. Prior to the auction, these two companies had negotiated over a potential merger. These negotiations had foundered. Both parties won a UMTS licence in the German auction. Had Telefonica failed to win a licence, the networks of KPN and Telefonica would have been largely complementary. Since Telefonica had won a licence, the networks of KPN and Telefonica were overlapping in Germany. As a result, Telefonica's negotiating position in possible follow-up negotiations was much stronger (Van Damme, 2002).

8.5 ITALY

The Italian UMTS auction took place in October 2000. Italy used a simple ascending auction with five UMTS licences of 10 MHz each. New entrants had an option to buy an additional block of 5 MHz at a reduced price. In the auction, bidders were ranked according to their bids. Each bidder that was not among the five current highest bidders had to raise its bid above the fifth highest or quit the auction. Winners had to pay their final bid, with the result that a game was introduced of trying to avoid being the winner with the highest final bid (Van Damme, 2002; Kruse, 2002).[9]

To prevent an uncompetitive auction, the auction design contained the rule that if the number of 'serious' bidders (as tested by various prequalification conditions) did not exceed the number of licences, the number of available licences could be reduced. However, if this rule were actually put into practice, it would result in a higher degree of concentration on the Italian market for mobile telephony (Klemperer, 2002). Consequently, Jehiel and Moldovanu (2001) characterize the rule as a 'rather naive feature' of the Italian auction design.

The Italian auction design was based on the design of the successful UMTS auction in the United Kingdom. However, the Italian auction was a good deal less successful, particularly in terms of proceeds for the Italian government. One reason may have been that, because of their experiences with previously concluded UMTS auctions, companies knew what parties were the strong bidders. According to Klemperer, expectations were therefore that the number of bidders would be disappointing, because weaker parties would not participate or would decide to make joint bids. A small number of bidders would then pose a greater risk of collusive or predatory behaviour (Klemperer, 2002).

It is also suggested that the lower proceeds in countries like Italy were due to the earlier UMTS auctions in the United Kingdom and Germany. Of course, the value of a UMTS licence was difficult to establish. Since bidders in the auctions in the United Kingdom and Germany could not take the course of auctions in other European countries as an example, they were particularly subject to the risk of the winners' curse, that is the risk that they would pay too much. Participants in these first European auctions might also have had incentives to demonstrate their intended leading role in the European mobile services industry and to gain a reputation for being tough. According to this explanation, the high proceeds in the United Kingdom and Germany, which were unexpected to many, might have caused bidders in other countries like Italy to leave no stone unturned to avoid the winners' curse. The lower proceeds in a country like Italy might then be regarded as a consequence of downward biasing (Kruse, 2002).

Eventually, there were only six bidders for the five licences available in the Italian auction. The six bidders were Omnitel (controlled by Vodafone), Wind (partially owned by France Telecom), Telecom Italia Mobile (TIM), Ipse (largely controlled by Spain's Telefonica and Finnish mobile operator

Sonera), Blu (a consortium, partially owned by British Telecom) and Andala (controlled by Hong Kong's conglomerate Hutchison Whampoa) (ITU, 2001; BBC News, 2000a). Among the six bidders were four incumbents and two new entrants. At least one new entry was therefore inevitable. In accordance with the auction regulations, the number of available licences remained fixed at five (Jehiel and Moldovanu, 2001).

A remarkable event during the Italian UMTS auction was the relatively early exit of Blu, the weakest and smallest incumbent, from the auction. Blu stated that it had withdrawn from the auction because of serious conflicts about financing between the Italian shareholders and the main foreign backer, British Telecom (Jehiel and Moldovanu, 2001). With five bidders left for five licences, Blu's withdrawal resulted in the end of the auction. Because of Blu's withdrawal, the proceeds of the auction – 12.2 billion euros – were a lot lower than the more than 25 billion euros that the Italian government had counted on (Information Age, 2006; BBC News, 2000b).

The Italian government then accused Blu and other participants in the auction of manipulation (Jehiel and Moldovanu, 2001). According to government officials, there had been collusion. They said that Blu had only participated to avoid invoking the rule reducing the number of licences, which would allow the other bidders to acquire a relatively cheap licence (Klemperer, 2002). The government threatened to cancel the auction while forfeiting the deposits. These deposits were about as high as the eventual licence prices. Eventually, however, the outcome of the auction was authorized (Jehiel and Moldovanu, 2001). The competition authority investigated the matter, but no violations of the auction rules or of the competition laws were found (Van Damme, 2002). Italy's highest administrative court ordered the Treasury Ministry to return the deposit – 1.7 billion US dollars – to Blu (The Industry Standard, 2001).

8.6 AUSTRIA

The Austrian auction of UMTS licences took place in November 2000. Austria used a simultaneous ascending auction. The design of the Austrian auction was equal to that of the German auction. Austria, too, offered 12 blocks of paired spectrum. The number of licences and the size of the licences had not been determined in advance and the number of UMTS licences could, in theory, range from zero to six (Jehiel and Moldovanu, 2001; Kruse, 2002).

A remarkable incident about one week before the start of the auction was a statement by Telekom Austria (TA), the biggest Austrian incumbent. In it, TA stated that it would be content with just two of the 12 blocks of frequency on offer and that, if the other five bidders adopted a similar attitude, 'it should be possible to get the frequencies on sensible terms'. However, in the same statement TA also made clear that it would bid for a third block if one of its rivals did. This statement might be regarded as proposing a collusive deal. It can also be taken as a threat to take measures if the other parties did not accept the offer. The competition authorities did not challenge Telekom Austria's statement (Klemperer, 2002; Van Damme, 2002).

Eventually, there were only six participants in the Austrian UMTS auction, while a maximum of six licences were on offer. Among the six participants were four GSM incumbents. The bidder parties were Connect, max.mobil, Mobilkom, 3G Mobile, Hutchison 3G, and Mannesmann 3G (Jehiel and Moldovanu, 2001; RTR, 2000).

Since there were only six candidates for at most six licences, the auction might have ended as soon as the reserve price was reached. The reserve price had been fixed at a fairly low level, thus creating a clear incentive for the six companies to split up the market with two blocks for each bidder, as TA had already suggested. However, after reaching the reserve price, the auction continued for several rounds. The reason may have been that the participants wanted to create the appearance of a competitive auction to prevent the government changing the regulations after all (Klemperer, 2002). Another possible explanation is that the participants were out to secure more capacity and reduce the number of licences. However, the auction was eventually concluded with six winners and with a relatively low price per licence (Jehiel and Moldovanu, 2001, p. 17).

Although Austria had copied the German auction design, the Austrian auction was far less successful than the German auction. Consequently, Klemperer says that 'when the Austrians copied the German design three months later, the firms had learnt to coordinate their behaviour during the auction, and it was the firms that won the Austrian round' (Klemperer, 2002). Although the auction had continued after reaching the reserve price, the proceeds were disappointing, at least in terms of government revenues (Kruse, 2002). The total proceeds of the Austrian auction were 832 million euros (ITU, 2001). Overall, it seems that the participants in the auction accepted Telekom Austria's offer and settled for two blocks of frequency 'on sensible terms'.

8.7 THE NETHERLANDS

In the Netherlands, the first questions facing the State Secretary for Transport were how many lots should be auctioned and whether a separate lot should be available to new entrants. The State Secretary opted for five lots of different sizes: two lots of 2×15MHz paired plus 5MHz unpaired, and three of 2×10MHz paired plus 5MHz unpaired. No separate lot was reserved for new entrants. She was then reproached from several quarters for making it very easy for the incumbent providers, since it would be easy for the five providers that were already active on the mobile-telephony market, that is KPN,[10] Libertel, Ben, Dutchtone and Telfort to divide the booty. New entrants, who still had to invest in their own network, would not be a match for the incumbent providers that would be able to make higher bids. Besides, the incumbent providers would not be incentivized to go to any extreme in an ascending auction. The five available lots would deprive the incumbent providers of the incentive to heavily overbid competitors. Besides affecting the competitive power in the market of mobile communication, the choice to auction five lots would also affect the National Treasury, according to the critics.

The State Secretary answered the question regarding whether mandatory national roaming had to be imposed in the negative. She said she expected roaming agreements to be concluded on a commercial basis. According to some, the State Secretary thus took an ill-considered decision and put new entrants fully at the mercy of the incumbent providers as regards roaming, deterring potential candidates. For example, during the consultation round on the design of the auction, MCI WorldCom already announced that it made its participation in the auction conditional on the roaming rights for new entrants (NRC, 2001). Certainty as regards roaming carries a lot of weight for a company without a GSM network that is seriously contemplating taking part in the UMTS auction, because the coverage that the company can offer its customers is decisive. Eventually the expected earnings are normative, both for the price that can be paid for the licence and for the investments that can be made to roll out its own UMTS network. Not obliging the incumbent providers to allow roaming would deprive new entrants that have managed to secure a UMTS licence in advance of the possibility of using the GSM networks of the incumbent providers, because in practice new entrants could not count on the voluntary cooperation of the incumbent providers. Although in this respect no direct indications were found of strategic behaviour by the Ministry of Transport or tête-à-têtes between the Ministry and KPN, advice of Dutch telecom regulator OPTA[11] about the auction structure was ignored and the State Secretary's lack of foresight is surprising.

The run-up to the auction was a mess. Until the auction actually began on 6 July 2000, it remained uncertain who was a candidate and who was not. Although initially ten applications for a licence were filed, the number kept changing. Several licence applicants withdrew at a later stage or entered into mutual mergers before the auction began. For example, Ben and the German T-Mobile International soon formed a partnership. Three other parties withdrew, one of them on the eve of the auction (Hutchison) and one (NTL Nederland) twenty minutes before the start of the first bidding round. Eventually, only six candidates remained for five lots.

This course of events raises doubts about the licence applicants' real motives. Remarkably, MCI WorldCom had not registered for the auction, although the company had participated in the talks of the Post and Telecommunication Consultative Body (OPT) as a discussion partner from the very beginning. Although MCI WorldCom had expressly reserved the right not to participate if roaming was not arranged satisfactorily, which was the case (see above), the researchers of Erasmus University Rotterdam who later assessed the auction openly doubted the company's motives. They also doubted the intentions of companies that had applied for a licence but soon abandoned their application. According to them, the non-applicant and the withdrawing applicants had in common that their aim was not to acquire a licence, but to acquire a particular negotiating position. All had an interest in limiting the competition during the auction by developing joint plans in advance. One of the consequences of this implicit collusion caused the auction not to yield the amounts the government hoped for. The UMTS licences were auctioned for a total amount of 2.68 billion euros, considerably lower than the 9.08 billion euros the government had expected to receive. The government mainly stood by and watched the game being played:

A number of things are remarkable in this course of events. In the first place, MCI WorldCom, one of the potential new entrants that had participated in the OPT consultations, did not register for the auction. MCI had announced that it would only be interested in participating in the auction on certain conditions (. . .). These conditions had not been met. It cannot be ascertained whether this was the real reason for not registering. Secondly, a few other parties (. . .) did register for participation in the auction, but cancelled their registration before the start of the auction. Thirdly, at one stage there were ten registered parties, five of which were incumbents and five were new entrants. However, this does not warrant the conclusion that the auction design was sufficiently interesting for new entrants, because parties had to register before June 5, 2000, and then had a month to prepare their final strategy. Market parties could also use this period to discuss forms of cooperation with each other. As a matter of course, a market party has a stronger position in such negotiations if it has also registered for the auction as an independent party. Having registered did not automatically mean that a party was interested independently in a lot. Negotiations between Ben and Deutsche Telekom had a visible result in this respect [*a partnership* – eds]. The other registered parties may eventually not have participated because they could not find a suitable merger partner. (Janssen et al., 2001, pp. 150–51)

On 5 July 2000, the day before the auction began, newcomer Versatel openly invited the other participants to enter into negotiations about access to their GSM network and cooperation in the UMTS market. In exchange, Versatel was prepared to give up its (further) participation in the auction. As the sixth participant, Versatel believed it was holding a trump card, expecting to be able to decide the outcome of the auction.

After all, if Versatel withdrew, the five remaining parties would simply be able to divide the five remaining lots between them. This would have forced the government to give the five GSM operators the licences for nothing, or almost nothing, because there would no longer be a price-inflating greater demand in comparison to the offer. If Versatel continued to bid seriously, the company could raise the others' costs by inflating the price. It soon became known why Versatel nevertheless took part in the auction as the *underdog*. In a press release, Versatel made no bones about the motives underlying the invitation:

> We are the sole independent bidder in the Dutch UMTS auction that can define the competitive outcome of the process. However, we would not like to end up with nothing whilst other players get their licences for free. Versatel invites the incumbent mobile operators to start negotiations immediately for access to their existing 2G networks as well as entry to the 3G market either as a part owner of a licence or as a Mobile Virtual Network Operator. (Versatel, 2002)

In the same press release, Versatel indicated that the company was serious and that it was prepared to do all that was needed to realize access to the UMTS market. By cooperating now, the competitors might save themselves a lot of trouble in the future: 'Versatel believes that there must be open access to mobile networks. This can be done through the courts, the ministry or by the companies themselves. Doing it now will allow them to reflect this situation in the valuation of licences in the auction' (Versatel, 2002).

It may be concluded from Telfort's reaction that Versatel's threat was taken seriously. At any rate, Telfort held a confidential discussion with Versatel on 6 July 2000. Opinions differ about the content of the meeting and about which party initiated it. According to Telfort, the invitation came from Versatel and the aim was to conclude a roaming agreement, in exchange for which Versatel would abandon further participation in the auction. According to Versatel, Telfort initiated the meeting and roaming was not discussed. Versatel said Telfort only asked why Versatel was still taking part in the auction. Versatel said it had explained the importance of participation and had referred Telfort to the auctioneer in case the explanation did not suffice. Both parties admitted, however, that the discussion was about the auction.

Whatever the content of the discussion and whoever initiated it, we may conclude from the course of the events that the parties failed to reach agreement. Shortly before the end of the auction on the twelfth auction day, 21 July 2000, Versatel received a confidential letter from Telfort. The auction amount was then 2.68 billion euros. In the letter, Telfort stated that Versatel was approaching its bid ceiling and that making higher bids was no longer in the interest of its shareholders. Telfort warned that Versatel's shareholders could hold the directors liable for such behaviour:

> Expert opinion indicates to Telfort that you will soon reach a bid level that is not in the interest of your company (. . .) The ulterior motive for such a bid must be that Versatel is attempting to raise its competitors' cost or to gain access to their 2G or 3G networks (. . .) Telfort will hold Versatel liable for all damages as a result of this (. . .). To conclude, Telfort intends to treat the matter as strictly confidential in the interest of the proper course of the auction. (Janssen et al., 2001, pp. 160–65)

On Sunday 23 July 2000, Versatel asked the State Secretary for Transport to exclude Telfort from the auction because of contravention of Article 7, paragraphs 1 and 2, of the Regulations on Auctioning the Right of Use of Radio Frequencies for IMT-2000. Article 7, paragraph 1, reads: 'A participant shall refrain prior to and during the auction procedure from agreements or conduct that hinder the competition to be created in the auction procedure.' By decision of 24 July 2000, the State Secretary refused the request, after which Versatel immediately objected to the refusal. Versatel's request to the auctioneer, made on the same day, to extend the duration of the following bidding round or to suspend the auction was also refused. The auctioneer also refused the request for making a proposal to the State Secretary to exclude Telfort. That same day, Versatel announced that it would not make a bid in the next round. This put a sudden end to the bidding process. The counter stopped at 2.68 billion euros. After the end of the auction, Versatel filed several notices of objection with the aim of having the bids on 24 July 2000, notably the bid by which Telfort outbid Versatel, declared invalid. By decision of 2 April 2001, the State Secretary declared the objections, dealt with as a bundle, unfounded (District Court of Rotterdam, 2002).

The State Secretary took the view that there was no 'conduct that hinders the competition to be created in the auction' within the meaning of Article 7, paragraph 1, of the Regulations on Auctioning the Right of Use of Radio Frequencies for IMT-2000. In this respect she deemed it important that there was unilateral behaviour, that is, the sending of a letter, to which, in her opinion, Article 7, paragraph 1, did not pertain. Because Versatel's freedom of action remained unaffected, the State Secretary felt there was no 'conduct that hindered the competition to be created in the auction'. Telfort's claim for liability was no reason for the State Secretary to take a different view, because in business practice demands are far from unusual. According to the State Secretary, it is not uncommon for a party to threaten litigation if the other party stubbornly persists in a particular stance or course of action. The State Secretary also took the view that there was no 'conduct that disrupts the proper or orderly course of the auction' within the meaning of Article 7, paragraph 2, of the Regulations on Auctioning the Right of Use of Radio Frequencies for IMT-2000. Art.7, par. 2, reads: 'During the auction, participants shall refrain from conduct that disrupts the proper or orderly course of the auction.' Did the letter disrupt the orderly course of the auction? According to the State Secretary, it did not. Excluding Telfort would therefore have been a disproportional sanction for merely sending a letter.

8.8   STRATEGIC BEHAVIOUR

In tables 8.1, 8.2, 8.3 and 8.4, the various entries for strategic behaviour and the different types of strategic behaviour that were presented in this chapter are summarized. Each table focuses on one of the countries that were discussed in this chapter. The entries for strategic behaviour that were most frequently used in the UMTS case study were intertwined relations and indispensable nature. The most dominant type of strategic behaviour that we came across in this case study is collusion.

Table 8.1   Germany

Entry	Strategic behaviour: type and description
Intertwined relations + bottleneck facilities	*Collusion.* MobilCom states in an interview that 'should [Debitel] fail to secure a licence [it could] become a "virtual network operator" using MobilCom's network while saving on the cost of the licence'.
Bottleneck facilities + intertwined relations Bottleneck facilities + intertwined relations	*Collusion.* Vodafone-Mannesmann and Deutsche Telekom are believed to have given the last digit of their bids a signal function. *Raising opponents' costs (to a certain degree)* Deutsche Telekom initially drives up prices, but stops doing so before weaker parties withdraw from the auction. It thus looks after the interests of the German government.
Indispensable nature	*Vertical foreclosure.* Telefonica strengthens its negotiating position towards KPN by securing a German UMTS licence.

Table 8.2   Italy

Entry	Strategic behaviour: type and description
Indispensable nature + rules and contracts + intertwined relations	*Collusion* Early withdrawal of Blu means the end of the auction and relatively low proceeds for the Italian government.
Rules and contracts + financial resources	*Threatening + strategic use of litigation.* The Italian government threatened to cancel the auction while forfeiting the deposits.

Table 8.3   Austria

Entry	Strategic behaviour: type and description
Intertwined relations + Indispensable nature	*Collusion.* One week before the auction, Telekom Austria states that it would be satisfied with just two of the 12 blocks of frequency on offer and that, if the other five bidders took the same stance, 'it should be possible to get the frequencies on sensible terms'. This might be seen as offering a collusive deal.
Bottleneck facilities + financial resources	*Threatening.* Telekom Austria states that it would bid for a third block if one of its rivals did so.

Table 8.4   The Netherlands

Entry	Strategic behaviour: type and description
Intertwined relations + indispensable nature	*Collusion.* Versatel invites other parties to negotiate about access to their network and indicates that it is willing to abandon its participation in the auction in exchange for that.
Indispensable nature	*Predation.* Versatel threatens to raise costs of competitors.
Rules and contracts	*Predation.* Telfort threatens legal damages claim.

Table 8.4 (continued)

Entry	Strategic behaviour: type and description
Indispensable nature	*Lobbying.* Although MCI WorldCom had not registered for the auction, it did take part in the consultations about the structure of the auction from the start.
Intertwined relations	*Collusion.* Ben and T-Mobile International form a partnership to strengthen their position in the auction.
Indispensable nature	*Feint.* Three parties initially register for the auction, but withdraw later. Two of these parties (Hutchison and NTL Nederland) withdraw just before the start of the auction.
Rules and contracts	*Strategic use of litigation.* Versatel tries to have Telfort excluded from the auction.

NOTES

1. For an overview of the European policy on UMTS, see also: European Commission (2002).
2. Decision 128/1999/EG of the European Parliament and the Council of 14 December 1998 regarding the coordinated introduction of the third generation of mobile wireless communication systems (UMTS) in the community, Official Journal of the European Communities, L 017, 1999.
3. Directive 97/13/EC of the European Parliament and the Council of 10 April 1997 on a common framework for general authorizations and individual licences in the field of telecommunications services, Official Journal of the European Communities, L 117, 7 May 1997.
4. France used a hybrid mechanism. It intended to allocate by means of a beauty contest, but changed its plans during the process.
5. Spectrum is paired because one interval is used to send and the other to receive information (Grimm et al., 2001). To be more specific, the term 'paired' 'refers to the fact that there are actually two intervals of 60 MHz each. One interval is used for sending signals from handsets to the network's fixed antennas (uplink), and the other is used for the downlink (network antennas to handsets). A bundle of uplink and corresponding downlink frequencies is collectively referred to as a paired frequency band' (Seifert and Ehrhart, 2004, p. 5).
6. Some UMTS auction designs included a rule regarding mandatory roaming. This means that GSM incumbents had to grant an entrant access (in exchange for a fee) to their networks while the entrant would build its own infrastructure (Jehiel and Moldovanu, 2001, p. 6).
7. In the context of the EU, incumbent operators or incumbents are defined as

'telecommunications organisations granted special and exclusive rights by Member States or public operators which enjoyed a de facto monopoly before liberalisation' (European Commission, 2000, p. 332).

8. 'Blocks are "abstract", i.e. the exact location of each block in the spectrum will be determined ex-post, to ensure that a bidder gets adjacent blocks' (Jehiel and Moldovanu, 2001, p. 8).
9. The Italian auction was a 'discriminatory' auction (see section 8.2.2).
10. KPN (Koninklijke PTT Nederland) is the former Dutch telecommunication monopolist, which was still partly owned by the Dutch State at the time of the UMTS auction.
11. OPTA (Onafhankelijke Post en Telecommunicatie Autoriteit) is the Dutch independent regulatory authority.

REFERENCES

BBC News (2000a), 'Eight bid for Italy phone licences', 24 August, http://news.bbc.co.uk/2/low/business/893012.stm, accessed 18 July 2007.

BBC News (2000b), 'Italy inquiry into mobile phones auction', 25 October, http://news.bbc.co.uk/2/low/europe/989462.stm, accessed 18 July 2007.

Bjuggren, P. (2003), 'The Swedish 3G beauty contest: a beauty or a beast? (A note on beauty contests and auctions as alternative means of allocating 3G rights)', paper for the annual conference of the International Society for New Institutional Economics, Budapest, Hungary, 11–13 September 2003, www.isnie.org/ISNIE03/papers03/bjuggren.pdf, accessed 26 April 2005.

District Court of Rotterdam (2002), LJN AF2578, TELEC 01/813-SIMO, 29 November.

European Commission (2000), *6th Report on the Implementation of the Telecommunications Regulatory Package*, Luxembourg: Office for Official Publications of the European Communities.

European Commission (2002), *Comparative Assessment of the Licensing Regimes for 3G Mobile Communications in the European Union and their Impact on the Mobile Communications Sector. Final Report*, Brussels/Luxembourg: European Commission, Directorate-General Information Society, http://ec.europa.eu/information_society/topics/telecoms/radiospec/doc/pdf/mobiles/mckinsey_study/final_report.pdf, accessed 26 April 2005.

Grimm, V., F. Riedel and E. Wolfstetter (2001), 'The third generation (UMTS) spectrum auctions in Germany', *CESifo Working Papers*, number 584.

Information Age (2006), 'Italia UMTS auction over, Blu may be fined', 9 February, http://license.icopyright.et/user/viewFreeUse.act?fuid=MzkxODcz, accessed 18 July 2007.

International Telecommunication Union (ITU) (2001), 'Status of IMT-2000 (UMTS) 3G mobile licensing in Western Europe', www.itu.int/ITU-D/ict/statistics/at_glance/_page.print, accessed 18 July 2007.

Janssen, M.C.W., A.P. Ros and N. van der Windt (eds) (2001), *De Draad kwijt? Onderzoek naar de gang van zaken rond de Nederlandse UMTS-veiling* (in Dutch) (*Lost the thread? A study into the course of events surrounding the Dutch UMTS auction*), Rotterdam: Erasmus University Rotterdam.

Jehiel, P. and B. Moldovanu (2001), 'The European UMTS/IMT-2000 license auctions', www.enpc.fr/ceras/jehiel/umts1.pdf, accessed 26 April 2005.

Klemperer, P. (2002), 'How (not) to run auctions: the European 3G telecom auctions', *European Economic Review*, **46**(4–5), 829–45.

Kruse, J. (2002), 'Competition in mobile communications and the allocation of scarce resources: the case of UMTS', *Diskussionspapier, Institut für Wirtschaftspolitik der Universität der Bundeswehr Hamburg*, (119), November, www2.hsu-hh.de/kruse/forschung/download/scarceresources.pdf, accessed 26 April 2005.

NRC (2001), 'Spelers UMTS veiling dicteerden de regels' (in Dutch) ('Players in the UMTS auction dictated the rules'), *NRC webeditie* (in Dutch) (*NRC web edition*), 30 August.

RTR (2000), 'UMTS auction to start on November 2, 2000 Telekom-Control completes preparations', *press release Rundfunk und Telekom Regulierungs-GmbH*, 31 October, www.rtr.at/web.nsf/englisch/Portfolio_Presseinfos_ nach+ Datum_PresseInfoDatum_PInfo311000?OpenDocument, accessed 18 July 2007.

Schmid, J. (2000), 'Fierce bidding surpasses amount paid in British wireless auction: German phone-license sale heats up', *International Herald Tribune*, 15 August, www.iht.com/bin/print_ipub.php?file=/articles/2000/08/15/auction.2.t_1.php, accessed 18 July 2007.

Seifert, S. and K. Ehrhart (2004), 'Design of the 3G spectrum auctions in the UK and in Germany: an experimental investigation', www.iw.uni-karlsruhe.de/ Publications/Final%2004-03-17.pdf, accessed 26 April 2005.

The Industry Standard (2001), 'Blu wins legal battle for return of UMTS deposit', 5 July, www.thestandard.com/article/0,1902,27714,00.html, accessed 18 July 2007.

Van Damme, E. (2002), 'The European UMTS auctions', *European Economic Review*, **46**(4–5), 846–58.

Versatel (2002), 'Versatel disappointed with Dutch UMTS auction tomorrow', Versatel press release, 5 July, Amsterdam: Versatel.

9. Microsoft

9.1 BACKGROUND: MICROSOFT IN EUROPE

Microsoft was founded by Bill Gates in Redmond, Washington, in 1975. Over time, Microsoft has managed to build up a very dominant position in the computer software market, worldwide as well as in the European Union. In August 1995, Microsoft introduced the Windows operating system (Microsoft, 1 August 2007). Currently, over 90 per cent of all personal computers run on Windows (CFI,[1] 2007, para 31). As we will see in this chapter, Windows' dominant market position plays a key role in the legal struggle fought in recent years between Microsoft and the European Commission, which is the subject of this chapter. Before entering into the course of this legal struggle, we will discuss a number of terms from the computer world that are needed to fathom the ins and outs of this sector.

As said, Microsoft is a producer of computer software. Software should be distinguished from the hardware of a computer. The hardware is the physical part of the computer, such as the processor, the printer and the screen. Companies that produce hardware are, for example, Compaq and IBM. Within the software, a distinction should be made between the operating system and the applications. Operating systems, such as Windows and Linux, are responsible for dividing the tasks that the computer has to perform and for allocating memory. In fact, the operating system coordinates activities between the hardware and the applications. Applications include, for example, graphics programs, word processing programs or Internet browsers (Tanenbaum, 2001, pp. 1–34).

The operating system controls the hardware of the computer by means of 'interfaces'. The applications and the operating system are also mutually connected by means of an interface. Finally, the operating system has an interface with the computer users, also called the computer environment. In the computer sector, these three interfaces of the operating system form crucial technical bottleneck factors. For example, the operating system can only function if it matches the hardware seamlessly. Since the majority of computers use Windows, hardware producers are strongly dependent on Microsoft. Likewise, the applications have to be compatible with the operating system. Given the popularity of Windows, producers of applications will be inclined to ensure that their applications can run on Windows. Finally, the operating system tends to determine the computer environment. A change of operating system leads to a different computer environment, which is why computer users will not easily switch over to a new operating system (Silberschatz et al., 2006, pp. 3–35; Van Wendel de Joode, 2003).

This chapter presents a chronological report on some of the highlights in the struggle between Microsoft and the European Commission: what stance is taken by the two parties, what arguments they adduce to account for their actions, how they react to each other and what the strategies, actions and reactions of the main competitors are. Over the last years, Microsoft has been one of the most important dossiers of the European Commissioner for Competition and much is at stake both for the Commission and for Microsoft.

9.2 DECISION OF THE EUROPEAN COMMISSION: ABUSE OF DOMINANT POSITION

9.2.1 Sun Lodges a Complaint

On 10 December 1998, Sun Microsystems lodged a complaint against Microsoft with the European Commission. Sun Microsystems is a competitor of Microsoft's, selling such products as server operating systems.[2] The complaint was directed against Microsoft's refusal to disclose information that Sun Microsystems deemed necessary to allow it to compete on the work group server operating system market (CFI, 17 September 2007, paras 6 and 7).

Subsequently, in February 2000, the European Commission launched a separate investigation against Microsoft concerning the incorporation of Windows Media Player in Windows.[3] The proceedings initiated pursuant to Sun Microsystems' complaint and to the Commission's separate investigation were subsequently joined under Case COMP/C-3/37.792 (CFI, 9 March 2005, para 5).

On 24 March 2004, the European Commission adopted a decision in Case COMP/C-3/37.792 – Microsoft (Decision 2007/53/EC). According to the Decision, Microsoft infringed Article 82 EC and Article 54 of the Agreement on the European Economic Area by reason of two abuses of a dominant position (Decision 2007/53/EC, Article 2):

1.   The first abuse concerned Microsoft's refusal to supply its competitors with 'interoperability information' and allow the use of such

information for the development and distribution of products in competition with Microsoft's own products on the market for work group server operating systems.[4]
2. The second established abuse consisted in the fact that Microsoft made the availability of the Windows client personal computer operating system conditional on the simultaneous acquisition of the Windows Media Player software.

In its decision of 24 March 2004, the European Commission imposed a record fine of 497 million euros on Microsoft for abusing its dominant market position in operating systems for computers (Decision 2007/53/EC, Articles 3–7). Until then, the highest European fine ever handed down for abuse of a dominant market position had been in 1991, when Tetra Pak, the Swedish packaging manufacturer, had to pay 75 million euros (Decision 92/163/EEC). In 2001, another very high European fine – 462 million euros – was imposed on Roche, the pharmaceutical company, but this was for cartel formation (Decision 2003/2/EC).

In addition to this fine, Microsoft had to put a 'stripped-down' version of its Windows system on the European market without Media Player software for audio and video within 90 days to give competitors a better chance. According to the Commission, the bundling of the Microsoft Media Player software for audio and video with the Windows operating system had to be regarded as a tie-in sale, which the European Union regulations on abuse of market dominance prohibit.

Besides, Microsoft had to release interface codes within 120 days to make competition on the market for servers possible. Releasing these codes to the competition should enable their products to communicate with Windows.

Finally, Microsoft was obliged to submit a proposal for a suitable monitoring mechanism to the Commission within 30 days. The mechanism should at any rate contain a 'monitoring trustee' that was independent of Microsoft. In this way, the Commission wanted to monitor to what extent Microsoft complied with the above-mentioned measures imposed. In the eyes of the Commission, to perform this task, the 'monitoring trustee' should have wide-ranging powers: for example, the trustee was to have access to Microsoft employees and to the source code of relevant Microsoft products.

9.2.2 Infringement of Intellectual Property?

Initially, Microsoft tried to come to terms with the European Commission to prevent these measures being imposed. Two years earlier, Microsoft had managed to limit the damage in the United States substantially by means of such a settlement. At the time, the issue in the US was the coupling of Internet Explorer with Windows, which pushed Netscape, a competing Internet browser, from the market (cf. Microsoft, 16 January 2008; Economist, 2 March 2002). However, on 18 March 2004, the European Commissioner for Competition Policy, Mario Monti, announced that he would not effect a settlement with Microsoft about the abuse of its dominant market position in personal computers. He argued that Microsoft not only harmed consumers, but that it also hampered innovation by abusing its market dominance. According to Monti, a decision was needed that would create a strong precedent (Monti, 18 March 2004). The competition warmly welcomed the news that the Commission would not make a settlement with Microsoft, because a settlement would have a far smaller precedent effect than a conviction, a fine and the measures imposed by the Commission for future behaviour.

The Computer and Communications Industry Association (CCIA), with which major competitors such as Netscape, Sun Microsystems, Apple, Oracle and Nokia were affiliated, declared that both competitors and customers were 'major beneficiaries' of this decision that would limit Microsoft's 'massive monopoly powers' (Black, 15 April 2004). On the other hand, Monti recognized that the imposed 497 million euro fine would have no deterrent effect on Microsoft, which at the time had some 50 billion euros in hand. However, according to him, the other measures did have a preventive effect. Besides, the Commission left undecided whether Microsoft would in the future be forced to put two versions on the market of each new product that it would integrate with Windows, as was now the case with the Media Player. The Commission stated that it would judge 'on a case-to-case basis', but that the decision established 'clear principles' for the future conduct of dominant companies (European Commission, 24 March 2004; Monti, 24 March 2004).

The sanctions imposed dealt a heavy blow to Microsoft's tried and tested corporate strategy in Europe, because this strategy was aimed at coupling more software to the dominant Windows (Economist, 31 January 2004). In a reaction, Brad Smith, Microsoft Senior Vice President and General Counsel, called the fine 'unfortunate' for Microsoft. He also stated: 'Under our proposals [. . .] every Windows PC would have included three competing media players. [. . .] In addition the settlement provisions that we offered would have applied worldwide [. . . not] only to the European Economic Area.' And he went on to say:

There is an important principle at stake in this case. We believe that every company should have the ability to improve its products to meet the needs of consumers. [. . .] It reflects a decision by an important governmental body to try to step into the marketplace [. . .] by trying to restrict the innovations themselves. [This decision] in effect requires us to produce a second version of our software, [. . .] reduce its quality, and yet make it available at the same price as the full-featured version. (Smith, 24 March 2004)

Microsoft announced that it would challenge the conviction by the Commission in the European Court of First Instance in Luxembourg. Microsoft also filed a request there for the suspension of the sanctions imposed by the Commission for the duration of the appeal (CFI, 22 December 2004, paras 40–41).

Microsoft argued that it could not have known that it was breaching the EU regulations, because the European Commission had entered a new area in tackling the abuse of market dominance in the software sector. However, according to European Commissioner Monti, the crack-down on Microsoft – the imposed record fine and other measures – was 'nothing new'. He stated that the European Commission had applied the 'normal' competition regulations. He also stated that a good market analysis applies just as much to the 'new' economy (Monti, 24 March 2004; Ballmer and Smith, 24 March 2004).

Another argument of Microsoft's was that the imposed measures infringed intellectual property. This argument concerned the European Commission's demand that Microsoft should release interface codes within 120 days. According to Monti, however, there was no question here of expropriating intellectual property. He pointed out that, on the basis of legal precedent, dominant enterprises that play a decisive role in the development of new technologies can be forced to release such information. He also stated that Microsoft might receive compensation for releasing the interface codes. Monti even argued that the non-releasing of information by Microsoft formed part of a wider strategy to oust competitors from the market (Monti, 24 March 2004; Smith, 24 March 2004).

The measures of the European Commission met with concern from the US. The US Department of Justice announced in a statement that it found the decision 'unfortunate' as well. The Department also said that the measures might give rise to unintended effects: 'Sound antitrust policy must avoid chilling innovation and competition even by "dominant" companies.' According to the US Department, the measures would be aimed at protecting competitors rather than ensuring that consumers would be able to benefit from new software products (Hewitt Pate, 24 March 2004).

9.3 MICROSOFT DEFEATED IN THE EUROPEAN COURT OF FIRST INSTANCE

On 22 December 2004, the European Court of First Instance turned down Microsoft's request to suspend the sanctions of the European Commission. This ruling of the Court dealt Microsoft a heavy blow. The Court held that Microsoft had not proved that the sanctions imposed by the European Commission caused 'serious and irreparable damage'. However, this ruling merely concerned the request to suspend the imposed sanctions during the appeal. A final ruling of the European Court of First Instance in Microsoft's appeal against the sanctions of the Commission was to follow (CFI, 22 December 2004, para 475).

Microsoft had meanwhile paid the 497 million euro fine. Microsoft also stated that it had made all preparations to implement the other imposed measures. The reaction of Brad Smith, Microsoft Senior Vice President, to the ruling of the European Court of First Instance, was: 'We will [. . .] comply fully with the court order' (Microsoft, 22 December 2004).

The European Commission reacted positively to the decision. Neelie Kroes, the new European Commissioner for Competition, was particularly satisfied that the measures imposed by the Commission were not suspended and now took immediate effect. She also stated the following: 'The ruling is important because it retains the effectiveness of the antitrust enforcement, in particular in fast-moving markets' (European Commission, 22 December 2004).

Competitors reacted enthusiastically to the European Court of First Instance's ruling. According to RealNetworks, a competitor of Microsoft's in the field of software for playing sound and image, the ruling was a victory both for the European Commission and for consumers. Dave Stewart, counsel to RealNetworks, felt that 'the court has taken an important step toward promoting robust competition in digital media, fostering technological innovation and giving consumers real choice' (TimesOnline, 22 December 2004). Andrew Gavil, Professor of Law at Howard University, added that 'this ruling goes to the heart of Microsoft's bundling strategy. So potentially, this is very significant' (Lohr and Meller, 23 December 2004).

9.4 MICROSOFT FAILS TO COMPLY WITH THE IMPOSED MEASURES

In March 2005, the struggle between the European Commission and Microsoft flared up again. The European Commission took the view that, until then, Microsoft had not complied with the measures imposed in 2004. The Commission warned Microsoft that it might get a fine of 5 per cent of its total turnover if it failed to cooperate. Microsoft's turnover in 2004 was 36.8 billion dollars, resulting in a maximum fine of 1.8 billion dollars (1.4 billion euros). The Commission gave Microsoft three weeks to answer questions (Meller, 18 March 2005 and 14 April 2005).

The European Commission's warning concerned the measure imposed in 2004 to the effect that Microsoft had to release interface codes, allowing competitors' hardware and software to communicate with the Windows operating system. According to European Commissioner Neelie Kroes, Microsoft failed to properly implement the measures to promote interoperability. The Commission also said that Microsoft refused to make interface codes available to makers of free open source software[5] such as Linux. According to a spokesperson for Ms Kroes, Microsoft still made it very difficult for competing software firms to gain access to technical documentation needed to establish whether it would be useful for them to buy a licence from Microsoft. Microsoft also obliged the competitors to buy all-in-one licences. Ms Kroes' spokesperson also said that, as a result, companies potentially also paid for items they did not need, that is if they needed only a small part of the source code. According to the Commission, the level of the royalties Microsoft asked was also unjustified (BBC News, 18 March 2005; Meller, 18 March 2005).

Another point of conflict was the role of the independent trustee who was to gather information for the Commission to see whether Microsoft complied with the imposed sanctions. Microsoft wanted a veto over the information it had to give the Commission, but this was unacceptable in the Commission's eyes. All in all, the Commission felt that Microsoft was frustrating the sanctions, whereas Microsoft stated that the Commission failed to react to Microsoft's proposals and was frustrating the matter (Meller, 14 April 2005).

Another problem was the naming of the Windows version without the Media Player, which Microsoft now had ready for the European market. Microsoft intended to call this version the 'Windows XP Reduced Media Edition'. However, the European Commission felt that this name would only deter potential buyers. After the Commission had rejected ten of Microsoft's suggestions for a name, the two eventually agreed by the end of March 2005 that the bare Windows version would be sold under the name 'Windows XP Home Edition N' (Meller, 22 March 2006; Microsoft, 28 March 2006). However, in March 2005 the Commission did not yet have an official opinion about the question as to whether Microsoft had complied with the demand to offer a bare version of Windows – without the Media Player (Meller, 22 March 2006).

9.5 SETTLING AS A STRATEGY

Over time, both Microsoft and the European Commission have had the support of several parties in their legal struggle. In March 2005, nine parties were granted the right to participate in Microsoft's ongoing antitrust case. The interveners on the side of the European Commission included RealNetworks and the Free Software Foundation Europe. Those on the side of Microsoft included the Association for Competitive Technology and Exor, a Swedish business software producer (CFI, 17 September 2007, paras 62 and 63).

During this struggle, Microsoft opted several times to come to terms with a party siding with the European Commission. Since 2000, Microsoft has managed to terminate several lawsuits by means of such a settlement before the Court had the chance to give a ruling. In this way, not only was a legal judgment prevented – and possibly harmful jurisprudence – but in some cases it also meant that a competitor was eliminated.

For example, in 2003 Microsoft effected a 750 million dollar settlement with AOL Time Warner, the producer of the Internet browser Netscape. AOL Time Warner took the view that it was too difficult to install Netscape in Windows. In addition to the financial settlement, AOL also obtained the right to use Microsoft's Internet Explorer on its sites free of charge for seven years, which led to an explosive increase in the number of Internet Explorer users (Microsoft, 29 May 2005).

In 2003, Microsoft also agreed a 1.1 billion dollar settlement with a group of Californian computer users, who argued that they had paid too much for their software because of Microsoft's monopoly position. Claims had to be filed before 8 January 2005. A salient detail of the settlement was that a large part was paid in vouchers, which the computer users could then use to buy computer hardware and software – of the Microsoft brand, of course (Microsoft, 10 January 2003; Flynn, 5 January 2005).

In November 2004, Microsoft reached a settlement with one of its biggest opponents, the top executive of the Computer and Communications Industry Association, for an amount of 9.75 million dollars, causing him to withdraw from the lawsuit between Microsoft and the European Commission (Buck, 24 November 2004). After the CCIA had withdrawn from the antitrust case against Microsoft, Nokia left the CCIA. However, in February 2005, Nokia struck a deal with Microsoft involving the downloading of music onto mobile phones (Economist, 19 February 2005).

Another competitor of Microsoft's that withdrew from the European Commission's lawsuit against Microsoft after a settlement was RealNetworks, a US software company. In October 2005, Microsoft settled with RealNetworks. RealNetworks is the producer of applications like the RealPlayer, a competitor of Microsoft's Media Player. According to RealNetworks, it was too difficult to install the RealPlayer in Windows. RealNetworks had brought a lawsuit against Microsoft in the United States in 2003 and participated in the European Commission's lawsuit against Microsoft and in a lawsuit in South Korea. After a 761 million dollar settlement, RealNetworks withdrew from these lawsuits. The settlement involved a payment of 460 million dollars and a cooperation agreement between Microsoft and RealNetworks worth 301 million dollars. This cooperation consisted in Microsoft supporting Rhapsody, RealNetworks' music service on MSN, Microsoft's digital community. In exchange, RealNetworks would point out the ease of use of the Windows Media Player to Rhapsody subscribers. In other words, the gist of this settlement was that RealNetworks accepted that Microsoft's Media Player could develop into a global standard and that the RealPlayer was bought off the market (Microsoft, 11 October 2005; Lohr, 12 October 2005).

9.6   THE STRUGGLE CONTINUES: APPEAL PROCEEDINGS AND NEW COMPLAINTS

In February 2006, a group of companies from the computer sector and the world of information technology (united in the European Committee for Interoperable Systems, ECIS, which includes IBM, Nokia, Oracle and Sun) filed a new complaint against Microsoft with European Commissioner Neelie Kroes. According to these companies, Microsoft had not yet properly implemented the existing agreements forcing Microsoft to practise openness about programs. They accused Microsoft of maintaining its monopolies and trying to extend its market dominance to other areas such as the Internet (ECIS, 22 February 2006).

In April 2006, a hearing took place at the Court of First Instance of the European Court of Justice in Luxembourg in Microsoft's appeal proceedings against the European Commission's decision from 2004. In Ms Kroes' view, the technical information that Microsoft had released until then was insufficient. By the end of 2005, the European Commission had already warned Microsoft that, from 15 December 2005, it risked a fine of a maximum of 2 million euros per day if it continued to refuse to share essential information about Windows with competitors. However, since Microsoft had scored a profit of 10 billion euros in 2005, it is doubtful whether Microsoft was impressed by this threat (Decision C (2005) 4420, Article 1; Microsoft, 2007).

During the hearing in April 2006, Microsoft deftly backgrounded the European Commission's findings regarding Microsoft's systematic refusal to supply technical data that competitors need for coordinating new software applications properly with Microsoft products. Microsoft managed to focus the hearing on the issue of intellectual property. This particularly concerned the question concerning which law should take precedence: competition law or intellectual property law. Ian Forrester, one of Microsoft's counsels, argued that providing the technical information would come down to giving away intellectual property (CFI, 17 September 2007, paras 267–74 and 283). Many parties followed the hearing with great interest. A spokesperson for ECIS, a lobby group of big IT companies, stated: 'It is no exaggeration to say that the IT industry's future development depends on the outcome of this case, because it will determine whether the IT industry develops according to the Microsoft model or to a competitive model'. From a legal perspective, Microsoft had pulled out all the stops (Vinje, 28 April 2006).

In July 2006, the European Commission imposed another fine on Microsoft, this time worth 280.5 million euros, a fine that corresponded with an amount of 1.5 million euros per day (Decision C (2006) 3143, Article 1). Microsoft immediately announced that it would appeal against this decision (Smith, 12 July 2006). The reason for this fine was that, according to the Commission, Microsoft had still not complied with the demand that it should provide competitors with sufficient technical information about the Windows operating program (Decision C (2006) 3143). The Commission threatened to raise the fine from 1.5 million euros per day to 3 million euros if Microsoft continued to protect the market (Decision C (2006) 3143, Article 3). In November 2006, Ms Kroes warned Microsoft again that the imposed fine from July 2006 would be increased if Microsoft did not provide the requested information within a few days. Microsoft then submitted technical data about the Windows operating program to European Commissioner Kroes at the last moment. In her reaction, the European Commissioner stated that she would decide later whether the supplied information was sufficient (Meller, 16 November 2006; Meller, 24 November 2006).

Recent complaints about Microsoft from the Commission and the competition concern Vista, the new Windows operating program. As early as March 2006, the European Commission warned Microsoft of potential competition problems with Vista, because Microsoft intended to build an Internet search machine and antivirus software into Vista. Cass, a consultant to Microsoft, reacted to the warning by saying that Microsoft simply provided for a consumer's need with this 'bundling' of products. 'To take an analogy used by the Commission itself, the fact that laces are sold separately from shoes does not demonstrate that shoe manufacturers are engaged in a tying practice by selling shoes only with laces. One must still consider whether there is demand for shoes without laces' (Microsoft, 24

April 2006). However, in October 2006, Microsoft announced that it would make changes to Windows Vista because of the European Commission's warning (Smith, 13 October 2006).

The companies that had filed a complaint against Microsoft with the Commission in February 2006 (see above) filed another complaint on 26 January 2007, this time about Vista. According to the competitors, Vista should be regarded as Microsoft's latest attempt to extend its monopoly over the Internet. The complaints were aimed particularly at the XAML language for the Internet, which was to replace html, the current standard language. According to the competitors, this XAML language was dependent on Windows and would therefore oust competing operating systems, such as Linux, from the market. The companies asked the Commission to take a decision as soon as possible regarding the complaint they had filed in February 2006 (ECIS, 26 January 2007).

9.7   MICROSOFT'S APPEAL DISMISSED

On 17 September 2007, the Court of First Instance of the European Court of Justice gave a ruling in Microsoft's appeal against the European Commission (CFI, 17 September 2007). In this ruling, the Court of First Instance dismissed practically all the points of Microsoft's appeal, thus upholding most of the Commission's decision. The Court concurred with the Commission in its conclusion that Microsoft abused its power position by on the one hand failing to provide interoperability information to competitors and on the other hand by the tied sale of Windows Media Player (CFI, 17 September 2007, paras 776, 813 and 1229). According to the Court, the Commission had not committed any errors in judging the gravity and the duration of the infringement. The Court therefore upheld the fine of 497 million euros (CFI, 17 September 2007, paras 1332, 1366 and 1367).

Microsoft's argument that its products are (partly) protected by intellectual property rights and that the decision leads to the 'giving away' of those property rights was no reason for the Court to quash the Commission's decision: according to the Court, the decision shows that the Commission assumed that Microsoft could invoke such rights (CFI, 17 September 2007, paras 283 and 284).

However, the Court annulled the obligation to appoint a 'monitoring trustee', because its powers are much wider than European law permits and because forcing Microsoft to bear the cost of this trustee is contrary to the European regulations (CFI, 17 September 2007, paras 1278–79).

European Commissioner Kroes showed herself very satisfied with the Court's ruling:

> The Court has upheld a landmark Commission decision to give consumers more choice in software markets. That decision set an important precedent in terms of the obligations of dominant companies to allow competition, in particular in high tech industries. The Court ruling shows that the Commission was right to take its decision. Microsoft must now comply fully with its legal obligations to desist from engaging in anti-competitive conduct. (European Commission, 17 September 2007)

However, Thomas Barnett, a top-ranking official at the US Department of Justice, voiced criticism of the Court of First Instance's ruling. According to him, the decision might harm consumers: 'We are, however, concerned that the standard applied to unilateral conduct by the CFI, rather than helping consumers, may have the unfortunate consequence of harming consumers by chilling innovation and discouraging competition' (Barnett, 17 September 2007).

The day after these statements, European Commissioner Kroes reacted unusually harshly to this foreign interference in European independent courts: 'I find it totally unacceptable that a representative of the American government criticizes an independent court outside its own jurisdiction. That is absolutely not done' (IHT, 19 September 2007).

In reaction to the Court's ruling, Microsoft itself indicated, through Senior Vice President Brad Smith, that Microsoft would comply in all respects with the ruling and the Commission's decision: 'It's clearly very important to us as a company that we comply with our obligations under European law. We'll study this decision carefully, and if there are additional steps that we need to take in order to comply with it, we will take them' (Microsoft, 17 September 2007).

Then, more than a month later, Microsoft announced that it would not appeal against the decision and two days later the announcement followed that also the appeal lodged against the 280 million euro fine dating from 2006 was being withdrawn (Microsoft, 22 October 2007; Microsoft, 24 October 2007). Erich Andersen of Microsoft's European Department of Legal Affairs explained this decision in the following terms: 'We believe it's important at this stage to focus all of our energies on complying with our legal obligations and strengthening our constructive relationship with the European Commission' (Microsoft, 24 October 2007).

These statements followed a dinner party between Steve Ballmer, Microsoft's CEO, and European Commissioner Neelie Kroes. According to Kroes, Microsoft would, from then on, comply with the Commission's demands, and the positive results of this should be visible in the following years (Lohr and O'Brien, 23 October 2007).

Even so, on 14 January 2008, the European Commission announced that it was initiating formal investigations against Microsoft in two cases of suspected abuse of a dominant market position. The first case was related to a complaint by ECIS, the European Committee for Interoperable Systems, which argued that Microsoft illegally refused to disclose inter-operability information across a broad range of products. The second case was based on a complaint by Opera, a competing browser vendor, which accused Microsoft of illegal tying of its Internet Explorer product to its dominant Windows operating system (European Commission, 14 January 2008). As might have been expected, the struggle between Microsoft and the European Commission continues.

9.8   STRATEGIC BEHAVIOUR

Table 9.1 summarizes the entries for and types of strategic behaviour that we found for Microsoft. Table 9.2 concentrates on the European Commission. Finally, in Table 9.3, the findings for Microsoft's competitors are presented. The most frequently used entry for strategic behaviour that we encountered in this case study is that of rules and contracts. Bottleneck facilities and indispensable nature were also used several times as entries for strategic behaviour. The strategic use of litigation is the most frequently occurring type of strategic behaviour in the Microsoft case study.

Table 9.1   Microsoft

Entry	Strategic behaviour: type and description
Bottleneck facilities	*Strategic behaviour using dominant market position: tie-in sale.* Microsoft made availability of Windows client personal computer operating system conditional on simultaneous acquisition of Windows Media Player software.
Rules and contracts + factor 'time'	*Strategic use of litigation and time.* Delay: Microsoft finds one excuse after another to postpone the implementation of the measures ordered by the European Commission. Besides, Microsoft appeals against the imposed measures. Microsoft carries out imposed measures as late as possible.
Rules and contracts	*Strategic use of litigation.* Microsoft tries to reach a settlement with the European Commission to prevent measures being imposed, because a settlement would have had less precedent effect than a conviction, a fine and the measures for future behaviour imposed by the Commission.

Table 9.1 (continued)

Entry	Strategic behaviour: type and description
Rules and contracts + factor 'time'	*Strategic use of litigation.* After the measures imposed on 24 March 2004, Microsoft stated that it could not have known that it was contravening the EU competition regulations, because the European Commission had allegedly entered a new area with its action against the abuse of market dominance in the software sector.
Indispensable nature + bottleneck facilities	*Raising opponents' costs.* Microsoft obliged competitors that wanted to buy licences from Microsoft to buy all-in-one-licences. As a result, they might be paying for matters they did not need, i.e. if they needed only a small part of the source code.
Factor 'time'	*Strategic use of time.* Microsoft had to come up with a new name for the stripped-down version of Windows. The European Commission refused Microsoft's first ten suggestions, including 'Windows XP Reduced Media Edition'.
Indispensable nature + bottleneck facilities	*Strategic non-disclosure of information.* Microsoft refused to provide its competitors with interoperability information and to allow the use of such information for the development and distribution of products in competition with Microsoft's own products on the market for work group server operating systems.
Bottleneck facilities + indispensable nature + rules and contracts	*Strategic use of litigation + strategic non-disclosure of information.* Microsoft argues that releasing interface codes would infringe intellectual property.
Indispensable nature	*Strategic non-disclosure of information.* Microsoft wanted a veto over the information it had to provide to the Commission. The Commission wanted this information to see whether Microsoft complied with the imposed sanctions.
Financial resources	*Divide and rule, buying off.* After a 761 million dollar settlement, RealNetworks withdraws from lawsuits against Microsoft. Besides, because of the settlement, RealNetworks' RealPlayer was, in fact, bought out of the market.
Financial resources	*Divide and rule, buying off.* Microsoft paid an amount of 9.75 million dollars to one of its biggest opponents, the top executive of the CCIA trade

Table 9.1   (continued)

Entry	Strategic behaviour: type and description
	organization, to withdraw from the court case between Microsoft and the European Commission.
Financial resources	*Divide and rule, buying off.* Microsoft effected a 750 million dollar settlement with AOL Time Warner, the producer of the Internet browser Netscape. AOL Time Warner took the view that it was too difficult to install Netscape in Windows. In addition to the financial settlement, AOL also obtained the right to use Microsoft's Internet Explorer on its sites free of charge for seven years, which led to an explosive increase in the number of Internet Explorer users.
Intertwined relations	Microsoft manages to tempt the USA to get involved in the conflict between Microsoft and the European Commission and to make negative statements about the actions against Microsoft.

Table 9.2   *European Commission*

Entry	Strategic behaviour: type and description
Rules and contracts	*Threatening.* Investigation against Microsoft + imposing measures on Microsoft + warning that a fine will be imposed if the imposed measures are not implemented.

Table 9.3   *Competitors*

Entry	Strategic behaviour: type and description
Rules and contracts	*Underdog.* Supporting the European Commission in its investigation against Microsoft.
Rules and contracts	*Package deal + strategic use of litigation.* In exchange for a 761 million dollar settlement, RealNetworks, an important competitor of Microsoft's, withdraws from lawsuits against Microsoft.
Rules and contracts	*Package deal + strategic use of litigation.* The chief executive of the CCIA trade organization, one of Microsoft's biggest opponents, receives an amount of 9.75 million dollars from Microsoft, to withdraw from the court case between Microsoft and the European Commission.

NOTES

1. CFI stands for Court of First Instance, which is one of the courts of the European Court of Justice.
2. Servers are powerful multi-user computers in office networks, which are accessed through so-called 'client PCs', PCs that are connected to these servers (Decision 2007/53/EC, recital 47).
3. Films and music can be played with the help of the Windows Media Player software. Competing products are, for example, Apple's QuickTime and RealNetworks' RealPlayer (Decision 2007/53/EC, recitals 121, 131 and 135).
4. 'Interoperability information' is defined as follows in Article 1 of the Decision: 'the complete and accurate specifications for all the Protocols implemented in Windows Work Group Server Operating Systems and . . . used by Windows Work Group Servers to deliver file and print services and group and user administration services, including the Windows Domain Controller services, Active Directory Services and Group Policy services, to Windows Work Group Networks' (Article 1(1) of the Decision). 'Protocols' are defined as 'a set of rules of interconnection and interaction between various instances of Windows Work Group Server Operating Systems and Windows Client PC Operating Systems running on different computers in a Windows Work Group Network' (Article 1(2) of the Decision) (Decision 2007/53/EC, Article 1).
5. Open source software is computer software for which the source code is made available to the customer. This permits users to use, change and improve the software, and to redistribute it in modified or unmodified form (Decision 2007/53/EC, recital 26).

REFERENCES

Ballmer, S. and B. Smith (24 March 2004), 'Transcript: Steve Ballmer/Brad Smith News Conference with U.S.-based Journalists Regarding European Commission Ruling', www.microsoft.com, accessed 29 January 2008.

Barnett, T. (17 September 2007), 'Assistant Attorney General for antitrust, Thomas O. Barnett, issues statements on European Microsoft decision', www.usdoj.gov, accessed 30 October 2007.

BBC News (18 March 2005), 'EU warns on Microsoft behaviour', http://news.bbc.co.uk, accessed 30 January 2008.

Black, E. (15 April 2004), 'Letter sent to Secretary of State Powell urging no intervention', www.ccianet.org, accessed 29 January 2008.

Buck, T. (24 November 2004), 'Critic of Microsoft received $9.75m after deal', *Financial Times*, p. 1.

CFI (22 December 2004), Case T-201/04 R, Order of 22.12.2004, *Microsoft v. Commission*, ECR 2004, p. II-4463. Summary also appeared in the *Official Journal of the European Union* 2005, C 69/16.

CFI (9 March 2005), Case T-201/04, Order of 09.03.2005, *Microsoft v. Commission*, not published in ECR, http://curia.europa.eu, accessed 26 October 2007.

CFI (17 September 2007), Case T-201/04, Judgment of 17.09.2007, *Microsoft v. Commission*, not yet published in ECR. For a summary, see: Curia, Press Release No 63/07, 17.09.2007.

Decision 92/163/EEC (24 July 1991), *Tetra Pak II, Official Journal of the European Union* 1992, L72/1.

Decision 2003/2/EC (21 November 2001), Case COMP/37.512 – *Vitamins*, *Official Journal of the European Union* 2003, L6/1.

Decision 2007/53/EC (24 March 2004), Case COMP/37.792 – *Microsoft*, *Official Journal of the European Union* 2007, L 32/23.

Decision C (2005) 4420 (10 November 2005), Case COMP/37.792 – *Microsoft*, not yet published in the OJ, http://ec.europa.eu, accessed 26 October 2007.

Decision C (2006) 3143 (12 July 2006), Case COMP/37.792 – *Microsoft*, not yet published in the OJ, http://ec.europa.eu, accessed 26 October 2007.

ECIS (22 February 2006), 'ECIS calls for halt to anti-competitive Microsoft practices', www.ecis.eu, accessed 30 January 2008.

ECIS (26 January 2007), 'ECIS media release: with Vista Microsoft continues its illegal practices', www.ecis.eu, accessed 26 October 2007.

Economist, The (2002), 'On the right track?', 2 March, pp. 59–60.

Economist, The (2004), 'Sir Bill and his dragons – past, present and future', 31 January, pp. 67–9.

Economist, The (2005), 'Business', 19 February, p. 7.

European Commission (24 March 2004), 'Commission concludes on Microsoft investigation, imposes conduct remedies and a fine', EU Press Release IP/04/382, http://europa.eu/rapid, accessed 20 January 2008.

European Commission (22 December 2004), 'Questions and answers – Order of the President of the Court of First Instance in case T-201/04 R – Microsoft Corp. vs European Commission', EU Press Release MEMO/04/305, http://europa.eu/rapid, accessed 28 January 2008.

European Commission (17 September 2007), 'Antitrust: Commission welcomes CFI ruling upholding Commission's decision on Microsoft's abuse of dominant market position', EU Press Release MEMO/07/359, http://europa.eu/rapid, accessed 30 October 2007.

European Commission (14 January 2008), 'Antitrust: Commission initiates formal investigations against Microsoft in two cases of suspected abuse of dominant market position', EU Press Release MEMO/08/19, http://europa.eu/rapid, accessed 25 June 2008.

Flynn, L. (2005), 'Few takes for payments from Microsoft settlement', *The New York Times*, 5 January, www.nytimes.com, accessed 30 January 2008.

Hewitt Pate, R. (2004), 'Assistant Attorney General for Antitrust, R. Hewitt Pate, issues statement on the EC's decision in its Microsoft investigation', 24 March, www.usdoj.gov, accessed 29 January 2008.

IHT (2007), 'Kroes lashes out at US official over Microsoft', *International Herald Tribune*, 19 September, www.iht.com, accessed 30 January 2008.

Lohr, S. (2005), 'Antitrust suit turns into a partnership for Microsoft', *The New York Times*, 12 October, www.nytimes.com, accessed 30 January 2008.

Lohr, S. and P. Meller (2004), 'Europe rejects Microsoft's bid to preserve bundling plan', *The New York Times*, 23 December, www.nytimes.com, accessed 30 January 2008.

Lohr, S. and K. O'Brien (2007), 'Microsoft is yielding in European antitrust fight', *The New York Times*, 23 October, www.nytimes.com, accessed 30 January 2008.

Meller, P. (2005), 'EU doubts efforts by Microsoft to comply', *International Herald Tribune*, 18 March, www.iht.com, accessed 30 January 2008.

Meller, P. (2005), 'Microsoft and Europeans argue over ruling', *The New York Times*, 14 April, www.nytimes.com, accessed 30 January 2008.

Meller, P. (2006), 'Europe reviews Microsoft's compliance with antitrust ruling', *The New York Times*, 22 March, www.nytimes.com, accessed 30 January 2008.

Meller, P. (2006), 'Europe warns Microsoft over compliance', *The New York Times*, 16 November, www.nytimes.com, accessed 30 January 2008.

Meller, P. (2006), 'Microsoft gives Europe antitrust documents', *The New York Times*, 24 November, www.nytimes.com, accessed 30 January 2008.

Microsoft (2003), 'Microsoft and California plaintiffs settle California class action lawsuits: settlement to benefit consumers and California schools', 10 January, www.microsoft.com, accessed 30 January 2008.

Microsoft (2004), 'Microsoft statement on European Union Court of First Instance Order on interim measures', 22 December, www.microsoft.com, accessed 20 January 2008.

Microsoft (2005), 'AOL Time Warner and Microsoft agree to collaborate on digital media initiatives and settle pending litigation', 29 May, www.microsoft.com, accessed 30 January 2008.

Microsoft (2005), 'Microsoft and RealNetworks resolve antitrust case and announce digital music and games partnership', 11 October, www.microsoft.com, accessed 30 January 2008.

Microsoft (2006), 'Microsoft statement on European Commission process: company accepts Commission name for version of Windows without Media Player', 28 March, www.microsoft.com, accessed 30 January 2008.

Microsoft (2006), 'Excerpts from opening statement on Windows Media Player: as presented by counsel for Microsoft before the European Court of First Instance', 24 April, www.microsoft.com, accessed 30 January 2008.

Microsoft (2007), 'Yearly income statements: FY 1985–FY 2007', www.microsoft.com, accessed 26 October 2007.

Microsoft (2007), 'Fast facts about Microsoft', 1 August, www.microsoft.com, accessed 20 January 2007.

Microsoft (2007), 'Microsoft statement regarding the European Court of First Instance's judgment in the EU/Microsoft case', 17 September, www.microsoft.com, accessed 20 October 2007.

Microsoft (2007), 'Microsoft statement on compliance with European Commission 2004 decision', 22 October, www.microsoft.com, accessed 26 October 2007.

Microsoft (2007), 'Microsoft withdraws two remaining appeals with the Court of First Instance', 24 October, www.microsoft.com, accessed 26 October 2007.

Microsoft (2008), 'A timeline of the US–Microsoft consent decree', 16 January, www.microsoft.com, accessed 29 January 2008.

Monti, M. (2004), 'Commissioner Monti's statement on Microsoft', EU Press Release IP/04/365, 18 March, http://europa.eu/rapid, accessed 30 October 2007.

Monti, M. (2004), 'Commissioner Monti's announcement on Microsoft', 24 March, the announcement is available as audio file at www.bbc.co.uk as attachment to the article 'Microsoft hit by record EU fine' of 24 March 2004.

Silberschatz, A., P. Galvin and G. Gagne (2006), *Operating System Concepts*, Hoboken, NJ: John Wiley & Sons.

Smith, B. (2004), 'Transcript: Brad Smith news conference with European-based journalists regarding European Commission ruling', 24 March, www.microsoft.com, accessed 20 January 2008.

Smith, B. (2006), 'Brad Smith press conference transcript: European Commission July 12 decision on fines', 12 July, www.microsoft.com, accessed 30 January 2008.

Smith, B. (2006), 'Brad Smith press conference transcript: announcement regarding release of Windows Vista in Europe and Korea', 13 October, www.microsoft. com, accessed 30 January 2008.

Tanenbaum, A. (2001), *Modern Operating Systems*, Upper Saddle River, NJ: Prentice Hall.

TimesOnline (2004), 'Court rules against Microsoft over fines', 22 December, www.timesonline.co.uk, accessed 29 January 2008.

Van Wendel de Joode, R. (2003), 'Concurrentie in de computerindustrie' (in Dutch) ('Competition in the computer industry'), in E. ten Heuvelhof, M. de Jong, M. Kuit and H. Stout (eds), *Infrastratego. Strategisch Gedrag in InfrastructuurGebonden Sectoren*, Utrecht: Lemma, pp. 149–66.

Vinje, T. (2006), 'ECIS media release – close of the Microsoft oral hearing Luxembourg', 28 April, www.ecis.eu, accessed 30 January 2008.

10. Analysis

10.1 INTRODUCTION

In the preceding chapters, we have given a detailed overview of many kinds of strategic behaviour as we found them in the case studies. In these case studies, we looked at various network-based sectors: electricity (Enron), telecommunication (UMTS and AT&T), IT (Microsoft) and aviation (open skies). In the process, we presented the developments in several continents (Europe and North America) and countries (including Italy, Austria, Germany, the Netherlands and the United States). In describing our empirical findings, we have focused on entries for and forms of strategic behaviour as we introduced them in Chapters 3 and 4.

In this chapter, we will draw conclusions regarding strategic behaviour in network-based industries, based on our case descriptions. We will discuss what entries for strategic behaviour are used pre-eminently as a basis for strategic behaviour in network-based industries and what dominant patterns of strategic behaviour ensue from the characteristics of these network-based industries. In the chapter about open skies we saw, for example, that the European Union negotiators used occasional arguments by suggesting that the United States had *de facto* cabotage rights in the European Union. In our view, such a form of strategic behaviour may just as well occur in non-network-based sectors and is therefore not particularly characteristic of network-based industries. However, if we look at an example from the AT&T case study, where market entrants used the incumbent's obligation to guarantee the utility character by focusing on profitable segments of the market (known as 'cherry picking'), we can rank this under the category of strategic behaviour characteristic of network-based industries. Microsoft's refusal to release interoperability information to the competition is also characteristic of network-based industries.

First, in section 10.2, we will discuss the dominant pictures of strategic behaviour in network-based industries as they emerged from the case studies. We will give an overview of the most meaningful examples and arrange them by the entries for strategic behaviour from Chapter 4. Then, in section 10.3, we will embed our empirical findings in the theoretical literature about strategic behaviour. This implies that we will specify the theoretical forms of strategic behaviour discussed in Chapter 3 for network-based industries. This section, too, is structured on the basis of the entries for strategic behaviour. Generating such a theoretical overview for network-based industries is no simple task, since no handbook in this field is available anywhere and knowledge is contained in a myriad of publications dealing with sub-aspects like oligopolist price agreements or regulatory capture. It also appears that forms of strategic behaviour found by different authors concern more or less the same subject or show overlap. We therefore wish to emphasize that this overview inevitably cannot be complete. Besides, some strategic behaviour mentioned under one entry may also occur under another entry.

10.2   DOMINANT PICTURES OF STRATEGIC BEHAVIOUR

10.2.1   Strategic Use of Control over so-called 'Bottleneck Facilities' and other Crucial Technical Facilities and Standards

A company that has considerable influence on the access to, and the use of, bottleneck facilities, other crucial facilities and technical standards can use this situation to weaken the competitive position of (potential) competitors (see also Chapter 4). Table 10.1 again lists the main forms of strategic behaviour from the case studies in which the bottleneck provided an entry and that are characteristic of network-based industries.

The AT&T case study presented a dominant picture of using bottleneck facilities as an entry for strategic behaviour. AT&T had taken over Western Electric by the end of the nineteenth century. The fact that AT&T subscribers were then forced to use Western Electric equipment strengthened Western Electric's market position immensely, which resulted in extra income worth millions of dollars for AT&T. AT&T also frequently exploited the bottleneck by blocking interconnection. AT&T had a very extensive long-distance telephone network and repeatedly refused to interconnect it with local independent carriers.

We found another explicit example of the strategic use of bottleneck facilities in the Microsoft case study. Over 90 per cent of all personal computers run on Windows, Microsoft's operating system. The interfaces of the operating system with the hardware of the computer, with the applications and with the computer environment are very important technical bottleneck factors in the computer sector. Microsoft cleverly used both this bottleneck and its dominant market position by refusing to release interoperability information to the competition. This greatly reduced the possibilities of competing with Microsoft.

Table 10.1   *Strategic use of control over so-called 'bottleneck facilities'*
and other crucial technical facilities and standards

Case study	Strategic behaviour: type and definition
Microsoft	*Tied sales* Microsoft made availability of Windows client personal computer operating system conditional on simultaneous acquisition of Windows Media Player software.
Microsoft	*Raising rivals' costs* Microsoft obliged competitors that wanted to buy licences from Microsoft to buy all-in-one licences. Thus, they also paid potentially for items they did not need, viz. when they only needed a small part of the source code.
Microsoft	*Strategic non-disclosure of information* Microsoft refused to supply interoperability information to its competitors and to allow the use of such information for the development and distribution of products in competition with Microsoft's own products on the market for work group server operating systems.
UMTS Germany	*Collusion* In an interview, MobilCom stated that 'should [Debitel] fail to secure a license [it could] become a "virtual network operator" using MobilCom's network while saving on the cost of the license'.
UMTS Germany	*Vertical foreclosure* Telefonica strengthened its negotiating position vis-à-vis KPN by securing a German UMTS licence.
UMTS Austria	*Collusion* A week before the auction, Telecom Austria said that it would be content with just two of the 12 blocks of frequency on offer and that, if the other five bidders adopted a similar attitude, 'it should be possible to get the frequencies on sensible terms'. This might be regarded as offering a collusive deal.
UMTS The Netherlands	*Collusion* Ben and T-Mobile International formed a partnership to strengthen their position in the auction.
Open skies USA	*Vertical foreclosure. Divide and rule + carrot and stick.* US concluded bilaterals with EU member states.
AT&T	*Vertical foreclosure* AT&T took over Western Electric.

Table 10.1   (continued)

Case study	Strategic behaviour: type and definition
AT&T	*Vertical foreclosure* AT&T refused to connect its long-distance network with local independent carriers.
AT&T	*Vertical foreclosure* Poor operating of 'Protective Coupler', poor service of AT&T.
AT&T	*Vertical foreclosure* AT&T denied MCI interconnection.

We saw a final dominant pattern of strategic behaviour with the bottleneck as an entry in the UMTS case study. The auctions demonstrated clearly that the companies that already had a GSM licence for mobile telephony stood a better chance of also securing a UMTS licence. Several times, a licence or the possession of a network was used strategically. We saw a fine example of using bottleneck facilities as an entry for strategic behaviour in the German UMTS auction. MobilCom stated in an interview that, if Debitel failed to obtain a licence, Debitel might become a 'virtual network operator' by using MobilCom's network and that Debitel would then at the same time be able to save the cost of a UMTS licence.

10.2.2   Strategic Utilization of Intertwined Relations with Government Agencies and Other Actors

As we discussed briefly in Chapter 4, many former monopolists in the network-based sectors show a high degree of bundling with the government. In many cases, all or part of these companies used to be state-owned. Strong political and financial ties and a high degree of government interference with the monopolist's day-to-day operations usually marked the relationship between the monopolist and the national government. Formally, the government and the incumbent are now expected to have completely separate networks. In practice, however, we see that the former monopolists still maintain close links with the national government and that they gratefully use them to pursue lobbying activities. Besides, it is also important for a national government that the incumbents are doing well, since these companies are important for the national economy because of their dominant market position. In the case studies, we have seen several times that these intertwined relations between national government and former monopolist were utilized as an entry for strategic behaviour (see Table 10.2).

In the Open Skies case study, there was a clear pattern of using personal

Table 10.2 Strategic utilization of intertwined relations with government agencies and other actors

Case study	Strategic behaviour: type and definition
Microsoft	*Using others as tools* Microsoft twice seduced the USA into interfering in the conflict and making negative statements about actions against Microsoft.
Open skies USA	*Protectionism* US initiated Fly American programme.
Open skies USA	*Rhetoric, occasional argumentation* US negotiators disconnected issue of foreign ownership and control from EU–US negotiations about an Open Skies Treaty. Besides, in the process, they used those they represented as an 'excuse'.
AT&T	*Political lobbying* AT&T manipulated the outcomes of judicial procedures (consent decree 1956) through political lobbying.
UMTS Germany	*Raising rivals' costs* Deutsche Telecom initially forced up prices, but stopped doing so before weaker parties withdrew from the auction. It thus promoted the interests of the German government.

networks. In the aviation sector, we see an immense mixing of interests of airlines with those of states. In the United Kingdom, we saw that it was in the interest of British Airways and Virgin Atlantic – and therefore in the interest of the British government – not to extend access to Heathrow for transatlantic flights any further. In the negotiations about the Open Skies Treaty, coupling to other issues on the government agenda is often used, such as the EU demand that the US scrap the 'Fly American' rule for US government employees and armed forces. The American negotiators were also put under strong pressure, particularly by the US Congress, to disconnect the issue of foreign ownership and control from the negotiations about an Open Skies Treaty. The argument used by the US Congress was that giving foreign nationals more power in the managerial decisions of airlines might pose a risk to national defence and security. All this resulted in a strongly politicized negotiating process.

The AT&T case study also demonstrates a clear pattern of personal networks. A study in 1959 by the American antitrust subcommittee of the House Judiciary Committee into the 1956 consent decree showed that

AT&T lobbied actively to get the government to suspend its 1949 suit without requiring AT&T's divestiture of Western Electric. The study even showed that a letter about this subject sent by the Secretary of Defense to the Attorney General had actually been prepared by AT&T.

Finally, in the Microsoft case study we saw that Microsoft managed to seduce the American government into interfering in the conflict with the European Commission and making negative statements about actions against Microsoft. For example, in 2004 the US reacted with concern to the measures imposed on Microsoft by the European Commission. The American Department of Justice announced that it found the sentence 'unfortunate' and stated that a healthy competition policy should avoid discouraging innovation and competition, even where dominant companies are concerned. In September 2007, the American Department of Justice expressed similar criticism of the ruling of the Court of First Instance of the European Court of Justice in Microsoft's appeal against the European Commission. The American Department of Justice stated that the ruling might harm consumers by chilling innovation and discouraging competition.

10.2.3   Strategic Use of Rules: Legal Rules and Contracts

In the case studies, we found several times that rules were used as an entry for strategic behaviour (see Table 10.3). They may be formal legal rules, but also, for example, policy rules, organizational rules and contracts. In many cases, rules and agreements were interpreted so as to serve an actor's self-interest. In some cases, the mere threat that rules would be used was enough to achieve the desired result. Many immense developments that have taken place in the regulatory structures of network-based industries in recent decades have created extra room for interpretation, since many rules are complex, some of them are dated and many of them are new and unknown.

The strategic use of rules is a picture that emerged clearly in the AT&T case study. We saw that AT&T pursued various legal actions to derail the 1974 antitrust suit of the US Department of Justice. AT&T's competitors also used rules strategically in many cases. MCI's private lawsuit, together with the antitrust suit filed by the US Department of Justice, heralded the end of AT&T's heyday.

Rules also play an important part in the case study about Microsoft. A dominant picture in the many-year legal struggle between the European Commission and Microsoft is that Microsoft tries to use the rules so as to limit the damage as much as possible. For example, Microsoft tried to reach a settlement with the European Commission to prevent sanctions being imposed. In the United States, Microsoft had successfully used such a settlement earlier. However, the European Commissioner for

Table 10.3   Strategic use of rules: legal rules and contracts

Case study	Strategic behaviour: type and definition
Microsoft	*Strategic use of litigation* Microsoft tried to reach a settlement with the European Commission to prevent measures being imposed, because a settlement would be less of a precedent than a conviction, a fine and Commission-imposed measures for future behaviour.
Microsoft	*Threatening* European Commission: Investigation against Microsoft + imposing measures on Microsoft + warning that a fine would be imposed if the imposed measures were not carried out.
Microsoft	*Underdog* Microsoft's competitors: supporting European Commission in its research against Microsoft.
UMTS Italy	*Threatening + strategic use of litigation* The Italian government threatened to cancel the auction while forfeiting the deposits.
UMTS The Netherlands	*Predation* Telfort threatened a legal claim for compensation.
UMTS The Netherlands	*Strategic use of litigation* Versatel tried to have Telfort excluded from the auction.
Open skies European Commission	*Threatening + strategic use of litigation* European Commission initiated actions for infringement of Community law by member states under Article 226 of the EC Treaty.
Open skies European Commission	*Threatening + strategic use of rule-making/litigation* European Commission obtained exclusive power to conclude air traffic agreements.
AT&T	*Strategic use of litigation* AT&T pursued various legal actions to derail the 1974 antitrust suit of the Justice Department.
AT&T	*Puppy dog* Independents (e.g. MCI) initiated various (civil) antitrust actions against AT&T.
AT&T	*Puppy dog* Hush-A-Phone Co. tried to break AT&T's monopoly through court action.

Table 10.3   (continued)

Case study	Strategic behaviour: type and definition
AT&T	*Puppy dog* Carter Electronics Corp. tried to break AT&T's monopoly through court action.
AT&T	*Threatening* Justice Department put pressure on AT&T by threatening antitrust suit.
AT&T	*Threatening* Judicial authorities demanded that AT&T provide interconnection.

Competition did not accept a settlement. Microsoft then appealed against its conviction by the Commission and filed a request for suspension of the sanctions for the duration of the appeal proceedings. However, the European Court of First Instance dismissed Microsoft's request for suspension of the sanctions. Eventually, in September 2007, the Court of First Instance declared Microsoft's appeal unfounded on almost all points.

10.2.4   Strategic Use of the Factor 'Time'

As we set out in Chapter 4, the time factor may be crucially important for making a product profitable and for the survival chances of newcomers to the market. This may be taken advantage of in several ways, for example by delaying legal procedures, postponing the implementation of rules as long as possible or making crucial information available as late as possible (see Table 10.4).

In the case of Microsoft, the time factor is highly relevant. During the legal struggle with the European Commission, we therefore saw that Microsoft always tried to postpone potential sanctions as much as possible. It was in Microsoft's interest to refuse to release interface codes as long as possible, since releasing these codes would make it possible for competing products to communicate with Windows. The longer Microsoft was able to prevent competition, the more time there was to consolidate Microsoft's position on the server market. Microsoft also tried to maintain the coupling of the Media Player software to Windows as long as possible. In this way, it became very difficult for other producers of software for playing sound and image, such as RealNetworks, to compete with Microsoft. Microsoft also used the time factor strategically with regard to the naming of the Windows version without the Media Player. It was a very long time before Microsoft and the

Table 10.4   Strategic use of the factor 'time'

Case study	Strategic behaviour: type and definition
Microsoft	*Strategic use of time* Microsoft had to come up with a new name for the stripped version of Windows. The European Commission refused Microsoft's first ten suggestions, including 'Windows XP Reduced Media Edition'.
Open skies EU	*Quid pro quo / package deal + threatening* EU negotiators linked approval of Open Skies Treaty to US proposals on foreign ownership and control.
Open skies UK	*Rhetoric, occasional argumentation* British government professed that it only wanted a 'truly open skies' agreement and presented this as the reason why the British were not yet satisfied with the outcome of the negotiations (e.g. in June 2004).
Open skies BA and Virgin Atlantic	*Rhetoric, occasional argumentation* BA and Virgin Atlantic rejected US proposals. The reason they gave is that the proposals did not truly open up markets.

European Commission reached agreement about an acceptable name, and the European Commission turned down Microsoft's first ten suggestions.

Perhaps somewhat less typical of the network-based industries is the use of the factor 'time' as an entry for strategic behaviour in the Open Skies case study. We saw that the European negotiators tried to put pressure on the American negotiators by linking approval of the Open Skies Treaty to US proposals on foreign ownership and control. The sooner the Europeans signed an Open Skies Treaty, the sooner the Americans would be able to obtain the long-desired access to Heathrow. The British government, British Airways and Virgin Atlantic tried to postpone the introduction of an EU–US Open Skies Treaty as long as possible to protect their privileged position at Heathrow. The main reason they gave for their disapproval of the provisional outcome of the negotiations was that this result did not truly open up markets.

10.2.5   Strategic Use of Financial Resources

In the case studies, we have seen several times that financial resources were utilized as an entry for strategic behaviour (see Table 10.5). A dominant picture in the Microsoft case study was that (potential) opponents were induced by means of financial settlements to withdraw from the legal struggle

Table 10.5   Strategic use of financial resources

Case study	Strategic behaviour: type and definition
Microsoft	*Divide and rule, buying off* After a 761 million dollar settlement, RealNetworks withdrew from lawsuits against Microsoft. Besides, because of the settlement, RealNetworks' RealPlayer was, in fact, bought out of the market.
Microsoft	*Divide and rule, buying off* Microsoft paid an amount of 9.75 million dollars to one of its biggest opponents, the top executive of the CCIA trade organization, to withdraw from the court case between Microsoft and the European Commission.
Microsoft	*Divide and rule, buying off* Microsoft effected a 750 million dollar settlement with AOL Time Warner, the producer of the Internet browser Netscape. AOL Time Warner took the view that it was too difficult to install Netscape in Windows. In addition to the financial settlement, AOL also obtained the right to use Microsoft's Internet Explorer on its sites free of charge for seven years, which led to an explosive increase in the number of Internet Explorer users.
UMTS Italy	*Threatening + strategic use of litigation* The Italian government threatened to cancel the auction while forfeiting the deposits.
UMTS Austria	*Threatening* Telecom Austria stated that it would bid for a third block if one of its rivals did so.
AT&T	*Vertical foreclosure* AT&T took over Western Electric.
AT&T	*Cross subsidization + vertical foreclosure* AT&T subsidized local operations by transferring to them money earned from long-distance services.
AT&T	*Strategic use of litigation* AT&T tried to exhaust MCI financially.

against Microsoft. In some cases, such a settlement resulted not only in an opponent giving up the legal struggle, but also in a competing product being bought out of the market, as the settlement with RealNetworks showed. The UMTS case study made clear how existing market parties – which are usually in a relatively comfortable financial position – could threaten to use financial resources to reach the desired outcome of the auction. Finally, we also saw in the AT&T case study that financial resources were employed in several ways, for example when Western Electric was taken over.

10.2.6 Utility Character and Rules

As we briefly discussed in Chapter 4, both the incumbent and new entrants to the market can take advantage of the essential utility character of infrastructures. Given the strong economic and societal dependence on these infrastructures, a company that holds this infrastructure has strong leverage over the regulator. However, new market parties can also use this utility character strategically, because an incumbent has an obligation to supply because of the utility function of infrastructures, whereas the newcomers choose geographical areas or services that are the most attractive from a profit perspective.

In many of the case studies, the strategic use of the essential utility character of infrastructures went hand in hand with the strategic use of rules (see Table 10.6). We found notable examples of this combination of utility character and rules in the case study about Enron, both in the various energy-market trading strategies and in the ancillary services strategies. The 'Fat Boy' strategy implied that Enron would falsely overschedule load in hour-ahead and day-ahead markets to profit from higher real-time electricity prices. Another example of a strategy based on both utility character and rules is 'Selling non-firm as firm energy'. This means that Enron would sell power as backed up by operating services, while in fact it was not. A final example from the Enron case study is 'Double selling', which meant that Enron was selling ancillary services twice in different markets.

The combination of utility character and rules also occurs frequently in the AT&T case study. A type of strategic behaviour that we often found in this case study is tying. For example, AT&T subscribers were not allowed to use telephones or other peripherals of competitors. Meanwhile, AT&T only offered products manufactured by Western Electric. However, we also saw that competitors of AT&T's used AT&T's obligation to fulfil the utility function, for example by trying to concentrate on the profitable geographical areas.

10.2.7 Rules and Time

As we can see in Table 10.7, combining the entry *rules* and *time* is obvious. Parties may greatly benefit from delaying legal procedures as long as possible. This is clear from the Microsoft case study. Microsoft repeatedly tried to put off implementation of the measures imposed by the European

Table 10.6   Utility character and rules

Case study	Strategic behaviour: type and definition
AT&T	*Tying* Customers were not allowed to use telephones and telephone equipment of competitors.
AT&T	*Tying* Customers were obliged to lease AT&T equipment; no ownership possible.
AT&T	*Tying* Customers were allowed to use telephones of competitor on condition of leasing and back-leasing.
AT&T	*Tying* Introduction of 'Protective Coupler', which customers had to rent.
AT&T	*Cherry picking* RBOCs picked out profitable urban areas.
AT&T	*Cherry picking / cream skimming* Satellite use by MCI.
Open skies USA	*Use of rhetoric, occasional argumentation* US refused to grant cabotage rights using the arguments of national security and lacking reciprocity.
Enron	*Energy market trading strategies* Enron traders used time to increase the earnings from the vital function that electricity provides *(export of Californian power, Ricochet, Fat Boy, Thin Man)*.
Enron	*Ancillary services strategies* Enron traders used vital and scarce services that were designed to ensure grid stability *(Get Shorty, selling non-firm energy as firm energy, double selling)*.

Commission. Microsoft also made maximum use of the available possibilities for appeal. We saw the same attitude in AT&T, which made a strategic use of litigation in order to exhaust its competitor MCI financially.

10.2.8   Bottleneck Facilities and Rules

A final combination of entry for strategic behaviour that we came across frequently in the case studies is that of bottleneck and rules (see Table 10.8). In the case study about Enron, this combination of entry was used

Table 10.7   Rules and time

Case study	Strategic behaviour: type and definition
Microsoft	*Strategic use of litigation and time* Delay: Microsoft found one excuse after another to postpone the implementation of the measures ordered by the European Commission. Besides, Microsoft appealed against the imposed measures. The time profit gained might strengthen Microsoft's position.
Microsoft	*Strategic use of litigation* After the measures imposed on 24 March 2004, Microsoft argued that it could not have known that it was breaching the EU competition rules, because the European Commission had entered a new area with its action against misuse of market dominance in the software sector.
AT&T	*Strategic use of litigation* AT&T waited and passively underwent judicial screening.
AT&T	*Strategic use of litigation* AT&T tried to exhaust MCI financially
AT&T judicial authorities	*Threatening* Justice Department put pressure on AT&T by threatening antitrust suit.

in the 'Congestion Relief Strategies'. An example is the 'Load Shift' strategy, which meant that Enron would schedule large demands for power to change prices and then buy or sell in the targeted market to take advantage of the price differential. The 'Wheel-Out' strategy meant that Enron was scheduling power over transmission lines that had been taken out of service in order to collect congestion revenues.

We also found the combination of bottleneck and rules several times in the UMTS case study. Companies often managed to make a clever use of the rules surrounding the UMTS auction. In Austria, we saw that Telecom Austria threatened to bid for a third block if one of its rivals did so. We find a final example of the strategic use of bottleneck and rules in the Dutch UMTS auction. Newcomer Versatel indicated that it might be willing to abandon participation in the auction, if other parties showed themselves willing to negotiate with Versatel about access to their network.

Table 10.8   Bottleneck facilities and rules

Case study	Strategic behaviour: type and definition
Microsoft	*Strategic use of litigation + strategic non-disclosure of information* Microsoft argued that releasing interface codes would infringe intellectual property.
Microsoft	*Strategic non-disclosure of information* Microsoft wanted to veto the information it had to provide to the Commission. The Commission wanted this information to see whether Microsoft complied with the imposed sanctions.
UMTS Italy	*Collusion* Early withdrawal by Blu meant the end of the auction and relatively low proceeds for the Italian government.
UMTS Austria	*Collusion* A week before the auction, Telecom Austria stated that it would be satisfied with just two of the 12 blocks of frequency on offer and that, if the other five bidders adopted the same attitude, 'it should be possible to get the frequencies on sensible terms'. This might be regarded as offering a collusive deal.
UMTS Austria	*Threatening* Telecom Austria stated that it would bid for a third block if one of its rivals did.
UMTS The Netherlands	*Collusion* Versatel invited other parties to negotiate about access to their network and indicated that it was prepared to give up participation in the auction in exchange.
UMTS The Netherlands	*Predation* Versatel threatened to raise competitors' costs.
UMTS The Netherlands	Although MCI WorldCom had not registered for the auction, it did take part from the start in consultations about the structure of the auction.
UMTS The Netherlands	*Collusion* Ben and T-Mobile International formed a partnership to gain a stronger position in the auction.
UMTS The Netherlands	Three parties registered for the auction initially, but withdraw later. Two of these parties (Hutchison and NTL Nederland) withdrew just before the start of the auction.

Table 10.8 (continued)

Case study	Strategic behaviour: type and definition
Enron	*Congestion relief strategies* Enron traders used the scarce yet vital transmission capacity to increase earnings in a variety of ways *(Load Shift, Death Star, Wheel-Out, Non-Firm Export, Scheduling Energy to Collect Congestion Charges)*.

10.3 STRATEGIC BEHAVIOUR: COMPARISON WITH THE THEORY

In Chapter 3, we have given a theoretical overview of various forms of strategic behaviour as we can find it in normal industries. In this section, we will focus this overview on the theoretical forms of strategic behaviour in network-based industries.

10.3.1 Strategic Use of Control over so-called 'Bottleneck Facilities' and Other Crucial Technical Facilities and Standards

Bottleneck facilities, which are so characteristic of network-based industries, lend themselves extremely well to *monopolistic behaviour*. As we discussed in section 3.1.3, monopolists are in a comfortable position. They are able to set their optimum production level themselves (Breyer, 1979, p. 554). In a monopoly, profit-maximizing behaviour will easily lead to a relatively high price and a relatively low output (Tullock, 1967, p. 224).

Besides, monopolists have few incentives to innovate, work more efficiently and be customer-oriented in their production (Martin, 1993; Horn et al., 1994). Consequently, in recent decades we have seen that pressure has arisen to break down the monopoly in network-based sectors. In particular governments and regulators will take initiatives to introduce competitors in the market. Some monopolists will not wait for such intervention to happen. They operate proactively. For example, the *lazy monopolist* (Hirschmann, 1970, chapter 5) knows that, in the long run, it will be unable to resist the pressure to break down the monopoly, and that it had better cooperate in lifting its monopoly, albeit to a very limited degree.

In many cases, the monopolist is able to do so without too much damage, because it still has other possibilities of harassing potential new competitors. One of these is the strategic use of bottleneck facilities by means of *compatibility standards* (Adams and Brock, 1982). Competitors that supply products that are not compatible with them do not stand a chance in the market.

Another form of strategic behaviour we may come across pre-eminently in network-based industries and that concentrates on the use of bottleneck facilities in (partly) hindering competitors is *vertical foreclosure*. Here, the monopolist monopolizes assets that are key to operating on the market. An example would be R&D results, or access to a monopolistic network. These companies are able to do so because they have special relations with, for example, the R&D institutes and the network operator, which date from the past.

Predation is another frequent form of strategic behaviour in network-based industries, as we often have an incumbent there with considerable market power and with decisive influence on the access to crucial bottleneck facilities (see also section 3.2.3). As we set out earlier, predation covers all aggressive, threatening attitudes that an enterprise with market power can adopt to prevent others from entering the market, or to force others to leave the market. *Bluffing* is one of these predatory tactics (Shapiro, 1989, p. 406). For example, in the UMTS case study we saw that incumbents managed to influence the actions of their competitors, because it seemed credible that the incumbent would carry out the threat.

Collusion is a final type of strategic behaviour that may be an appealing option for companies in network-based industries and that may be accompanied by the strategic use of bottleneck facilities (see section 3.1.3). For example, the management of a network is an extremely suitable means to convince other parties that they may gain advantage by colluding. In the UMTS case study, there appeared to be several collusive deals, with access to a network being employed as a means of negotiation to influence the attitude of other auction participants during the auction.

10.3.2 Strategic Utilization of Intertwined Relations with Government Agencies and Other Actors

As said, incumbents and government in network-based industries tend to have a rather exceptional relationship. The bundling between government and former monopolist offers several points of departure for strategic behaviour. Emmons states that companies in network-based industries operate, so to say, in two arenas: the commercial and the political arena (Emmons, 2000) (see also section 3.2.1). In comparison with other companies, the incumbent has an advantage not only in the commercial arena, but also in the political one. This gives rise to a paradoxical situation. On the one hand, national governments have frequently stated in recent decades that they wish to reduce political interference in former monopolists. On the other hand, we see such interference in fact increasing in some respects, as is clear, for example, from the growing state support.

The so-called *golden share* also reflects the paradoxical relationship between incumbent and government. In fact, a golden share constitutes a veto right, which means that governmental permission is necessary in case of important decisions, such as to engage in a strategic alliance. Paradoxical about such a golden share is that it is a means for the government to keep a grip on the incumbent, but that it also enables the incumbent to use the government as a tool. In June 2002, the European Court of Justice ruled that national governments would no longer be allowed to maintain a golden share in former state-owned companies, except when it served a national strategic interest.[1]

In network-based industries, the special relationship between incumbent and government is often marked by a high degree of information asymmetry. The principal (i.e. the government) has less information than the agent (i.e. the incumbent) and, as a result, suffers a comparative disadvantage. An incumbent may use its information advantage by providing incomplete information, offering information either too late or too early, or offering information at an aggregation level favourable to itself (Owen and Braeutigam, 1978, p. 2). As we set out in section 3.3.3, this information asymmetry may lead to *adverse selection* and *moral hazard*. In the event of adverse selection, the principal does not make the optimum choice, because the agent has supplied inadequate information about its starting position, capacities or possibilities. Forms of adverse selection that we may find pre-eminently in the network-based industries are *strategic price-setting* and *strategic standard-setting*. This means that the incumbent makes clever use of the fact that the regulator is not aware of actual cost prices or technical requirements.

Although adverse selection and moral hazard may cause the relationship between government and company to look formally like a principal–agent relationship, they may actually lead to 'regulatory capture'; the regulator is captive to the regulatee. An extreme effect of regulatory capture that may occur in network-based industries and in which bundling with the government is employed as an entry for strategic behaviour is *using the agency as a cartel manager* (Owen and Braeutigam, 1978, p. 2). In this tactic, the agent exploits a general concern of the principal, namely that the company it regulates will fail, with the attendant consequences of a decline in service provision. The regulator is then vulnerable because accusing fingers will soon be pointed at the regulator. The regulator will want to prevent this at any price. An extreme consequence may be that the regulator allows the sector to control itself. This may degenerate into a collusion which has actually been endorsed by the regulator.

10.3.3 Strategic Use of Rules: Legal Rules and Contracts

Although it may seem inconsistent at first sight, liberalization in many cases in network-based industries went hand in hand with *re-regulation*, or 'the reformulation of old rules and the creation of new ones' (Vogel, 1996, p. 3) (also see section 4.2.4). Vogel (1996) states that, as a result, 'we have wound up with freer markets and *more* rules. In fact, there is often a logical link: liberalization requires reregulation' (Vogel, 1996, p. 3). For example, autonomization of companies tends to be accompanied by new rules, if only because it is not self-evident for a privatized utility company to be willing to work out its utility function in practice. As in section 10.3.2, we may also conclude here that there is a clearly paradoxical development, or, in Vogel's words: 'A movement aimed at reducing regulation has only increased it' (Vogel, 1996, p. 5).

One consequence of the immense changes that have taken place in the regulatory structures of network-based industries is that they create considerable room for strategic behaviour. It often turns out in practice that rules encourage strategic behaviour rather than curbing it. How can this be explained?

Strategic behaviour is difficult to interpret in law. Some say that legal authorities or institutions that take a juridically relevant decision *digitize* the analogue world of social perception. Because, in the application, law has only two binary concepts available: legal (unmistakably in accordance with the law) or illegal (unmistakably in conflict with the law). The *transformation* of extralegal behaviour to legal defined categories causes problems, including loss of meaning (Schuyt, 1982). Even in its morally or socially most precarious variants, strategic behaviour is not tantamount to unlawfulness. Strategic behaviour, especially relevant in a context of practical applications in the real world of a game-theoretical situation, is a social-science category and as such legally meaningless (De Jong and Stout, 2003). Bohne, a German legal sociologist, has labelled this type of behaviour that takes place in the periphery of the law, but not *within law*, as '*extralegal*' (Bohne, 1981). This concept is sometimes defined as neither a priori in conflict with the law, nor a priori in accordance with the law. So long as a behaviour is ranked under this category, the behaviour is legally (as yet) without meaning (De Jong and Stout, 2003).

In many cases, the parties that suffer the disadvantages of strategic behaviour will be inclined to invoke regulators or legal authorities to remedy their predicament and to correct the perceived detrimental strategic behaviour. Yet, quite often, regulatory and legal authorities have no easy job dealing with such conduct, for lack of substantial information on the matters at hand. Many actors that benefit from an extralegal situation will seek to postpone a judicial decision as long as possible, allowing them to continue their behaviour. So long as the judgment 'white' (lawful) or 'black' (unlawful) has not been passed, the parties concerned can even see this type of behaviour as normal or completely understandable behaviour arising from self-interest. What monopolist can be expected to give up its dominant position voluntarily and help its competitors to increase their market share? (De Jong and Stout, 2003).

Should a regulator or, for example, a court eventually take a decision, this creates clarity about the legal point of contention. However, this need not mean that it puts an end to the strategic behaviour. The game can, as it were, continue forever, although the legal decision has somewhat changed the playing field (De Jong and Stout, 2003).

10.3.4 Strategic Use of the Factor 'Time'

In network-based industries, the factor 'time' often seems to benefit the incumbent. A company that already has a strong position in the market sees its position, so to speak, growing stronger almost automatically. This phenomenon is sometimes referred to as the Matthew effect (also see section 4.1). The term was first used by the American sociologist Merton to indicate that well-known and prominent scientific researchers receive recognition for their findings more easily than less known scientists (Merton, 1968). Today, the term is used particularly in the context of the welfare state to indicate that social public spending proportionally benefits the higher social classes in the first place (Deleeck, 1983). The same phenomenon often occurs in network-based industries: 'the rich get richer and the poor get poorer'.

The important role played by the time factor in network-based industries is due partly to the *time-to-market* effect. Time to market – that is the time needed to put a product on the market – is crucial in these industries, which are marked by very rapid technological developments. Dealing strategically with the time factor may bring great advantages. As a result, organizations will try to take actions that may delay the business operations of other organizations. Meanwhile, they can use the time gained to consolidate or strengthen their own market position.

The time factor can also be used as an entry for strategic behaviour by using the *salami tactics*. This means that an incumbent tries to stretch a situation more and more to its own advantage. In this case, the incumbent tries to achieve its aim through several intermediate steps rather than tabling all demands at the same time. In retrospect, the attitude of many incumbents during the liberalization process of network-based industries might also be qualified as a salami-style attitude, because the incumbents often played an important role in realizing the liberalization arrangement. In itself, it is not surprising that many governments involved the incumbents in the process, given their knowledge and experience and their often considerable interest in the market. However, the involvement of the incumbents has also enabled them to safeguard their own interests in the design of the liberalization arrangement. As a result, many liberalization arrangements offer room for strategic behaviour, and incumbents have managed to make clever use of this room.

Finally, the time factor plays an important part in network-based industries because of the long construction time of infrastructure networks. In the past, incumbents have usually invested a great deal of time and money in the construction of a network. Some of these costs are *sunk costs*, which cannot be recovered to any significant degree. On the other hand, the incumbent that has the network of course has strong leverage over newcomers.

10.3.5 Strategic Use of Financial Resources

The sunk costs from the preceding section also play a role in the entry offered by finance. Incumbents in particular are often in a position in which they can use financial resources as an entry for strategic behaviour. Network-based industries are highly capital-intensive. A company that wants to gain a foothold in these industries must invest up-front and create a market as soon as possible. Besides, investments tend to be recouped only in the longer term. As a result, companies need deep pockets to play a part in these industries. Unlike the incumbent, entrants usually do not (yet) have extensive financial resources, a physical network or an impressive customer base. As a result, they face a disadvantage that they cannot always overcome.

10.3.6 Utility Character and Rules

The utility character of network-based industries is protected by rules. This combination of utility character and rules offers possibilities for strategic behaviour both for incumbents and for newcomers.

Incumbents in the utility world tend to be burdened with obligations from the past as monopolists, such as the duty to provide *universal service* or the duty to provide less profitable services. Newcomers are not bothered by this and can afford to build up a portfolio containing only commercially attractive activities, also called *cherry picking* or *cream skimming* (Bos, 1995). In fact, this is a form of the better-known *free riding*.

Traditionally, the established company performs a number of activities from which the newcomer also benefits. For example, some of the fruits of political lobbying or advertising may accrue to the sector as a whole, while the incumbent alone bears the costs.

On the other hand, the incumbent may also benefit from the utility character of network-based industries, because society cannot do without the services of these industries. Since the incumbent usually controls a large part of the market, this dependence strengthens its position. The utility function has also become manifest in strong government interference, from which the incumbent may, in turn, benefit, as we saw in section 10.3.2. Finally, the duty of universal service provision has also brought advantages for the incumbent, because it has resulted in the incumbent building up an immense customer base, which has given it a head start over market entrants.

10.3.7 Rules and Time

As far as the strategic use of rules and time is concerned, the ex-monopolist may gain great advantage by *strategic use of litigation* (Owen and Braeutigam, 1978, p. 2). It institutes a great many proceedings with the regulator, prolonging them as long as possible. Underlying this strategy is the assumption that legal processes and the time they take benefit the incumbent. There are two reasons for this. First, because of its size, it is less dependent on the decision in the case than the newcomer, whose survival may depend on it. Second, the incumbent is more able to bear high proceedings costs than the entrant is, because to the former these costs will constitute a modest part of its total operating costs, while to the latter they may form a considerable part of the total costs. Finally, an incumbent may also make clever use of the combination of rules and time by means of a *sleeping patent*. Such a patent only has value because it denies competitors access to technology (Gilbert, 1981).

The practice tends to be that an incumbent offers several utility products for different markets and that it therefore has to deal with several regulators. In this situation, the better-informed companies are in a position to opt strategically for those regulators where they see the best possibilities for themselves, a strategy called *forum shopping*.[2]

A final way of using the combination of rules and time strategically is *labelling* situations. This means that parties seek to get those terms and concepts of reality accepted that offer them the best chance of success. In interactions with a regulator, labelling may have far-reaching consequences. For example, giving a form of behaviour a particular label makes it fall into a particular legal category, as a result of which

the behaviour falls – or does not fall – within the competence of a particular court, falls – or does not fall – under a particular act of law and
is – or is not – permitted. Lakoff (2000) demonstrates that the use of
language is highly determinant for processes of labelling. Language is
an important tool in the process of sense-making (Lakoff, 2000; pp. 9
and 41). Those who manage to get their language, their vocabulary and
their metaphor accepted to describe a situation or a process have won
the first battle.

10.3.8   Bottleneck Facilities and Rules

Like the utility function, the bottleneck is protected by rules. These rules,
too, can be used as an entry for strategic behaviour. In this context, *access*
and *interconnection* play an important role, as we saw in the AT&T case
study. The European Access Directive[3] defines access for electronic communications as follows: 'the making available of facilities and/or services,
to another undertaking, under defined conditions, on either an exclusive
or non-exclusive basis, for the purpose of providing electronic communications services.' The same directive defines interconnection as follows:
'the physical and logical linking of public communications networks used
by the same or a different undertaking in order to allow the users of one
undertaking to communicate with users of the same or another undertaking, or to access services provided by another undertaking.' Since the
incumbent is often one of the few companies or even the only company
in a specific network-based sector that has a network, it can make life
very difficult for its (potential) competitors by thwarting access and interconnection. For example, it may hamper access to the local loop or hinder
access to physical infrastructure such as buildings. Finally an incumbent
can also use the bottleneck by means of high or excessive interconnection
fees.

10.4   CONCLUSION

The case studies in this book have shown that strategic behaviour is a
common phenomenon in network-based industries. This is an important
finding, because an actor that displays strategic behaviour normally acts
out of self-interest. In many cases, this self-interest does not match more
generally accepted interests or aims, such as creating a level playing field or
protecting the quality and price of products and services.

We have observed strategic behaviour in all relationships possible
between the various actors in network-based industries. For example,

strategic behaviour occurs between (potentially) competing companies, such as between an incumbent and an entrant. Strategic behaviour may also occur between companies and regulators and in the relation between companies in different links of the production chain. Besides, we have found that strategic behaviour can take a variety of forms. In this book, we have discussed six categories of entries for strategic behaviour that are characteristic of network-based industries. In addition, we have shown that not only the entries, but also the forms of strategic behaviour that we find in network-based industries and that use these entries differ from those in the normal industries. Consequently, strategic behaviour in network-based industries requires a particular approach. In Chapter 11, we will discuss what counterarrangements may be employed to counter strategic behaviour in network-based industries or to limit its adverse effects.

NOTES

1. *European Commission v. Portugal* (Case C-367/98); *European Commission v. France* (Case C-483/99); *European Commission v. Belgium* (Case C-503/99).
2. For a discussion of the phenomenon of forum shopping, see for example Rubin et al. (2001) and Bell (2003).
3. Official Journal of the European Communities (24 April 2002, L108/11), Directive 2002/19/EC of the European Parliament and of the Council of 7 March 2002 on access to, and interconnection of, electronic communications networks and associated facilities.

REFERENCES

Adams, W. and J. Brock (1982), 'Integrated monopoly and market power: system selling, compatibility standards, and market control', *Quarterly Review of Economics and Business*, **22**(4), 29–42.

Bell, A.S. (2003), *Forum Shopping and Venue in Transnational Litigation*, Oxford and New York: Oxford University Press.

Bohne, E. (1981), 'Der informale Rechtsstaat. Eine empirische und rechtliche Untersuchung zum Gesetzesvollzug unter besonderer Berücksichtigung des Immissionsschutzes', in Ernst E. Hirsch and M. Rehbinder, *Schriftenreihe zur Rechtssoziologie und Rechtstatsachenforschung*, Vol. 49, Berlin: Duncker and Humblot.

Bos, D.I. (1995), *Marktwerking en Regulering* (in Dutch) (*Competition and Regulation*), The Hague: Ministry of Economic Affairs.

Breyer, S. (1979), 'Analyzing regulatory failure: mismatches, less restrictive alternatives, and reform', *Harvard Law Review*, **92**(3), 549–609.

De Jong, M. and H. Stout (2003), 'Strategic behaviour and the law: how legal authorities deal with factual strategic behaviour of former monopolists', *International Journal of Technology, Policy and Management*, **3**(1), 38–55.

Deleeck, H. (1983), *Het Mattheuseffect. De Ongelijke Verdeling van de Sociale Overheidsuitgaven in België* (in Dutch) (*The Matthew Effect. The Uneven Distribution of Social Public Spending in Belgium*), Antwerp: Kluwer.

Emmons, W. (2000), *The Evolving Bargain. Strategic Implications of Deregulation and Privatization*, Boston, MA: Harvard Business School Press.

Gilbert, R. (1981), 'Patents, sleeping patents and entry deterrence', in S. Salop (ed.), *Strategy, Predation and Antitrust Analysis*, Washington, DC: Federal Trade Commission, pp. 205–70.

Hirschmann, A.O. (1970), *Exit, Voice and Loyalty: Responses to Decline in Firms, Organizations, and States*, Cambridge, MA: Harvard University Press.

Horn, H., H. Lang and S. Lundgren (1994), 'Competition, long-run contracts and internal inefficiency in firms', *European Economic Review*, **38**(2), 213–33.

Lakoff, R.T. (2000), *The Language War*, Berkeley, CA: University of California Press.

Martin, S. (1993), 'Endogenous firm efficiency in a Cournot principal–agent model', *Journal of Economic Theory*, **59**(2), 445–50.

Merton, R.K. (1968), 'The Matthew effect in science. The reward and communication systems of science are considered', *Science*, **159**(3810), 56–63.

Owen, B.M. and R. Braeutigam (1978), *The Regulation Game, Strategic Use of the Administrative Process*, Cambridge, MA: Ballinger Publishing Company.

Rubin, P.H., C. Curran and J.F. Curran (2001), 'Litigation versus legislation: Forum shopping by rent seekers', *Public Choice*, **107**(3–4), 295–310.

Schuyt, C.J.M. (1982), *Ongeregeldheden. Naar een Theorie van de Wetgeving in de Verzorgingsstaat* (in Dutch) (*Irregularities. Towards a Theory of Legislation in the Welfare State*), Address, University of Leiden, Alphen aan den Rijn: Samson Uitgeverij.

Shapiro, C. (1989), 'Theories of oligopoly behavior', in R. Schmalensee and R.D. Willig (eds), *Handbook of Industrial Organization*, Vol. 1, Amsterdam: Elsevier Science Publishers, pp. 330–414.

Tullock, G. (1967), 'The welfare costs of tariffs, monopolies and theft', *Western Economic Journal*, **5**, 224–32.

Vogel, S.K. (1996), *Freer Markets, More Rules: Regulatory Reform in Advanced Industrial Countries*, Ithaca, NY: Cornell University Press.

11.   Counterarrangements

11.1   INTRODUCTION

The case study chapters and their analysis in the previous chapter show that strategic behaviour frequently occurs in infrastructure-based sectors. In many cases, strategic behaviour has serious consequences, not only for the configuration of the market, but also for market parties, end consumers and governments. Market parties can tell immediately by their corporate performance, final consumers are faced with higher prices or a less reliable service provision, and governments find important policy targets being missed.

Strategic behaviour pays. This may be the foremost explanation for the ubiquity of strategic behaviour. What this behaviour will lead to and how it will be judged in the longer term is unclear yet, but these strategic winners do not always suffer negative repercussions in the longer term for their strategic behaviour. Memories are short and once the strategic game has been won, it is simply a matter of 'new round, new chances'. Strategic behaviour pays also because the counterforces tend to be weakly organized. Dixit (1996) has shown that the multiple principal problem leads agents to receive various incentives working at cross-purposes. This problem occurs especially in public sector environments and makes the strength of principal stimuli to agents extremely weak and the attainment of ideal outcomes out of reach. This does not imply that regulatory intervention is totally impossible, but economic theory has had a very hard time bridging the gap with practical organizational behaviour (Laffont and Tirole, 1993). The complexity of administrative context is such that it has thus far been infeasible to include this empirical wealth in the theory of institutional economics. The way in which price caps and sharing returns have been dealt with, has been patchy at best. We believe that our interdisciplinary approach has brought us a few steps closer to offering a workable approach to fine tuning regulatory incentives against strategic behaviour, although optimality is an unachievable target in complex systems replete with transactions costs.

In this chapter, we describe five arrangements that are meant to either counter strategic behaviour or mitigate its effects. Henceforth, we will call these arrangements 'counterarrangements' (ten Heuvelhof et al.,

2003). As we saw in the case study chapters, strategic behaviour has both tangible and less tangible manifestations, which, besides, can merge diffusely. In view of this, it would not be recommendable to employ just one type of counterarrangement, with one clearly ordered structure. This would be ineffective because of the amorphous character of strategic behaviour. We will therefore discuss several counterarrangements, parts of which will overlap, or which may even be mutually exclusive. It may be expected that good results can only be achieved with the help of counterarrangements at different aggregation levels using diverse 'countering methods'.

In sections 11.2 to 11.4, we will deal with three well-known counterarrangements: competition engineering, skimming returns and consumer protection. Experience has now shown that the effect of these counterarrangements is limited. In sections 11.5 and 11.6, we will introduce two new counterarrangements that may be more effective. They are an internal arrangement and an external one: hybrid governance and the regulator.

Hybrid governance is a special form of corporate governance. Corporate governance concerns the way an enterprise is governed and the way this governance is accounted for. The term 'hybrid' refers to the hybrid legal design of corporate governance: not merely hard law, not merely soft law, but an intelligent mix of hard and soft law. The idea behind hybrid governance is that an enterprise's institutional design can moderate the incentives for strategic behaviour, can actively stimulate the safeguarding of public interests, while at the same time societal costs entailed by government interference can be avoided.

Although regulators in themselves are a familiar arrangement, the form we propose here to combat strategic behaviour is radically different from the way regulators fulfil their role in general.

11.2   COMPETITION ENGINEERING

The idea behind competition engineering as a counterarrangement is that competition can be influenced by government policies. Competition engineering can combat potential strategic behaviour because the more competitors there are, the fewer chances strategic behaviour will have.

Competition engineering has two variants. The passive variant is facilitating. This variant concentrates on realizing the optimum conditions within which competition can develop. In the active variant, competitors are actually put in the market.

11.2.1 Passive Variant

The passive variant regulates the designing of a *level playing field*. Competition does not develop automatically. An incumbent has such an advantage over potential newcomers that, without further measures, these newcomers will rarely manage to gain a position in the market as serious competitors of the incumbent. This is why a level playing field needs to be created that offers better chances of fair competition. Regulators, supported by statutory rules, have to design such a level playing field. When creating a level playing field, the legislator and the regulator will seek, for example, to cut the ties between the incumbent and other relevant actors. Examples include the earlier mentioned opportunities, such as the self-evident access that incumbents have to bottleneck facilities and the relations between incumbent and relevant governments, such as departments, administrators and regulators. The case studies show that vertical ties are not cut completely. The reason why they are not has undoubtedly to do with the position and efforts of the incumbent in the preparatory process for the institutional change. The incumbent is an established and deep-rooted party that, of course, will play its role in the consultation and negotiation process that should lead to the new institutional structure (Emmons, 2000). It will realize that the more, and the more intensive, relations it maintains with other actors, the stronger its position will be in the new competition struggle. The incumbent will put forward in the debate that the desired quality of service provision demands a certain technical integrity (Van Twist et al., 2000). Radical severance of all vertical relations would take insufficient account of this need for technical integrity.

The incumbent's efforts tend to lead to a halfway result of this preparatory process. For example, the incumbent continues to form part of the holding company of which the other companies from the production chain also form part. Another possible outcome is that the incumbent continues to own important bottleneck facilities. Even if all these relations had been cut, there would be historically developed mutual relations between organizations and between people, preventing a complete separation.

The consequences of these ineffective outcomes of the decoupling process were clearly visible in the strategic games in the case studies. Although the close relations from the past have formally been weakened, in practice incumbents appear to be able to derive benefit from these historically developed links. Much strategic behaviour starts with exploiting these relations. Entrants do not have these contacts and thus have a serious disadvantage. Repeatedly, the playing field appears to be not level on this point.

If it is a given that incumbents cannot be decoupled completely from other organizations and from bottleneck facilities, then it is imperative to seek the realization of a level playing field in a different way. Rather than trying to sever the relations radically, it is imperative to seek to continue these relations on a certain level, with the entrants also entering into these relations. All competitors – both incumbent and entrants – then have these relations. Although the players will be bundled then, the *playing field* will be *level*. In concrete terms, for the institutional design of the bottleneck facilities this would mean that the companies that use these facilities own them and/or exploit them jointly. This also guarantees the technical integrity.

11.2.2   Active Variant

Although the playing field may be completely level, it remains to be seen whether any entrants actually show up that have the courage to start competing with the *incumbent*. A more active form of *competition engineering* is to not wait and see, but actually to put a competitor in the market. Two variants are imaginable. In the first place, the incumbent can be split up into several organizations that start competing with each other (Ten Heuvelhof and Van Twist, 2001). The splitting up of the American AT&T had elements of this. AT&T was cut up into seven *Baby Bells*, which were given the monopoly of local telephony and the new AT&T, which, in competition, would start operating on the market for long-distance telephony (see Chapter 7). In retrospect, this split-up formed the prelude to a second wave of changes aimed at introducing market forces, meant to create competition also on the local networks. The idea was that local telephone companies would also gain access to the long-distance market and other local networks that clearly and irreversibly opened up their own, local markets (Temin and Galambos, 1987).

In the second place, a government itself can start enterprising, thus adding an extra competing company to the market. This creates the situation of the competing public organization (Ten Heuvelhof and Van Twist, 2000). The form it is given requires a great deal of attention; in the first place, because a government is not accustomed to enterprising, certainly not in competition; in the second place, because a government is not only a party in a market, but also lays down the rules and is the regulator. This inevitably triggers a debate about the desirability of hybrid companies and the appearance of an entanglement of interests.

Although splitting up an incumbent and/or adding a competing public organization will increase the number of competing players, it will not end strategic behaviour. At best, these changes will steer the transition process to an open market into a new phase. For example, the market configuration will shift from a monopoly to a duopoly or perhaps an oligopoly, but it should be remembered that these configurations, too, are fertile breeding grounds for strategic behaviour. However, these changes offer opportunities for designing counterarrangements against strategic behaviour. These changes can be used particularly to make up for a part of the regulator's information disadvantage in comparison with the incumbent. The competing public organization can enable such a regulator to find out more about the minute details of the business operations and market developments in the sector. It becomes easier for the regulator to gather inside information. Armed with this information, it can intervene more effectively. The increase in the number of players also offers possibilities for introducing benchmarking systems that may incentivize companies in the sector to boost their performance.

11.3 SKIMMING RETURNS

Successful strategic behaviour improves a company's position. In some cases, the strategic behaviour immediately results in having fewer competitors or in the possibility of charging higher prices. The company may also be able to manoeuvre itself into a position that offers the prospect of a relatively easy future, for example a future without competitors or a future with a powerless regulator. Anyway, the advantages to itself that a company is able to realize will sooner or later pay off in higher returns. This assumption underlies all counterarrangements that follow from the financial parameters of the strategically behaving company. Where market forces fail to operate fully, strategically operating companies will succeed in realizing excessive profits. The knowledge that these will be skimmed anyway will act as a brake on this strategic behaviour.

Currently these arrangements are used mainly in those links of the production chain where a (natural) monopoly survives after liberalization. Examples included the setting of tariffs for transport over the electricity networks. The arrangements can also be used in the links where there are excessively high prices because of the absence of sufficient competition.

11.3.1 Rate of Return

This family of counterarrangements has two variants. The first variant is *rate of return regulation* (Bos, 1995). This regulation determines a maximum return. The regulator establishes how much capital the enterprise has invested and indicates what it regards as a reasonable return on this capital invested. The enterprise then determines the price it has to charge its consumers to reach that return.

Two main drawbacks are attached to this counterarrangement. First, the company is left with hardly any incentives to produce efficiently, because all efficiency profit leading to a return higher than the established return will be skimmed off. This is a serious drawback, even more so because the aim of promoting competition is to create that incentive. The second drawback is caused by the fact that the regulator has to establish the invested capital. This is difficult for the outsider that every regulator will be. Here, the regulator has to pay for its information disadvantage in comparison with the company. We may safely assume that companies that are able to behave strategically because of their information advantage will succeed in pulling the wool over the regulator's eyes also on this point. At any rate, the company will lack the incentive for sober investment, because all investments are taken into account to fix the permitted return. Instead, the company will feel an incentive to overinvest. The company may do so from the need to deliver perfect services, but it should always ask itself whether the extra costs warrant the reaching of the ultimate degree of perfection (Breyer, 1982). Rate-of-return regulation deprives the company of the incentive to make such a trade-off.

11.3.2   Price Regulation

The second variant is price regulation. The regulator fixes a *price cap*. If this price cap is in force for a longer period, an automatic annual adjustment will take place for inflation, for example, and for a productivity increase that is considered reasonable. The advantage of *price cap* regulation over *rate-of-return* regulation is that the company continues to feel the incentive to produce efficiently, because all it manages to realize in cost price that is lower than the price it can charge will accrue to the company. However, also in this case the regulator will continue to have its information disadvantage, which makes it difficult to fix the right price cap. The company that wishes to use its information advantage strategically has more possibilities under price cap regulation than it has under a regime of rate-of-return regulation, because it is able to profit from its information advantage also in the process between price and return. A consequence of strategic behaviour that may arise in the event of price cap regulation is underinvestment. Once the regulator has fixed the price cap, the company will have an interest in keeping costs as low as possible, because all it manages to realize in cost saving will accrue to the company. In some cases, its information disadvantage will keep the regulator from discovering and preventing underinvestment.

11.4 CONSUMER PROTECTION

Conceivably, the adverse effects of the strategic behaviour will eventually affect the final consumers of the services and products. They either pay excessive prices or receive insufficient quality. This is even more problematic because the services provided are so vital to the consumers. This means, for example, that they do not have the option to buy nothing if they dislike the price/quality ratio. This is why the doctrine of consumer protection has been developed. Now that consumers cannot refrain from buying nor have the freedom, or have hardly any freedom, to choose other suppliers, they deserve extra protection, goes the basic idea behind consumer protection. To make consumer protection an adequate arrangement, three preconditions have to be met: the market must be transparent, the switching costs must be low and the legal protection must be adequate.

11.4.1 Transparent Market

First, it is important for the market to be transparent. This may seem obvious, but actually consumers in markets where they used to have no possibility of selecting a supplier themselves and where they do now, have a poor picture of the differences between suppliers. This is partly due to the suppliers themselves, many of whom offer too much, irrelevant and hardly comparable information. The fact that not all consumers are equally well informed deserves special attention. The well informed consumers are able to select suppliers in a way that serves their interest. However, the companies, in their turn, appear to be able to shift the disadvantages they suffer to their poorly informed consumers (Boone and Potters, 2002).

11.4.2 Low Switching Costs

In the second place, low switching costs are necessary to allow consumers to benefit from the operation of market forces. It must be simple for a consumer to switch to another provider. This goes for any investments in equipment that a consumer needs to make, the length of notice periods and other obstacles.

11.4.3 Adequate Legal Protection

Finally, it must be possible to handle complaints procedures quickly and cheaply. If the length and the cost of a complaints procedure keep the consumer from turning to complaints agencies, it will be very unattractive to do so. This is especially true of minor problems and, consequently, minor complaints. A *small claims court* is an interesting idea in this connection (Ybema, 2002).

The attraction in the idea of consumer protection is that the arrangement fits in with the eventually envisaged level, that is the consumer. The disadvantage is that a good deal of strategic behaviour can no longer be traced when the service reaches the consumer. Much of the strategic behaviour takes place far upwards in the production chain and remains invisible to the consumer. A more structural protection of consumers would therefore be a good supplement. An interesting idea in this context is the possibility of *empowered public interest groups (PIGs)* (Ayres and Braithwaite, 1992, p. 54 ff). PIGs are given a heavy, institutionalized position in the process of designing the operation of market forces. However, the design of these PIGs deserves a great deal of attention to prevent them from degenerating into querulous and powerless little groups of dissatisfied users. It is necessary, for example, for a PIG to receive all the information exchanged between relevant organizations (Ten Heuvelhof and Van Twist, 2001, p. 4). This idea has been elaborated in hybrid governance, the internal arrangement discussed below.

11.5   HYBRID GOVERNANCE

11.5.1   Hard Law and its Restraints

Much is usually expected of the law as regards controlling strategically operating enterprises. The idea is that laws and regulations can enforce 'decent' market behaviour and, for example, prevent cheating. Of course, this is not strange, because statutory rules are naturally and pre-eminently meant to regulate behaviour. However, 'regulation can make matters worse' (Noll, 1989, p. 1262). Capturing by organized groups, for example the incumbent, may result in regulation that harms competition and provides opportunities for strategic behaviour. Owen and Braeutigam (1978) refer to many varieties of strategic behaviour in the regulatory process, for example the strategic use of information, strategic use of litigation, strategic use of innovation, and so on. However, there is also empirical research showing that capturing may be overcome (Derthick and Quirk, 1985).

The fact that regulation may work out poorly also follows from an analysis at a deeper level. How do laws and regulations work? They affect behavioural alternatives of entrepreneurs and can limit these alternatives in such a way that undesirable behaviours are no longer an option. In the context of strategic behaviour, they are notably instrumental laws, laws aimed at realizing government policy, for example a particular economic order or social distribution. In the literature, this type of law is occasionally referred to as 'purposive law of the interventionist state' (Teubner, 1983, p. 240). This restraint can take place in several ways: directly, by imposing a direct legal obligation; examples would be the enterprise with 'substantial market power', which is subject to heavier requirements than its competitors, or the duty to negotiate with a competitor about access to crucial networks and facilities. Behaviour can also be restrained indirectly, that is by attaching binding rules to a licence, for example. Examples include the supply licence for electricity.

According to modern theoretical insights, instrumental legislation and regulation offer only very limited possibilities for influencing societal processes (Nonet and Selznick, 1978; Teubner, 1983, 1989 and 1992). An important explanation for this is the self-referentiality of social systems. Examples of social (sub)systems are: society, the state, the church, the law, science, the economy and the political system. Self-referential systems are closed to the environment in their operation, with the result that realizing changes from the (political) environment is difficult. This self-referentiality causes social systems to reproduce themselves continuously: the system itself determines observation, the selection of what is relevant and the giving of meaning to information. The system thus proves itself and demonstrates the relevance of its own interpretation continually. However, this does not mean that social systems cannot change. Systems can vary their internal operation. They construct their environment by themselves and observe changes in it. They do not adapt themselves to objective changes in their environment, because their perception is subjective.

The only way external signals can enter the system is by offering the system elements for self-reproduction. An example will clarify this. Many companies are not spontaneously inclined to account for the adverse external effects they cause to their environment. The problem as such does not match the self-reference of the economic system. Only when levies affect the cost–benefit analysis are environmental problems observed in the economic communication. Another example concerns price and quality effects of a licence.

In a market sector, the customer should be central and the customer's wishes should determine the definition of quality. The interaction between demand and supply determines the quality to be realized eventually. The customer imposes requirements on quality, the providers react by offering a particular quality at a particular price. This leads to the trade-off between quality and price. Public-law instruments such as licences are not a substitute for this process, because the essence of a licence is that it is a unilateral legal act on the part of the administrative body that wants to bring about a legal consequence. The will of the applicant concerned does not matter. The essence of a market is that it facilitates a bilateral process between customer and supplier. This process results in agreements between customers and suppliers encompassing a trade-off between quality and price. Since the will of the licensor will not adequately represent the customer's will, an efficient allocation of resources – which the parties set out to achieve – is disturbed. Having customers themselves inform the provider of their wishes directly would achieve a better match with the market process (Ten Heuvelhof and Stout, 2005).

11.5.2   Soft Law and its Possibilities

Evidently, the effects of instrumental legislation are limited. 'Soft law' might offer a solution. The term 'soft law' refers to quasi-legal instruments that do not have any legally binding force, or the binding force of which is somewhat 'weaker' than that of traditional 'hard law'. A promising arrangement based on the model of soft law is the institutional anchoring of standards of decency, rules aimed at realizing values like fairness, openness, honesty, reliability; these are values that, if realized, keep the entrepreneur from strategic behaviour (Stout, 2007a and 2007b).

The core of institutional anchoring is that intended values are realized, not with the help of compulsive rules of behaviour, but by the way the organization is designed. In other words, the point is that incentives should be built into the structure of the organization that help the organization to display desired behaviour or renounce undesirable (strategic) behaviour.

Of course, the arrangement must not be non-committal. It should be prevented from eventually only involving good intentions. The arrangement should also have teeth and, if necessary, be enforced with the help of coercion. This requires having rules of soft law accompanied by rules of hard law. The application of rules of soft and hard law should be balanced and should alternate. Of course, the use of hard law should be limited to (tails of) processes, because setting material standards with the help of legal rules alone has proved to be useless. We speak of *hybrid governance* because of the combination of soft and hard law.

Institutional anchoring has the following advantages:

- It utilizes the self-reflective capacity of the organization instead of frustrating it in the way normal legislation does.
- It reinforces competition as a mechanism for promoting the efficient fulfilment of public duties.

● Institutional anchoring fits in with the growing tendency to anchor good conduct in the philosophy of corporate social responsibility.

The key question is how to arrive at adequate institutional anchoring. How can values and standards within a certain enterprise be reinforced in such a way that they lend support in preventing and combating strategic behaviour? We cannot give a general answer to this question. It depends on the legal structure chosen, which has been provided for in the legislation on legal persons, and this differs from one country to another. Each nation has its own specific corporate forms, with its own rules and restraints. It is therefore relevant whether we are dealing with, for example, the Dutch Naamloze Vennootschap (NV), the German Aktiengesellschaft (AG) or the British Limited Corporation (Ltd). To stick to these three examples, there are major differences between the institutional structure of an NV, an AG and a Ltd. They particularly concern the bodies of the enterprise and the way the tasks and powers within the enterprise are distributed over and between these bodies.

In spite of the differences, there are basic similarities. In addition to its legal personality, the modern business corporation has at least three other universal legal features: transferable shares (shareholders may change without affecting its status as a legal entity), perpetual succession capacity (its possible continued existence despite shareholders' death or withdrawal), and limited liability (including, but not limited to, the shareholders' limited responsibility for corporate debt).

The following arrangement for institutional anchoring is based on the Dutch Naamloze Vennootschap (NV), the common company structure for utility industries in the Netherlands. Values and standards can be anchored at three levels: the executive board, the supervisory board and the shareholders' meeting.

Executive board level
Companies can establish a code for their own sector with the intention of committing the executive board to a number of rules of behaviour. This code should primarily contain rules with regard to processes (agents, subjects, methods). The crux of the matter is to set up a permanent consultative circuit in which stakeholders participate (government, supervisory directors, users and social organizations). A consultative circuit of this kind will be sufficiently dynamic and flexible to deal with the special nature of strategic behaviour.

Through its participants, the consultative circuit will also exhibit a responsive capability and will be able to pick up social signals, an indispensable quality with a view to the dynamics of the debate. By virtue of its composition, the circuit is so transparent that its decision making can be traced, which not only makes it possible to check outcomes but also legitimizes them to a certain extent. The way in which the rules come into being is in itself a good basis for compliance.

The responsibility of companies in the public sector should not be limited to the creation of the code but should include its implementation. For example, the civil effect of the code can be realized by getting the board to report on compliance in its annual report. The obligation to report brings with it the obligation to explain why certain rules from the code have not been observed, for instance. It would then be up to the shareholders to form an opinion on this matter. After all, the general meeting of shareholders is the body to which the annual report is submitted for assessment. It could express its discontent about the report in terms of its willingness to approve the annual accounts, which means that the response to a failure in compliance need not be without a sanction.

Supervisory board level

The supervisory board should be composed of interests other than the company's profitability. How can this be achieved? Flexible, socially oriented arrangements are the most appropriate way of achieving this, such as an appointments policy geared towards recruiting supervisory directors from a wide spectrum of interests; wise men and women with a great many years of experience in social functions. This basic profile for a supervisory director can be laid down in the Articles of Association.

The level of the shareholders' meeting

The shareholders' meeting can play an important role in representing public interests. While it is true to say that shareholders are only interested in the profitability of the company and therefore in the share profit to be gained, the interests that shareholders represent, or believe they should represent, are determined by the shareholders themselves. Shareholders as individuals could choose to allow themselves to be led by more idealistic motives. Given that public interests are best represented by those who are directly involved, we propose that those with a vested interest in a public interest, that is private interest groups (PIGs; also see section 11.4.3) such as environmental or consumer organizations, should be given the opportunity to purchase shares. Since it is not realistic to suppose that non-commercial organizations have sufficient funds to purchase shares, companies should meet private interest groups part of the way in this respect. They might do so by issuing shares at reduced prices. This would enable the shareholders' meeting to grow into a forum for weighing up public interests and would allow socially acceptable trade-offs to be made between interests.

Trade-offs that take place in this way are both public and transparent, and can therefore be verified. In this way, strategic behaviour that might harm public interests stands no chance of success.

The process of making shares available to private interest groups in this way could also be laid down in the Articles of Association. This applies equally to the distribution of shares among the various categories of shareholders.

It is essential that the relationship between public-interest shareholders and private commercial shareholders should not be left to chance. The way the shares are distributed provides opportunities to incorporate incentives for efficiency. If the representatives of public interests were to be given 51 per cent of the shares and the private shareholders 49 per cent, this would kill two birds with one stone. The private influence would still provide an incentive strong enough to realize high efficiency, while the 51 per cent public share would still safeguard the serving of public interests.

The above leads us to the following conclusion. As we saw in 11.5.1, traditional legal rules do not suffice to curb strategic behaviour. The only way external signals can enter the system is by offering the system elements for self-reproduction. This can be achieved with hybrid governance, with incentives built in to the governance of the enterprise in such a way that the enterprise, as it were automatically, refrains from strategic behaviour.

11.6 REGULATORS[1]

Network-based industries in the USA have traditionally been organized as private enterprises, and private monopolies and oligopolies are common. In the US, regulators were brought in as a countervailing power. Within such settings, heroic battles were fought in the last century between private companies and regulators, for example in the telecoms sector (Temin and Galambos, 1987) and the aviation sector (Vietor, 1995). In Europe, more or less parallel to privatization, regulators were recently set up following the American example to supervise private monopolies and oligopolies and safeguard public values at stake in these sectors.

Apparently, the institutional design, organization and working methods of these regulators are widespread concepts, but their effectiveness is disputed. More specifically, regulators should be strictly independent; they should apply clear rules laid down at the political level, and their working methods should be transparent. Independence, rule-based operation and transparency are undeniably part of a cast-iron democracy mantra, but it is doubtful whether these principles will automatically suffice to curb the excrescences of strategic behaviour in the network-based industries.

Below, we will explore for each of these principles what risks are involved in interpreting them too literally. We will also explore reinterpretations of these principles that may be more effective, without affecting their essence.

11.6.1 Independence?

Independence allows for impartial action without reducing information asymmetry

A regulator should be strictly independent (De Ru and Peeters, 2000). It should be able to make its decisions independently. Independence ensures that a regulator need not worry about a possible backlash of its decision against itself. Independence translates into a great distance from the players in the field.

But how effective is strict independence? To what extent does strict independence help to curb strategic behaviour? One of the main reasons why strategic behaviour is so rampant and proves to be so difficult to fight is the information disadvantage of the regulator vis-à-vis companies in the sector. The regulator has to familiarize itself with the capillaries of the companies; it has to study cost–price calculations and decide whether the returns earned are reasonable. The regulator must have 'state of the art' technical know-how, operate on at least the same level as the companies that have a potential advantage because of the commercial incentive they feel to build up, and maintain a technological head start. In practice, this is rare if not impossible (Ten Heuvelhof and Stout, 2003).

The regulator depends on other players for its information. Information is an asset. To acquire it, the regulator has to open itself up to others and give up its strict independence.

For example, in its day-to-day operations, OFTEL, the British regulator, actually proved to be highly dependent on other actors, also for obtaining information (Hall et al., 2000, p. 8). OFTEL proved to be highly dependent not only on other regulatory actors, but on a large variety of industrial players with divergent interests, including consumer organizations. In our case studies on Microsoft and AT&T, we observed similar phenomena for the European Commission and American regulators.

Reducing information disadvantage by intensive contact with the field

Of course, much information asymmetry can be removed by a statutory obligation to supply information. Supported by legislation, the regulator can oblige companies to provide the relevant information. However, this does not remove the asymmetry. The information that the regulator obtains in this way is 'need to know' information. In addition to that, there is 'nice to know' information. The regulator can only obtain this type of information by operating in the field and by seeking the vicinity of the important players. This is how the regulator can build up the required intelligence.

The opening up of markets offers a good starting point for a strategy to increase the regulator's knowledge. Although it is very difficult for the regulator to reduce its information disadvantage in the regulator–monopolist relationship, it has more possibilities available in a market that is open, however limited the degree of openness may be. Entrants faced with an aggressive defensive incumbent will be inclined to seek the support of the regulator. This support will be materialized by providing company information that is difficult to come by and by qualitative comment on 'need to know' information provided by the incumbent. For example, OFTEL proved to be less dependent on BT for its information when more companies appeared on the scene. (Hall et al., 2000, pp. 136 and 206). The European Commission was informed of Microsoft's strategic actions by its competitors and suppliers of complementary facilities.

In general, one can say that independence should be safeguarded in *structural independence*. At the institutional level, the regulator should be truly independent. But in policy and work processes, the regulator should adopt an outward focus and move into the field. Distance is a dangerous strategy and 'being there' a dire necessity. The regulator should work alongside the companies; they should be on committees together, do research together, carry out pilot projects together and conduct evaluations together: in short, *process bundling*. In these work processes, the information that the regulator needs to make up some of its disadvantage will flow freely.

11.6.2 Rules?

There are two reasons for having the regulator operate on the basis of, and within, clear rules established by politicians. The first is that the inspected companies have a right to know what is permitted and what is not. They make big investments and play the game with brinksmanship. This is fair only under the condition that the rules in force are clear. The second is that, in many cases, regulators have been given autonomy from political superiors. If these political overlords still want a grip, they will get it by fixing clear and detailed rules and ordering the regulator to operate within the framework of these rules. This is how the minister can still deliver on his political responsibility.

Strict enforcement is hard to combine with negotiating and process bundling
Clear and detailed rules should be complemented by strict enforcement.
The regulator should therefore supervise compliance with these rules and
enforce them strictly in the event of non-compliance. However, the regulator as an enforcement machine is bound to provoke tensions. Hall et al.
have convincingly demonstrated that much of the regulator's work takes
place in bargaining processes. Negotiations will proceed more smoothly if
they take place harmoniously. Strict enforcement that works out unfavour-
ably for companies with which the regulator will have to negotiate again
at a later stage will not improve the atmosphere in those negotiations.
Likewise, the desired process bundling described above will be arduous if
the regulator repeatedly spoils the atmosphere by strict enforcement (Hall
et al., 2000, p. 203).

**Enforcing rules requires a long lead time at odds with immediate effective
action**
Supervising compliance with rules and enforcement demands a long lead
time. It usually takes some time for the regulator to establish an infringement of rules. The regulator will then first try to put the norm-deviant
company back on the right track with mild measures. These will be followed by formal cautioning, which may eventually be followed by formal
enforcement actions. Strategic behaviour of the norm-deviant company
may considerably prolong this period. The company may at least lodge an
objection and an appeal, which will take a few months. It will have even
more possibilities of gaining time. For example, it may create the impression that it is willing to fulfil the requirements set by the regulator, whereas
in reality it is not. Both the Microsoft and AT&T cases have shown this
convincingly. It may also try to gain support among third parties for a
somewhat more lenient treatment by the regulator.

However, companies are sensitive to quick decision making, particularly
in the transition period. New companies venture into the market and it is
important for them to gain customers quickly. In transition periods, new
products and services will be launched in the market. The market for these
new products and services still has to be divided. Strategic behaviour that
induces customers to choose one particular company instead of another
pays off handsomely, especially during this period. A slow response to
such behaviour makes it even more attractive.

Task competence for regulators
To enable regulators to operate more effectively, they need to be given
more scope than the rules allow them (Ten Heuvelhof and Stout, 2003).
They should be given more possibilities of acting *ex ante*. Proactive action

is not only desirable, but even necessary. The concept of task competence might be suitable here. The task description might be to guarantee proper competition. This will give the regulator great freedom of action, as long as it takes place in the context of its task performance.

11.6.3 Transparency?

Transparency facilitates checks and creates certainty for norm addressees
Regulators should be transparent (De Ru and Peeters, 2000). It should be clear to the outside world how regulators deal with the market parties, how they interpret the rules they have to enforce, what criteria they apply, what sanctions they impose and what their priorities are. Such transparency is necessary for two reasons. The first is that political authorities want to know how the regulator operates. The second is that the companies falling under the regulator want to know what they can expect. What does the regulator monitor? What does it take a grave view of and what does it turn a blind eye to? They can request this transparency to obtain legal certainty (De Moor-van Vugt, 2001, p. 5).

However, transparency hampers unexpected and surprise action
The question is to what extent transparency improves the regulator's position in the arena in which it operates. What matters to the regulator's position is its information disadvantage compared with the companies in the field. Although it is inevitable for a regulator to lag behind the companies as regards the whole of the available information, a regulator has a natural advantage on one point in the information portfolio: its own mode of thought and its actions. What does it focus on? What does it pay special attention to? It should cherish its advantage on this point. The question is therefore how desirable transparency is. The ultimate consequence of full transparency would be that the regulation no longer holds any surprises for the inspected companies. However, regulation should never be fully predictable, because complete predictability makes it very easy indeed for a strategically operating company to thwart the regulator and prevent it from making 'accidental discoveries'.

Transparency exposes the regulator to information disadvantage
The regulator can even undo much of the information disadvantage by not making clear what information it has actually available. It will be obvious to companies that the regulator knows less than they do. However, not knowing exactly how much less the regulator knows weakens their strategic advantage. If companies are uncertain, they will prefer to be safe rather than sorry and keep a safe margin about what the regulator knows.

Transparency can all too easily undermine this, because it allows companies to find out exactly what the regulator knows and attune their actions accordingly.

It will be more difficult to repent and change course for organizations with maximum transparency than for organizations that feel less spied upon. Organizations with maximum transparency realize that their change of course will not go unnoticed by the outside world and that it will provoke criticism of the actions performed in the past. In the light of this change of course, it will be difficult to defend the old, abandoned course. The learning organization will at least suffer serious loss of face. In short, organizations are entitled to their own domain, screened off from the outside world. Some discretion towards organizations stimulates learning processes and eventually benefits the quality of the organization's operations.

Ex post accountability
The solution to the dilemma is to shift the emphasis from transparency to subsequent accountability, which, of course, involves a certain transparency. The regulator should be able to account at a later stage for its actions and its failure to take action, for its choice of priorities and posteriorities and for the criteria it uses. These accountability processes can be in line with two traditions. The first is that of enforcement under administrative law, in which the administration nearly always has some discretionary powers. The standard provision in administrative regulations is: 'the board *can* . . . .'. The point here is that the regulator is left some scope and that it may be asked afterwards to account for the way it used its discretionary scope. This rule should be coupled to the task competence suggested above to replace traditional regulations. The regulator would then be asked afterwards to account for the way it interpreted its task competence.

The second tradition is enforcement under penal law. Organizations that have duties and responsibilities in investigating criminal offences and prosecuting suspects have always had plenty of scope to operate and build up an information position. They are not obliged to provide maximum transparency beforehand and, as regards prosecuting in individual cases, they have many possibilities to follow their own line of action. Of course, they have to account for their actions afterwards, although this may be to a limited circle of authorities.

11.6.4   New Regulation?

A regulator that is given the scope to operate in the way outlined above is better able to address strategic behaviour. Its being intertwined in processes enables it to gain information. This information helps it to make up for its information disadvantage. Although this will not completely undo the information asymmetry, it will reduce it. Allowing the regulator to operate in opacity reduces the effect of the remaining information disadvantage even further.

Containing the disadvantages of a regulatory risk
Although this may sound attractive, there is a downside to such changes that deserves to be mentioned. Without closer attention being paid to them, such changes would imply a regulatory risk (Parker, 2003, pp. 85–6) for the market parties. In addition to their 'normal' commercial uncertainties, companies now also face uncertainties arising from this regulatory risk. Like every other risk, this will put up costs. Regulation in the UK has been described as 'a discretionary system where negotiations and personality are becoming its most important feature'. It is turning into a 'game' between industry chiefs and regulators because regulation does not provide a clear and certain set of rules within which the industry can take economic decisions. Rather, investing in influencing regulators and changing the rules of the game are becoming an industry in themselves, consuming resources and increasing the burden of regulation (Veljanovski, 1991, p. 26). This regulatory risk is dealt with in the literature as something that should be avoided at any price. On the other hand, the lesson of this book is that 'any price' is too high a price. When deciding about a possible reduction of the regulatory risk, the government should weigh the extra cost of a certain regulatory risk for companies against the advantages of fewer possibilities for strategic behaviour. This will create a more balanced picture.

The government might allow the regulatory risk to continue to exist on a selective basis. This would be possible because the regulator uses these options only with respect to companies that behave strategically. It should apply the 'traditional' norms towards the other companies.

11.7 CONCLUSION

Strategic behaviour is difficult to catch. It cannot be proven clearly. In many cases, it can only be observed in the course of time, afterwards, when the 'picture is complete'. It changes rapidly and behaviours used in one form can be continued in a different form. If this were otherwise, it would probably not amount to strategic behaviour. This means that high demands are imposed on the counterforces. Strategic behaviour is typically the behaviour of intelligently operating actors that are reflective, act contingently and are able to hide their actions and underlying motives.

Only actors that are equally intelligent, know the sector inside out and can, in turn, also be smart when they have to, are able to resist it. It is the regulator that has to realize the promises of the operation of market forces and contain the strategic behaviour of the parties concerned. However, the case studies demonstrate that this is successful only to a very limited extent. This is why we have suggested two alternative types of arrangement in addition to the traditional counterarrangements of competition engineering, skimming returns and consumer protection. They are *hybrid governance* of 'hard law' and 'soft law', and regulators with higher degrees of freedom in their actions. We have briefly set out the advantages and disadvantages of using either of them. The use of these arrangements is unlikely to make all strategic behaviour a thing of the past and it is questionable whether that is desirable. The reason is that the great and many institutional changes that have taken place in these sectors were, and are, also meant to incentivize companies to start operating more cleverly and accurately. Offering room for strategic behaviour fits in with this, although strategic behaviour should not be allowed to take on forms that undo the advantages of the changes.

NOTE

1. Section 11.6 is based on E. ten Heuvelhof (2006).

REFERENCES

Ayres, I. and J. Braithwaite (1992), *Responsive Regulation*, New York: Oxford University Press.
Boone, J. and J. Potters (2002), 'Transparency, prices and welfare with imperfect substitutes', discussion paper, Tilburg: CentER.
Bos, D.I. (1995), *Marktwerking en Regulering* (in Dutch) (*Competition and Regulation*), The Hague: Ministry of Economic Affairs.
Breyer, S. (1982), *Regulation and its Reform*, Cambridge, MA: Harvard University Press.
De Moor-van Vugt, A.J.C. (2001), *Toezicht achter Matglas* (in Dutch) (*Regulation Behind Frosted Glass*), The Hague: Boom Juridische Uitgevers.
Derthick, M. and P.J. Quirk (1985), *The Politics of Deregulation*, Washington, DC: The Brookings Institution.
De Ru, H.J. and J.A.F. Peeters (eds) (2000), 'Toezicht als nieuwe vorm van over-heidsbemoeienis ingekaderd (in Dutch) ('Regulation embedded as a new form of government intervention'), in *Toezicht en Regulering van Nieuwe Markten* (in Dutch) (*Supervising and Regulating New Markets*), The Hague: SDU Uitgevers, pp. 3–18.

Dixit, A.K. (1996), *The Making of Economic Policy: A Transaction–Cost Politics Perspective*, Cambridge, MA: MIT Press.

Emmons, W. (2000), *The Evolving Bargain. Strategic Implications of Deregulation and Privatization*, Boston, MA: Harvard Business School Press.

Hall, C., C. Scott and C. Hood (2000), *Telecommunications Regulation, Culture, Chaos and Interdependence Inside the Regulatory Process*, London: Routledge.

Laffont, J.-J. and J. Tirole (1993), *A Theory of Incentives in Procurement and Regulation*, Cambridge, MA: MIT Press.

Noll, R.G. (1989), 'The politics of regulation', in R. Schmalensee and R.D. Willig (eds), *Handbook of Industrial Organization*, Vol. 2, Amsterdam: Elsevier Science Publishers, pp. 1253–87.

Nonet P. and Ph. Selznick (1978), *Law and Society in Transition: Toward Responsive Law*, New York: Harper Colophon Books.

Owen, B.M. and R. Braeutigam (1978), *The Regulation Game: Strategic Use of the Administrative Process*, Cambridge, MA: Ballinger Publishing Company.

Parker, D. (2003), 'The dynamics of regulation: performance, risk and strategy in the privatized, regulated industries', in E.F.M. Wubben and W. Hulsink (eds), *On Creating Competition and Strategic Restructuring*, Cheltenham, UK and Northampton, MA, USA: Edward Elgar, pp. 69–101.

Stout, H.D. (2007a), 'Safeguarding public interests in liberalized utilities sector, the Dutch case', paper for the EGPA 2007, Annual Conference, Madrid, Spain, 2007 EGPA Annual, Study Group XI Regulation and Management of Public Utilities.

Stout, H.D. (2007b), *Weerbare Waarden. Borging van Publieke Belangen in Nutssectoren* (in Dutch) (*Defensible Values. Safeguarding Public Interests in Utility Sectors*), The Hague: Boom Juridische Uitgevers.

Temin, P. and L. Galambos (1987), *The Fall of the Bell System. A Study in Prices and Politics*, Cambridge: Cambridge University Press.

Ten Heuvelhof, E.F. (2006), 'New dilemmas in regulating critical infrastructures', *International Journal of Critical Infrastructures*, **2**(2–3), 160–70.

Ten Heuvelhof, E.F. and H.D. Stout (2003), 'Telecom: Sluwe Bedrijven, Geslepen Toezicht' (in Dutch) ('Telecom: Sly Companies, Smart Regulation'), *Bestuurswetenschappen*, **57**(6), 532–3.

Ten Heuvelhof, E.F. and H.D. Stout (2005), 'Concurrentie in elektriciteit' (in Dutch) ('Competition in electricity'), *Openbaar Bestuur, Tijdschrift for Beleid, Organisatie & Politiek*, **15**(11), 14–20.

Ten Heuvelhof, E.F. and M.J.W. van Twist (2000), 'Nieuwe markten en de rol van de overheid' (in Dutch) ('New markets and the role of the government'), *ESB dossier 22 June 2000*, D 28–D 32.

Ten Heuvelhof, E.F. and M.J.W. van Twist (2001), 'Competition engineering door ontbinding van de incumbent' (in Dutch) ('Competition engineering by dissolving the incumbent'), *Tijdschrift Privatisering*, **8**(2), 4–7.

Ten Heuvelhof, E.F., M. de Jong, M. Kuit and H. Stout (2003), *Infrastratego, Strategisch Gedrag in Infrastructuurgebonden Sectoren* (in Dutch) (*Infrastrategy, Strategic Behaviour in Infrastructure-based Sectors*), Utrecht: Lemma.

Teubner, G. (1983), 'Substantive and reflexive elements in modern law', *Law & Society Review*, **17**(2), 239–85.

Teubner, G. (1989), *Recht als Autopoietisches System*, Frankfurt am Main: Suhrkamp Verlag.

Teubner, G. (1992), 'Regulatory law: Chronicle of a death foretold', *Social Legal Studies*, **1**, 451–75.

Van Twist, M.J.W., M.B. Kort, E.F. ten Heuvelhof, M. Kuit and H.D. Stout (2000), 'De regulator aan zet. Concurrentieverstoring in nutssectoren als strategisch spel met techniek als inzet' (in Dutch) ('Competition distortion in utility sectors with technology as the stakes'), *Tijdschrift Privatisering*, **7**(5), 13–17.

Veljanovski, C. (1991), *Regulators and the Market: An Assessment of the Growth of Regulation in the UK*, London: Institute of Economic Affairs.

Vietor, R.H.K. (1995), *Contrived Competition, Regulation and Deregulation in America*, Cambridge, MA: Harvard University Press.

Ybema, G. (2002), *Economisch Statistische Berichten*, 7 June, 450.

Index